PORTRAIT OF
NORTH WALES

PORTRAIT OF NORTH WALES

Michael Senior

ISBN: 0-86381-726-2

Cover design: Sian Parri
Cover illustration: Bwrdd Croeso Cymru
Black and white illustrations: Bwrdd Croeso Cymru

First published in hardback: Robert Hale & Co. 1973
Second edition in paperback: Gwasg Carreg Gwalch 1987
New edition: Gwasg Carreg Gwalch 2001

Gwasg Carreg Gwalch, 12 Iard yr Orsaf, Llanrwst, Wales LL26 0EH
☎ 01492 642031   🖷 01492 641502
✆ books@carreg-gwalch.co.uk   Website: www.carreg-gwalch.co.uk

Acknowledgements

I should like to thank Denis Bruce, Richard Griffith, and Ednyfed Hudson Davies, for lending me books, and the following for their kind permission to publish quotations: Professor Gwyn Jones and Professor Thomas Jones, translators of the *Mabinogion*; the Trustees of the late Dylan Thomas and J.M. Dent & Sons Ltd.

An extract from *Pieta* by R.S. Thomas is reprinted by permission of Granada Publishing Ltd.

An extract from *The Burning Tree* is reprinted by permission of Faber & Faber Ltd.

About the author

Michael Senior was born in Llandudno, in north-west Wales, in 1940, and in spite of education in England and extensive travels in Europe, Africa and South America, he has never been permanently resident anywhere other than in North Wales. There he farms in a small way and writes (a wide variety of material including poetry and plays), publishing, among other things, articles on local history and topical problems in newspapers and magazines. His national publications to date include seven full-length books, and locally he is the author of 'Conwy, The Town's Story', 'Caernarfon, The Town's Story', 'The Conwy Valley, Its Long History', 'Llandudno's Story', 'Anglesey, The Island's Story', 'Meirionnydd's Story' and 'Llŷn, the Peninsula's Story'.

In his spare time he is much involved in the conservation movement in the Conwy area and the Snowdonia National Park, and with local affairs in general, which brings him constantly into touch with the reality of the condition of North Wales and its inhabitants today.

Contents

Preface to the Second Revised Edition

When I first wrote *Portrait of North Wales* I was thirty-two. I had had some literary success before, but this was my first nationally commissioned publication. It was to be part of the publisher Robert Hale's *Portrait* series of regions of Great Britain. I had been trying to sell a book about Crete, but this came up instead. My agent asked if I could write a book about North Wales, because Hale had a slot. I could of course, and did.

There are probably few experiences quite like the publication of your first book. Comparison of books with children is traditional. But those grow up, grow apart, grow old. A book is an object in the physical world – the smell of it, the size and shape of it, for instance, being among its qualities. On publication it has become something removed from the words and thoughts which gave rise to it.

I wrote it fast, sometimes doing a chapter a day. Something of the spontaneity of this shows through, I think. It has the feel of being quite a breezy book. The leg-work required for the research took place in parallel, involving much travelling, and this has proved a valuable habit to have formed. I still believe (some thirty publications later) that when you are writing about places a few words, perhaps as few as half a dozen, scribbled on the spot, are worth much more than any amount of academic scholarly research.

In the Preface to the first revision I wrote: ' . . . I am struck by how little needs to be amended. Overall the impressions I recorded then have remained remarkably true, a sign I suppose of North Wales's characteristic resilience in the face of the pressures of change'.

That was in 1987. I am both happy and surprised to report that I want to say much the same thing now, as I write this in the year 2000. Not that I am in any way against change. Change itself has been the agent of the richness which we see around us. Time itself is change. It is North Wales's power to remain true to itself throughout this process, its characterising differentness, that I wish to celebrate.

I was worried then – both in the 1970's and the 1980's – about the possible effects of new forms of infrastructure on the region's personality. I expressed some qualms about the most obvious of these, the new A55, with the words: 'What we may say with a measure of confidence is that not all the effects of the road (if indeed any) will be beneficial'. The Conwy tunnel was at that time (in 1987) being built, the western bypasses not complete, but I already knew that the construction of the eastern section had led to a rise in burglary. I cast doubts on the likelihood of success of the road's main aim, that of attracting industry. As I write this today in June 2000 the vast Hotpoint factory in Llandudno-Junction still stands empty. No doubts the effects of 'Objective One' funding (still at present to take place) will do something to revitalise North Wales's traditionally slack economy. If so this will simply underline the fact that the North Wales road failed to do this.

My main concern was the likely change in the population, but here perhaps I failed to take adequately into account the extreme resilience of the identity of the original residents. They have, after all, not left; they have over the course of centuries been largely unaffected by the long-standing fashion for country cottages; with the radical change in emphasis which the foundation of the Welsh Assembly has brought about – from central to regional government – there is now in general in Wales a firmer sense of Welshness, a sense of living somewhere with its own identity, which I now see can counterbalance the increase in the spread of an incoming population.

Of course the new road is useful. I use it all the time. There is something almost luxurious about having a motorway on one's doorstep. In terms of tourism however it cannot be as economically productive as it perhaps appears. The fact that you can get here from places as far away as Birmingham, for the day, and back, cannot do much to fill Llandudno's vast number of hotel beds. The coach parties that disgorge in such quantities in Conwy are a misleading sign of abundance. They only have an hour there. They are doing North Wales in a day.

Reactions to being by-passed also vary. Abergele at once responded by brightening up and becoming lively. Conwy has taken much longer than expected to revive, after having been so long besieged by traffic, but is now gradually shedding its run-down image. Penmaenmawr on the other hand has gone from bad to worse, and is at present largely boarded up. No doubt an injection of capital will counteract some of this blight, but what is mainly needed is a new attitude.

'The fact is,' I wrote in 1987, and am happy to repeat now, 'we have retained more of what is valuable than we have lost, and done more of that than many other formerly attractive parts of Britain. It is still true to say that so far, at any rate, North Wales has benefited rather than suffered from its elements of change.'

Michael Senior
Glan Conwy
June 2000

Introduction

Gwynedd and Powys

Time is change. Without change we should hardly be aware of the passing of the thousands of years. Perhaps resistance to change is a way one can measure the element of difference between one place and another. Just as the old red sandstone has been scraped away, the limestone scarred and smoothed, the granite outcrop largely unmodified – as-it-was-then almost indistinguishable from as-it-is-now – so the degree to which a place resists, or reacts to, the passage of time is what gives it its present character, its appearance, and its distinction from somewhere else.

Certainly it is hard to describe what North Wales is except in terms of the past of which it is composed – by saying, for instance, that it differs from South Wales in the extent to which it has been unaffected by change. And the same for Wales as a whole: one is inclined to say that it is a patch of Britain which has somehow not gone the same way, or at any rate not at the same speed.

Anyone setting out to say what Wales is will find at once that it is easier to say what it is not. It is not a geographic unit, the piece of Britain's coastline lying between the great estuaries of the Severn *(Hafren)* and the Dee *(Afon Dyfrdwy)*. If it were no more than that it would be something equivalent to East Anglia. Nor is it to be defined historically, as the subject of a political agreement (and several disagreements) between Llywelyn the Great and the kings of England. That brief recognition of independence had been reversed within two generations. It is perhaps the land inhabited by the Welsh, but they are equally hard to define, being neither an ethnic group nor, completely, a linguistic one. Perhaps the best negative by which to describe it is the simplest one. It is not England.

Too close to England ever to be free of the influences which, after all, have been felt at greater distances, it has always been too different from her ever to let those influences have much effect. It may be that mistakes made in the sixth century led to the isolation of Wales, but one feels that it would have become so anyway, isolated by nature and habit even within an untouched Celtic Britain. The traditional view is that the English stole the rest of the country from the Welsh. They say in Wales that the Welsh have stolen so much land from the English that they have had to pile it up into mountains.

What actually happened? During the first thousand years before Christ there was considerable movement of people throughout Europe, in the course of which the group of tribes which had in common a culture which became known as Celtic (and who are therefore grouped together as The Celts) spread from central Europe in all directions, until they or their culture (since archaeology finds it hard to say which) became dominant in Europe from the Black Sea to the north-west of Spain. Since the earliest examples of this culture so far discovered were in western Austria, the Rhineland and the Danube Basin, it is presumed that that is where they came from. They came to Britain in waves – the first one perhaps being pushed outwards through Europe by the second – and brought with them the Iron Age. The first main wave arrived probably during the fifth century BC, and the second main wave during the third. These dates are of course rough guides merely, archaeology provides only a hazy outline which one tries, for the sake of order, to make into a shape.

When the Celts came they were not entering an empty country. Britain had been invaded two thousand years before, and probably a few times in between, and even before that it was not uninhabited. The pattern which they imposed however, is the one which remains significant to the British Isles. The Gaelic-speaking, first-wave Celts occupied Ireland. Scotland (originally occupied by a slightly mysterious people whom history is content to label as Picts) was invaded by them later across the Irish Sea. The Brythonic-speaking Celts, now consigned to Cornwall, Wales and Brittany, occupied the rest of Britain.

Even to the Romans the political position of Wales was unlike that of the rest of the island, and this difference was even more apparent after they had gone. Saxon invasions had already begun to be felt in the east and south of Britain, by the time the Roman withdrawal started in 383. But in the west the terror which came from the sea was the Irish, who (either unaware or unconcerned that they were attacking a fellow sub-branch of the same linguistic and cultural group) swept across North Wales and, by about AD 395, occupied the whole of the country between Afon Conwy and the Dee *(Afon Dyfrdwy)*.

Resistance to the Irish at this time probably had a decisive effect on British history. It meant that the attention of some of the most capable men available (in what was, it seems, a time in which they were scarce) was concentrated on the north-west coast. When the last legionaries left in about 407, Cunedda, a military leader who had been summoned from the north to rescue the invaded area, settled down with his army to guard North Wales against invasion from the west, sadly unaware of what was coming at them from behind, his descendants continued blindly to pursue this policy, and by the time his great-grandson Maelgwn died (a man who, in strength of character, power and wealth, was one of the few Brythonic kings capable of restoring unity and resisting the invasion), in about 547, Ida had founded the kingdom of Bernicia on the east coast, and Aelle was about to do the same with Deira just below it.

In the meantime, in what appears from here to be all too much like another part of the forest, Britain had had a nominal high king in the person of Vortigern *(Gwrtheyrn)*. From about 425 to about 461 he held what seems to have been a rather shaky power. The Saxon attacks had become a serious problem from about 410. The Picts, or possibly a confederation of northern tribes, were also causing him trouble. Vortigern

(Gwrtheyrn) lacked the mobility and the forces to fight a war on two fronts, and settled for what, superficially, seems a diplomatic compromise. He employed the Saxons to fight the Picts. As with all devastatingly simple expedients, it was easier to say than to do. Since he was unable to pay them (possibly they had already contributed to his lack of wealth), he had to offer them land. The immigration problem had started.

When they came the Saxons prophesied that they would occupy the country for three hundred years. Though this estimation, made in about AD 450, seems to have been an unduly modest one, it was, to the succeeding generations of Celts, an ominous indication of their intention. Within a few years the supposed mercenaries had broken their agreement; they claimed that the monthly supplies were too small, and since Vortigern *(Gwrtheyrn)* was in no position to satisfy them they set about devastating the island.

Possibly there was at some time a reversal. Possibly nationalism stirred for a time, a glimmer of revival promising a return to pre-Roman Celtic nationhood. Possibly the check on Anglo-Saxon advances between 514 and 547 means something more than the bare facts allow. Procopius and a later German chronicler record that Angles were emigrating from Britain to France in 531. Possibly there was the Battle of Mount Badon. Possibly there was Arthur.

What we know is that it did not last. If Arthur existed he was dead by 540. Ida's Bernicia joined with Aelle's Deira to form Northumbria, and between 552 and the end of the century the Brythonic Celts were defeated at Old Sarum, at Barbury Down, at some site in Buckinghamshire, at Dyrham and at Catterick. Finally a defeat at Chester divided the Welsh Cymry from their closest allies, the Cymry of Strathclyde and Cumbria. From then on Wales was isolated by the kingdom of Mercia, which eventually expanded, under Offa, to border with Northumbria in the north and Wessex in the south.

The rest is anything but silence, but since a large amount of subsequent history is visible to the naked eye we shall be dealing with it later. I thought it was well to dispose of the first thousand years or so in potted form (and seldom has so much been pushed into so small a pot) to give a preliminary answer to the question 'What is Wales?' Some of what has been outlined here will be filled in in more detail as it occurs on the spot. To give some idea of the form in which this, among other things, will be done, I shall now try to answer the question 'What is North Wales?'

North Wales does not need to be artificially divided for the purposes of this book. Historically, geographically, culturally, even prehistorically and geomorphologically, it divides itself. It falls naturally and inevitably into four main sections.

The land between the rivers Conwy and Dee *(Afon Dyfrdwy)* is the country of invasions. Romans camped in it. Irish tribes swarmed across it. English earls annexed it. English kings invaded it repeatedly. The Welsh retreated from it, reoccupied it, raided the borders from it, rebelled in it, and never quite let it go.

Across Afon Conwy is the inner sanctuary – the massif which has come to be known (in English) as Snowdonia, *Eryri* in Welsh. Traditionally and historically this is the place of retreat, the mountain fastness which no Roman, Saxon or Norman had the courage or the ability to penetrate. The raiders pursued by retaliation had only to cross Afon Conwy with their cattle (and other people's) and their kinsfolk and disappear into the hills.

Anglesey *(Ynys Môn)* is an island in a very true sense, despite its proud bridges. Even today there are said to be people who have never crossed the Straits to the mainland. As an island it has developed a character of its own and, looking and feeling unlike any other part of Wales, also behaves accordingly. It is not hard to imagine why the druids made it the centre of their religion; nor why the Romans felt that until they had conquered Anglesey *(Ynys Môn)* they were not safe in Britain.

The Llŷn peninsula sticks out from the country like a finger, and retains the independence which its position of extremity gives it. Sparsely inhabited now (at one time, to judge by the hill-forts and stone hut circles, the most popular settlement in ancient Britain), it is a Welsh-speaking land, characterized by stone, stone walls, stone-scattered fields, stone cottages; a land mostly of farmers and of almost tribal interrelationship; enclosed, rock solid, quite unaffected by the existence, incongruously, of the well-to-do yachtsmen's resort of Abersoch on the one hand, and on the other a holiday camp.

Grouping together these extremities, the island and the peninsula, we are then left with that southern block of North Wales which lies between the Ffestiniog valley and the Mawddach estuary, the country known as Ardudwy. It is somewhere along the lower valleys of this attractive, wooded area, that (with a countryside gradually growing mellower and milder) North Wales becomes Mid-Wales.

When the Romans came a tribe called the *Ordovices* occupied the part of North Wales south of the Vale of Llangollen; and two tribes called the *Venedotae* and the *Deceangli* occupied, respectively, Anglesey *(Ynys Môn)* and Llŷn on the one hand, and the country between Afon Conwy and the Dee *(Afon Dyfrdwy)* on the other. The first of these main areas (the territory of the *Ordovices*) had become the Kingdom of Powys by the end of the 'Dark Ages'; while the second had already been established as the Kingdom of Gwynedd (a name connected with the name of the *Venedotae* tribe) by Maelgwn in the sixth century. Although divided during the Middle Ages into further subdivisions known as *cantrefi*, Gwynedd and Powys remained the main divisions of North Wales until Edward I imposed the English county system in 1284. The situation has reverted now to something closer to Edward's original.

Although it was some centuries before the full effect of

English domination began to be felt, Wales had been the object of curiosity, and the cause of some wonder and amazement, to outside observers, since early times. A long pedigree of awed visitors contributed their Portraits of North Wales. Giraldus Cambrensis, in the 1180s, included the north in his *Itinerary*, although he only spent eight days there, as against a month in the south. Leland's descriptions, in the 1530s, seem to have introduced Wales to the national consciousness – Ben Jonson mentions Penmaenmawr in one of his plays – and with the Welsh part of Camden's *Britannia* (1586), Wales was officially on the map. Although Dr Johnson visited Snowdonia in 1774, travelling with Mr and Mrs Thrale, he had little to say about it. The mountains were apparently not as barren as he had expected. The size of the castle impressed him. Boswell was disappointed that he kept no notes or journal.

Pennant's *Journey to Snowdon*, in 1781, is the first accurately observed, objectively recorded description. It was followed quite soon by the advent of the romantic attitude. Wordsworth's 'Prelude' ends in Snowdon, and the next decade saw the publication of *Wild Wales*. Perhaps Borrow is archetypally the romantic traveller, amazed that the simple natives are so wise, seeing towering crags around him wherever there was a piece of rock, and overawed on every possible occasion by the mystery, the wilderness, the strangeness on every hand.

But though these explorers looked in, and went away to express their views, Wales had only to a limited extent looked out. After the Union indeed, the members of the great Welsh families found themselves welcome at the Tudor court. (To a great extent the anglicization of the Welsh aristocracy which resulted from this determined that the place of exclusively Welsh culture should be among the simpler people). But it was perhaps not until the great roads came that North Wales found itself becoming a part of the English political body. It was not so much that it entered the outer world, as that the outer world entered it.

It was originally, of course, an economic impetus which set it off. The slate industry demanded better transport, and in 1802 Lord Penrhyn built a turnpike which connected Capel Curig with the port near Bangor, along the route of what is now the Nant Ffrancon pass. The commercial importance of the Irish mail led to a series of Parliamentary committees, which finally resulted in the commissioning of Thomas Telford to find an acceptable route from London to Holyhead. Making use of Lord Penrhyn's enterprise, he drove what is now the A5 through the mountains. Telford's other road from Chester connected to it in the 1830s, and in 1848 was joined by a railway.

The invasion was then complete.

A note on the language

The Celtic languages are a group which compose one of the subdivisions of Indo-European. They are again subdivided into two groups, Gaelic and Brythonic. Welsh is one of the Brythonic ones. As with other sub-divisions of languages, the two conform to the *p* and *q* characteristics, and Welsh in this case is the *p* language, Irish being the *q*. That is to say, just as the *q* in the Latin *quinque* is a *p* in the Greek version of the word, *pente*, so the Welsh for five is *pump*, and the old Irish *coic* – the *c's* having once, apparently, been *q's*.

There are many points of resemblance between Welsh and other European languages, although they are admittedly not readily apparent. The words which look familiar are, however, mostly borrowed: *pont* (bridge); *ysgol* (school); *eglwys* (church), *llyfr* (book), *mur* (wall), *ffenestr* (window), and others, are due to the Roman occupation and the long survival of the Latin language as the dominant language of learning and of the church.

Welsh is one of the last widely spoken examples of a Celtic language. It is so robust and vigorous that I cannot believe that it will ever die, though this is the fear of many. In some ways it is the very proximity of the country to its powerful neighbour that has kept the language alive. Political coercion stamped out the Irish language almost completely (except in the islands), and attempts to revive it can never restore it to its former natural state. The same sort of campaign failed in Wales. Cornish was last spoken in the eighteenth century, and Manx and Gaelic are not exactly thriving. Welsh is still the language of Wales, and there are many good reasons why it should remain so. The Irish are separated by a patch of sea, and so are in no danger of being mistaken for just another lot of provincial Englishmen with funny accents. Much that is characteristically Welsh is closely tied to the health and life of its language. Without the language the country might be able to retain its sense of identity, its independence of mind, its self-awareness, and perhaps its cultural outlook, but it would do so less securely.

Welsh has undergone a process of transformation, like any other language, so that it is now quite hard for many a modern Welsh speaker to understand Dafydd ap Gwilym, the fourteenth-century poet, for instance. Modern Welsh came into existence during the sixteenth century, rather like modern English.

It is not only a hard language to learn, but it looks it. The spelling puts a lot of people off. It is very important to remember that the letters, particularly the vowels, do not always have the values which they have in English. A glossary is provided at the end of this book containing the more important of the words which occur in the text. Many of the place-names in Wales have meanings, and where this is the case they will appear in the glossary.

The main points in which the pronunciation of Welsh differs from that of English are as follows:

Ch One of the letters of the alphabet. It is hard, as in Scottish *loch*, not as in English 'church'.
Dd Also one of the letters of the alphabet. Pronounced as *th* as

18

in 'this' and 'that' – not as in 'thought'; Welsh has a *th* for this.

F   Pronounced like *v*.

Ff   Another member of the alphabet. Pronounced like English *f*.

G   is always hard, as in 'given'.

Ll   This one (again a letter included in the alphabet) always seems to cause the most trouble. Put your tongue in the position of sounding the letter *l*, as for instance if you were about to say 'long'. Now emit a passage of air through the tongue without voicing the letter – that is, without sounding the '*ler*' sound but going straight on to the 'ong'. If you have done this successfully you have now said *llong*, which means 'ship'.

Rh   Ordinary *r* is rolled more strongly than in English. *Rh* (also an alphabetic letter) is pronounced more strongly still. The *h* is sounded, as it is supposed to be in the English words 'what' and 'why'. One way of getting round the difficulty is to put the *h* first, *hr*, which sounds very much the same.

Th   Again in the alphabet, this is soft (as in 'both'), never as in 'this'.

U   A misleading letter, pronounced like *i*. Thus *pump* (five) is pronounced 'pimp'. It can also be a long *i* sound; *du* (black) is pronounced 'dee'.

W   Another significant variant: it is pronounced somewhat like double *o*, but varies between the double *o* of 'booth' and the double *o* of 'book'. You never quite know which one it is going to be, and so it to some extent invalidates the claim that Welsh is a phonetic language. (The letter *y* also does this.) *W* can be used as in English, 'wall, 'swell', etc.

Y   Something like an English *u*, as in 'funny'. This seems to be its commonest sound, but it has two others: an *ee* sound, as in 'clean', and *i* sound as in 'sin' (in which respect it doubles with Welsh *u*). Unfortunately you have to take a guess. *Yn* (in): pronounced 'un'. *Dyn* (man): pronounced 'deen'. *Bryn* (hill): pronounced 'brin'.

To make up for the extra letters, there are some missing. Thus the letter J, much to the embarrassment of all the Joneses, does not occur in the Welsh alphabet. Neither do K, Q, V and X.

Pronunciations of diphthongs sometimes present some problems. Briefly, *ae*, *ai*, and *au* are all pronounced (usually) as the *ei* in 'height'. *Ai* is sometimes shortened to sound like the *e* in 'let'. *Ei* and *eu* include a dark *u* sound before an *i* sound, producing something like the French *eui* as in *deuil*. *Oe* and *oi* are as the *oi* in English 'boil'.

The rule regarding stress is quite simple: it is normally placed on the penultimate syllable. There are exceptions, which are stressed on the last syllable, but these are not often encountered.

Part One

DISPUTED TERRITORY

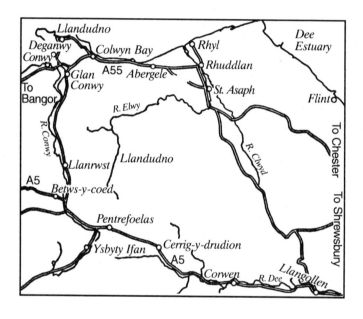

One

BORDER COUNTRY

'Quiet mysteries were in progress behind those tossing horizons: the West, as ever, was retreating with some secret which may not be worth the discovery, but which no practical man will ever discover.' E.M. Forster, in *Howard's End*, looks out at Wales from the Shropshire foothills, and sees it as sheltering a reality inaccessible to the hard-headed people of his book. They were looking across a temperamental frontier, a borderland of the mind.

The sense of brooding, of something lurking on the horizon, characterizes the journey west from the border towns. Approaching, one glimpses the looming heights, senses the distant presence of a different climate, a different sort of structure of the earth and sky. The approach is made, almost inevitably, from one or other of two border towns, Chester or Shrewsbury, the very existence of which is inextricably involved with the fact of being on the borders of Wales.

Borderland it has always been, a land poised between realities, full of promise, expectancy, uncertainty, which give to all states of transition a quality of unreality and excitement. It was always in dispute, the cause of wars and quarrels, the battleground on which the larger question of Wales was fought out so long. Marcher Lords and marauding Princes marched persistently backwards and forwards across it, driving each other's cattle, burning each other's farms. No treaty survived for long against the unbalancing influence of this traditional opposition of points of view. Even the characters which lurk in the background of local lore have something of this ambiguity about them. Both real and legendary, they somehow manage to be at the same time the factual figures of British history and the outsized figments of Celtic imagination.

Perhaps the commonest way of approach, prosaically but

quickly in a car, is by the A5 out of England, and the border county of Shropshire. When one has passed through Chirk and drops towards the valley of Llangollen, the border has been well and truly crossed, and it is safe to say, drifting into a wider and more rolling landscape, that this is Wales at last.

Llangollen is on the Dee *(Afon Dyfrdwy)*, that is to say that fine salmon river flows right through it, and probably the existence of the town is due to the fact that the flow narrows slightly at this point, allowing it to be crossed. The bridge which crosses it is said to date from the fourteenth century, so that the town is clearly well-established. Its present form, solid and concentrated, is probably due to the wool-industry which flourished here for a time, now being replaced by tourism as the current reason for the town's existence.

The praises of Ruskin and Browning, and of George Borrow (who complimented the natives on their 'very good English'), are largely forgotten now. It is not travellers' tales which brings people to Llangollen. This quiet, grey town is now famous all over the world as the home of the International Eisteddfod.

This improbable event, started by a handful of enthusiasts on a small scale, has blossomed during the last thirty years into something which can have no equivalent anywhere. It is to folk dancing and singing what the United Nations is to politics. No respectable country can afford to be without a team there. The result is a plethora of national costumes for a week every July, during which the small, unassuming town is invaded by languages and cultures it would never normally have dreamt of. The effect is extraordinary; Dylan Thomas's description of it is no over-statement of the sight which every year confronts the surprised visitor:

Here, over the bridge come three Javanese, winged, helmeted, carrying gongs and steel bubbles. Kilted, sporraned, tartan'd, daggered Scotsmen reel and strathspey up a side-street, piping hot. Burgundian girls, wearing, on their heads, bird-cages made of

23

velvet, suddenly whisk on the pavement into a coloured dance. A viking goes into a pub . . .

The eisteddfod field itself is in the valley at the back of the town, under the hill of Dinas Brân with its imposing ruins – appropriately, as we shall see, a likely contender for the Castle of the Holy Grail. It is altogether a setting which would make a meeting of the undertakers' union seem romantic. Being dedicated to music, dance and song, this gathering of colourful people has every advantage. Music pours out of the giant marquee (one of the world's largest) and drowns the chattering in strange tongues of the excited competitors, which itself, though it might not help much towards the building of a tower of Babel, is an experience one seldom gets in such an intensified form, and certainly would never expect in a quiet Welsh valley.

This is the only international eisteddfod, and should not be confused with either the National Eisteddfod (which takes place once a year, moving from town to town and alternating between the north and south), or with the many local eisteddfodau (the plural) which occur, like annual festivals, in towns and valleys throughout Wales. An eisteddfod is essentially a competition, the national one being (at least according to the official view, which many people would dispute) of some importance in the cultural life of the country, since it sets a standard by which literature and music may be kept to a traditionally high level. The National Eisteddfod, and the local ones, are exclusively Welsh affairs, frequented by Welsh speakers (with a popular and much-used translation service for others); and through them many of the language's rigid literary forms have been preserved in an unbroken tradition since the Middle Ages. Anyone who penetrates at all far into North Wales will find for themselves that Welsh is a living language, both in the rural areas and in the seats of learning; and the point does not need to be stressed.

Eisteddfodau in some form have, it would seem, always taken place in Wales. The name itself was certainly applied to one held in Carmarthen in 1450. Before that the gatherings at which bardic contests took place were simply part of Welsh cultural life, and seem to have had no definite name. The word is simply the noun from the verb 'to sit' (*eistedd*), and means a session, and hence a meeting. Possibly originally it referred to meetings of elders, and certainly it was assumed, when the revival of interest in Celticism started at the end of the eighteenth century, that the druids would have called their meetings by this name.

They may or may not have done so, of course, since there is no evidence on the question; but unfortunately the image of what a druid was became elaborated by the imaginations of the romantics, with the result that the philosophers described by classical authors have become transformed in everyone's mind into something rather over-picturesque. The result is the strange spectacle of school-masters and clergymen in long white robes, which incongruously dominates the annual National Eisteddfod. Whether or not druidism was ever anything which could correctly be called a religion, the rituals of romantic paganism which decorate the eisteddfod today are particulary ironic, in view of the fact that the Archdruid himself is very often a minister of the church. The confusion which has arisen somewhere in this development is between bards and druids. The eisteddfod is the bardic festival, the opportunity for professional (and nowadays amateur) bards to compete against each other, like football teams.

Besides this present-day phenomenon, Llangollen is lucky enough to have two important links with the past. Both are well worth inspecting, sharing as they do in the town's attractive setting. One is the castle of Dinas Brân which dominates the valley, and indeed can be seen for miles around. The other is the Abbey of Valle Crucis.

Valle Crucis is at the back of the town, and one of the routes out of Llangollen goes near to it. This, on a fine day, is the more exciting way to go, although as far as scenery is concerned it is a choice of superlatives. Whether one prefers the greeness of clothed valleys, or the spaciousness of bare uplands, both are at their best in the next part of the journey into Wales. Crossing the river here takes you over the high ground in a north-westerly direction. The Horseshoe Pass. Its name will need no explanation to anyone who has been over it, since the wide curve which loops round a large empty valley is a very recognizable shape. It is a high, moorland route, often blocked in winter. Whether or not one goes this way will of course depend on the intended destination; as a route to Llandudno, for instance, it is as quick, and possibly shorter. You would miss the long journey down towards the coast through wooded valleys and beside frothing rivers; you would gain the airy openness of the pass, and some very extensive views.

About a mile and a half (2.4 km) out of the town on the road to the Horseshoe Pass, below the road on the right, is Valle Crucis Abbey. Enough remains of it to give an impression of what a stately building it once was. Founded in 1200, the monastery was Cistercian. For centuries it was the burial place of local princes, one of the main centres of the religious life of North Wales, and, as one can see at a glance, a place of some wealth and standing. However simple life may have been in country places during the Middle Ages, the power and majesty of the church dominated both the community and the landscape.

It is called Valle Crucis after a cross which probably stood here when the Abbey was built, and, now no more than a short pillar, stands here still. It may be found a little farther up the valley, close to the road. It is inscribed with the pedigree of somebody called Eliseg, a king of Powys, and although the inscription is not now legible it at one time was, and the generally agreed reading of it reveals that Eliseg traces his ancestry to some quite remarkable people. Maximus occurs, the Romanized Spanish-born general who declared himself Emperor and drained Britain of fighting men to challenge the alternative Emperor in France, in the early fourth century.

Vortigern *(Gwrtheyrn)* is also there, the native king to whom the Saxon invasion happened, and of whose unhappy flight we shall find further traces elsewhere. Clearly anything could be deduced from such an inscription, which is probably more indicative of the self-importance of the royal family of Powys than of any historical relationships; but Geoffrey Ashe, the 'Arthurian' historian, argues convincingly that some of the names indicate a period of British-Saxon inter-marriage in the fifth century. This, if it could be more substantially proved, would be an interesting glimpse into an otherwise dark period of history.

Dinas Brân also belongs to that disputed territory, the area of time where history and legend merge in an unclear horizon. Something about it as one sees it from the valley suggests mystery, and even when one walks among its stones, real and substantial enough, this characteristic remoteness from reality is still strong. It has been left untouched by the green-grass-bank, marked-path, keep-off-the-grass treatment, and stands, with all its antiquity intact, ruinous, untended, magnificently crumbling, allowing scope for speculation and imagination. Attempts to delve into its known history produce the same quality: an elusiveness of fact.

Set impregnably on a high, round hill, it is further insulated against the outside world by a large-scale system of ditches and ramparts. Parts of the walls still stand, the remains of gate-towers and possibly a barbican to the east, to the south the base of a tower mid-way down the wall and, among the more intact items, a passageway which was the original entrance. The position of the Great Hall, on the south side, can be identified; it has two tall windows looking out over the Dee valley *(Dyffryn Dyfrdwy)*. The view from this vantage point is superb, a spread of fields and woods laid out below on three sides, fading into a haze of uplands.

What, then, is the nearest one can come to an historical fact about this archaic craggy fortress, with its fine position and palatial proportions? Probably that Gruffudd ap Madog issued the charter of Valle Crucis from there in 1270; and therefore, one supposes, it was inhabited at least till then. From about 1282, it is known, the castle started to become neglected; its owner then, John de Warrenne, favoured his new castle at Holt. The design of Dinas Brân, as it remains now, points to an origin in the early thirteenth century. Legend however suggests something much older.

The story of the Norman outlaw Fulk Fitz Warine, a character similar in some ways to Robin Hood, as preserved in a thirteenth-century French romance (*Fouke Fitz Warin*), deals among other things with the adventures of knights at 'Chastiel Bran', our Castell Dinas Brân which, it mentions, had already been set on fire and destroyed. In the romance, the castle is associated with wonders. What these were probably remains a mystery, as none who went to see them came back, except one. This element connects the story with others then evolving, which became the legends of the Holy Grail.

The name Brân, which simply means 'crow', is traditionally held to be the name of an individual, Dinas Brân: 'Brân's Stronghold'. Who was Brân?

Probably the oldest record of him which we have is in the *Mabinogion* story of 'Branwen'. The manuscript is of the fourteenth century, the material, according to some authorities, dating from about 1060. Brân is the king of Britain, and his most notable attribute is the possession of a magic cauldron, capable of bringing the dead back to life. It is this cauldron which is generally agreed to be one of the original prototypes of the Holy Grail. Brân's ability to bring about rebirth gives him rather more the character of a god than of an earthly figure. His other qualities, as described in 'Branwen', confirm this.

The story adds that Brân's head was buried on the White Mount in London; as long as it remained there it would protect the island against invasion. It is interesting to find that the shrine of Brân has in fact been perpetuated on the hill of the

28

White Tower, where the presence of the ravens – there is little distinction between raven and crow – is sometimes said to perform a similar protection.

The legend of the Grail grew from these primitive beginnings to its full form during the late twelfth century. Two of the stories of this period name the owner of the holy vessel as Bron. When Malory finally drew together the strands, he worked from several different sources. Grail Castle had throughout been called by many names, even sometimes within the same work. Such confusion is the result of re-working varied originals, themselves subject to the interpretations of copiers. But when the castle which houses the Grail first occurs in Malory's saga, when Sir Launcelot comes on it by chance and is shown the holy vessel, it is called Corbin. 'And so he departed, and rode till he came to the castle of Corbin.' The name is repeated several times during the tale of the birth of Galahad. A second time, later in the story, Launcelot comes upon it accidentally again, and again Malory names it for a few chapters consistently. He was translating in these passages, from the French prose *Lancelot*, written between 1215 and 1230. One would therefore expect the otherwise unexplained name 'Corbin' to be an old French word; and in fact it is. It is the old French for crow or raven. The city or castle of Corbin means the same as Dinas Brân.

Thus we have three reasons for supposing a connection between this splendid castle and the Holy Grail. The similarities between *Fouke Fitz Warin* and Grail stories; the fact that it was Brân who possessed the original Celtic mystic vessel; and Malory's equating Grail Castle with Brân's stronghold.

When the first Grail seeker, Chrétien de Troyes' Perceval, happened in the courses of his wandering to be riding down a river valley, and entered Grail Castle because he could find no place to cross the river, might that in fact have been the Dee *(Afon Dyfrdwy)*? At any rate the description of the castle suits this majestic ruin. 'One might search,' says Chrétien, 'as far as Beirut, without finding one as noble or as well situated.'

Should one now remain on the same side of the river as the Grail seeker, and instead of passing on farther into Wales by Telford's London-Holyhead road, choose to cross the Horseshoe Pass, it would eventually lead down through the wooded and round undulating country of Denbighshire. The towns of both Rhuthun and Denbigh *(Dinbych)* are passed through, pleasant and sturdy places which exhibit a good sense of town planning, their public buildings having a proper consciousness of civic hierarchy.

Ruthin Castle, much of which is modern, covers a long period of history. Edward I, in whose time it was rebuilt, granted it and the town to the Greys, a family who will be mentioned again. The castle went through the customary change of hands during the Civil Wars; and is now celebrated for its medieval banquets and other large-scale functions.

Between Rhuthun and Denbigh *(Dinbych)* stretches the Clwyd valley *(Dyffryn Clwyd)*, good farming country of more English rather than a typically Welsh type, flat meadowland with pasture and shelter which much of Wales would envy. The castle at Denbigh *(Dinbych)* has a slightly more sensational history than that of Rhuthun, although neither have the historical importance of Rhuddlan or Conwy. Queen Elizabeth gave it to the Earl of Leicester, with unfortunate results for the whole of North Wales, which suffered from the high-handed greed of that wilful favourite.

Charles I paid a hasty visit to Denbigh Castle after the telling defeat of Rowton Moor, which can hardly have been the happiest days that sad, losing monarch enjoyed. Denbigh *(Dinbych)*, however, suffered on his behalf a prolonged siege during the rest of the Civil War, and won for itself the distinction of being the last Royalist stronghold to fall.

Although it is probably hardly aware of the fact, Denbigh *(Dinbych)* was the birthplace of at least one Famous Person. Henry Morton Stanley is best known as the American journalist who made a correct presumption somewhere in the African jungle. He was actually a Welshman called John Rowlands, but was probably quite glad to have forgotten the fact. His parents were unmarried, the father dying soon after Stanley was born. In 1847, aged six, he went to the workhouse at St Asaph. It was not until he had gone to sea and arrived in New Orleans that his life really started. He was adopted by a broker there, and took his name.

Beyond Denbigh *(Dinbych)*, one comes down to St Asaph (and the north coast with the main approach from Chester), coming to St Asaph down the valley of a stream called Elwy. G.M. Hopkins, a lover of Wales, wrote a poem called 'In the Valley of Elwy', in which while the scenery is approved, the people come in for a sharp Jesuitical reproof:

> *Lovely the woods, waters, meadows, combes, vales,*
> *All the air things wear that build this world of Wales:*
> *Only the inmate does not correspond:*
> *God, lover of souls, swaying considerate scales,*
> *Complete thy creature dear O where it fails,*
> *Being mighty a master, being a father and fond.*

Was it this area one wonders, that he refers to in his great masterpiece, 'The Wreck of the Deutschland'?

> *Away in the loveable west,*
> *On a pastoral forehead of Wales,*
> *I was under a roof here, I was at rest,*
> *And they the prey of the gales;*

There is something ironic in the fact that the largest town in North Wales, Wrexham, is so easily avoided whichever direction one takes. But this is convenient, since large towns and industrial areas are not exactly characteristic of North Wales, and in many ways Wrexham is in North Wales only geographically. We have, in the meantime, left it behind. And

Telford's road, the A5, from which we diverged to pass down, the Clwyd valley *(Dyffryn Clwyd)*, continues up the Dee valley *(Dyffryn Dyfrdwy)* from Llangollen, winding among the beautiful Berwyn hills. Eventually Dinas Brân is out of sight, and the country changes slightly. It is sad to see the once soft, bracken-clothed slopes of the Berwyn mountains now partly planted with coniferous trees. By contrast the indigenous hardwoods, birch and scrub oak, can still be seen along the river itself. Glyndyfrdwy, meaning simply the valley of the water of the Dee *(Afon Dyfrdwy)*, is the name not only of the valley here but of the next village on the road. This is the country of Owain Glyndŵr, anglicized (by Shakespeare and others) as Owen Glendower; and in fact it was from the valley that he took his name.

Glyndŵr has all the makings of a popular hero, and it is hardly surprising that legends have gathered the aura of the supernatural about him. He was the Che Guevara of his period, the inspiration and guiding force of a nationalistic rising, which he propelled with the vigour and persistence of a true guerrilla leader, the power of the common people behind him.

It began with the reign of Henry IV. Glyndŵr lived comfortably and peacefully on his estates until then, and through the descriptions of his bard, Iolo Goch, we see him basking in the luxuries of a Wales which, by his own idealism, he was to help destroy. Circumstances which in themselves seemed slight, being no more than a quarrel with his neighbour over some land, led to his being denounced as a traitor. The neighbour was the powerful Marcher Lord, Lord Grey of Ruthin, who happened to be a favourite at Court. When, through a trick of Grey's, Glyndŵr was more or less outlawed, he was at once proclaimed by his supporters as Prince of Wales. It all happened within a short space of time, in the year 1400, when he was already about 41.

The country was ready for something to happen. English domination since Edward I's conquest had not been harsh, but there were signs that under Henry it would be harsher. In the meantime the bards had kept alive a spirit of patriotism, which possibly had been assisted by sympathy for the deposed king, Richard II, and suspicion of the usurper. All they lacked now was a leader, and Owain, a descendant of princes, was a man to appeal to them. He raised the standard of the dragon, symbolic to the Welsh of their revival as a nation – an imagery stemming from the legend popularized by Geoffrey of Monmouth two and a half centuries before: that the red dragon, the native dragon, though it seemed for the time being to be losing, would one day recover, and drive out the dragon of the Saxon invaders.

But Owain was not to be the prince they had so long been hoping for, prophesized by the bards. In fact they were to have to wait a little longer, until the day when Henry Tudor raised the standard of the red dragon on the field of Bosworth. With hindsight, probably, a legend professes to foretell this. The Abbot of Valle Crucis was one morning walking alone in the Berwyn hills, in the mists of daybreak. Suddenly Owain Glyndŵr appeared, also alone. 'You have risen early, Father,' he said. 'No,' said the Abbot sadly, 'it is you who has risen early, by a hundred years.'

Glyndŵr started by invading and burning, on Fair Day, Lord Grey's town of Rhuthun, almost completely destroying it. From there started a long causal chain. The ravages and burnings, and reprisals, of the rebellion might, at first, have been no more than another outbreak of border trouble. The Welsh exercised their usual advantage, their ability to take to the hills. When the King at last arrived in North Wales, there was no sign of Owain or his army. Owain had mobility on his side, and in fact his appearance at places so far apart soon gave him a reputation for magic in the eyes of the bewildered English. It might still have been no more than this guerrilla skirmishing, if he had not had the vision of a fanatic – the concept of an independent Wales, with its own Church and universities, and a determination to act to bring it about –

which could hardly fail to draw popular support. For five years his successes seemed to promise that he would create in Wales his ideal vision.

For a time, he did, in effect, rule much of Wales. He established a court at Harlech, and called his own Parliament. Henry IV was in no strong position. Owain had the support of Sir Edmund Mortimer (of the House of York), and the Earl of Northumberland, and the three of them agreed to an arrangement by which Britain would be divided between them. The King of France had concluded a treaty with Owain as Prince of Wales, and sent a fleet to help him. Henry knew only too well that kings are not omnipotent, and probably remembered how he himself, Henry Bolingbroke, had come by the crown.

With an unpredictable suddenness the tide of war turned, and once turned it ebbed from Owain's glamorous successes with a rush. With typical courage he kept alive the remnants of hope in his scattered forces, but his helpers faded away; and he himself vanished. He lived for some years as an outlaw, refusing a pardon from Henry V, and no one quite knows how or where (or if) he died. All that was left was a country weaker and more bloodstained than ever, the charred homesteads and bereavements of unsuccessful rebellion, the great heroic optimism collapsed into ash.

Beyond Glyndyfrdwy the road passes through the town of Corwen, once in the heart of Glyndŵr territory, now of no great note. It was here, in 1789, that the first of the present type of national eisteddfodau was held, owing largely to the enthusiasm and persistence of a local man, Thomas Jones. The Corwen eisteddfod took place in the Owain Glyndŵr Hotel, and was a much less pretentious affair than its successors of the late eighteenth century. By 1792 a notorious promoter of Celtic revivalism, who named himself Iolo Morganwg, had contrived to add to the literary and musical competition the 'Gorsedd', the ceremonial which survives in the annual event today.

Iolo Morganwg, who did much to awaken an interest in old Welsh literature, also did much to cast doubts on its authenticity. From his library came many of the original manuscripts from which people such as Lady Charlotte Guest translated the ancient bards into good early-Victorian English. Unfortunately some of these were later found to have been 'improved' by Iolo, a competent and scholarly forger, so that much which was taken for a long period to be the genuine matter of early Welsh is now known to be an elaborate fraud.

Beyond Corwen the road begins to rise, having to climb out of one valley in order eventually to drop down into another. Around Cerrigydrudion a change in the countryside takes place. Suddenly you are aware that it has become open, wind-blown, and spacious. At some point now the mountains come into sight, their far-off presence promising or threatening, but unmistakably the ultimate goal of a journey. Spread out peak beside peak, even at this distance they are an imposing gathering of giants. These are not the Himalayas – or even the Alps, but (as closer experience of them will reliably confirm) they are as awesome, as magnificent, as serene or terrible, as any mountains even travellers more intrepid than those breasting a rise on the A5 are likely to encounter. To people returning the first sight of the mountains (banks of Atlantic cloud gigantically catching on their high summits, streaks of pale sun marking the contrasts of their flanks and the valleys which gash them) is the first assurance that they are back in Wales. To many it is what Wales means. The mass which rises now in the west is the heartland, the hard but solid backbone, accounting for much which would otherwise be unaccountable in the race which for so long has lived between them and the clouds.

George Borrow (a ghost so persistent on Telford's great Holyhead road that his opinionated voice is not drowned even by the uncouth noise of the internal combustion engine) walked the twenty miles from Llangollen to Cerrigydrudion, stopping here and there to air his Welsh on the way. And on arrival at the Inn had energy and breath enough to address the landlady in a most improbable way. Sometimes one can hardly believe him.

> 'Madam!' said I, bowing to the lady, 'as I suppose you are the mistress of this establishment, I beg leave to inform you that I am an Englishman walking through these regions in order fully to enjoy their beauties and wonders. I have this day come from Llangollen, and being somewhat hungry and fatigued hope I can be accommodated here with a dinner and a bed.'

Nor was she stuck for a reply.

> 'Sir!' said the lady getting up and making me a profound curtesy, 'I am as you suppose the mistress of this establishment, and am happy to say that I shall be able to accommodate you – pray sit down, sir.'

Modern travellers should not take this as being typical of these parts. It would be a mistake to conclude that Cerrigydrudion is a very formal place.

Beyond Cerrigydrudion and at a point near Pentrefoelas the land starts to tilt, the streams to drain down towards Afon Conwy and its valley, and another chapter.

Two

NORTH COAST

From the northern approach in the area of Flint there are fine views of England. You look out across wide tidal water, and see a green, dappled country dabbed by patches of sun; rural, light, overlooking the sea. It looks a pleasant enough place.

It is in fact the Wirral peninsula, and this water (or, if the tide is out, these acres of mud) is the River Dee *(Afon Dyfrdwy)*.

The railway follows this approach; the main roads take a more direct line. Consequently for most people Flint is a place they have been through in a train. The area around is partly industrialized, and offers no great attractions. Flint has a castle, set firmly over the town on a rock. It was built along with so many others by Edward I, but never figured prominently in his campaigns. Perhaps this part of Wales was too close to Chester to be argued over seriously.

It was at Flint Castle, however, that Bolingbroke, come from Chester, encountered Richard II, come from Conwy, a meeting which resulted in the abdication of the latter and the transformation of the former to Henry IV (Part I). It must have been an even sadder little scene than that described by Shakespeare, in *Richard II*, with the curt direction: 'Wales. Before Flint Castle.' This was perhaps Flint's only moment at the centre of the historical stage.

Rhuddlan, by contrast, was in the thick of things from the start. It had been of interest to earlier kings than Edward, having been occupied successively by the forces of Harold, William the Conqueror, Henry II and King John. It was, almost traditionally, a staging post for attacks launched into North Wales. It was perhaps inevitable that Edward would eventually find himself there; but it was by an indirect route that events led to his arrival, and the building of the present magnificent castle.

Edward was on crusade when he succeeded to the throne of England, in 1272. He returned to England in 1274, and held a belated coronation. It was the custom to demand the attendance of the King of Scotland and the Prince of Wales, to pay homage to the new king. Scotland and Wales were in the tribute-paying circumstances of less powerful kingdoms wishing to retain some independence of rule. Llywelyn ap Gruffudd (grandson of Llywelyn the Great) refused to attend the coronation. It happened that at that time a plot against his life had been uncovered, the conspirator being none other than his brother Dafydd. When found out Dafydd crossed the border, along with a fellow-plotter, the Prince of Powys. And Edward welcomed them in England. Llywelyn refused to pay the levy of three thousand marks which he had paid annually to Henry III. The animosity which had always existed between the two men thus reached its crisis.

Edward launched a well-planned and well-prepared invasion of Wales in 1276. His three-pronged attack involved an army which had cost him £23,000 to gather and equip. He himself went with the northernmost contingent from Chester. When in the summer of 1277 Edward pressed forward into north-west Wales to the extent of being able to move his headquarters from Chester to Rhuddlan, he had taken the first step towards conquest.

Gaining Rhuddlan, he fortified it strongly, building the castle which is now there. With its round towers and double entrance, it was the prototype for the later great ones, but simpler in structure. Much of it has now gone, largely owing to demolition which took place when the Parliamentarians finally won it in the Civil War. Sandstone was used in places, particularly on the outer bottom surface: and this, having now quite worn away, has given it a decayed and crumbling look.

From Rhuddlan (which was then a port) Edward was able to send ships along the coast, and his troops arrived by sea in Anglesey *(Ynys Môn)*, where the inhabitants fled to the mainland. Llywelyn was thus confined to the mountains. By

November he was short of food, and the situation began to look bleak. He gave in.

For a time there was peace. The Treaty of Aberconwy, 1277, deprived Llywelyn of rule over Wales east of Afon Conwy. The inner part of the Kingdom of Gwynedd he was allowed to keep. His brother, Dafydd, who had marched with the English attack, was given overlordship of the eastern area as a reward for his support. But English officials and English inhabitants of the borough of Rhuddlan remained. Unfortunately they behaved badly.

> *When anie cometh to Rhutlan with merchandise, if he refuse whatsoever anie Englishman offereth, he is forthwith sent to castell to prison, and the buier hath the thing, and the King hath the price: then the souldiours of the castell first spoil and beate the partie, and then cause him to pay the porter, and then let him go.*

Ironically, it was Dafydd, changing sides again, who started the revolt. He called on Llywelyn to help him, and the Prince of Wales crossed Afon Conwy. For a short time in 1282 there was a revival of hope. Llywelyn besieged Rhuddlan, and the King marched hurriedly north to relieve it. But it was more than the Welsh Prince could do to fight a war on so many fronts. While trying to muster his failing forces in the south, he was killed. He was killed while riding back with a small party from a reconnaissance trip. They ran into a band of English soldiers, one of whom thrust his lance through Llywelyn without knowing at all what he had done. It was only later that the dead man was recognized, and Llywelyn's head was cut off and sent to the king. It was afterwards displayed on a spike at the Tower of London.

Dafydd succeeded as leader, forlornly, fighting a lost war. After Llywelyn's death the course of the war went against the Welsh. Their morale had died with their leader. A contemporary poet expressed their bitterness:

Little good it did me to be tricked
Into leaving my head on, with no head on him.
A head which, falling, made panic welcome;
A head which, falling, made it better to give up;
A soldier's head, a head for praise henceforth;
A leader's head, a dragon's head was on him,
Head of fair, dogged Llewelyn; it shocks the world
    That an iron stake should pierce it.

           (Gwyn Williams' translation, from his anthology
                             'The Burning Tree')

Dafydd was captured in June 1283, and the war was over. Edward and his Queen, Eleanor of Castile, now made Rhuddlan for a time their home. From there the king set about bringing order to the newly-conquered country. He planned the line of castles along the coast which would establish and retain control. Flint and Rhuddlan were to be followed by Conwy, Caernarfon, Beaumaris and Harlech. By the Statute of Rhuddlan, 1284, Wales was given a written constitution. The Principality was formally confiscated, and subjected to the Crown. The Clwyd valley *(Dyffryn Clwyd)* was granted to the Marcher Lord, Lord Grey, whose descendant was to give rise to Glyndŵr's revolt. The bulk of Wales was retained by the king.

The Statute of Rhuddlan gave the new Crown territory its laws. The English county system (introduced to England by William the Conqueror) was to form the framework of government. A Justice for North Wales was appointed, and administration and order were the responsibility of a sheriff for each county. The State was to replace the tribal system of justice. Family feuds, previously the rule, were no longer acceptable. Now all disputes had to go before the Courts. English Criminal Law was to be applied, together with the 'hue and cry' method of capture.

Edward called a Parliament at Rhuddlan to institute this legislation. A plaque marks the site, in the High Street, where his 'Parliament House' stood.

Afon Clwyd, which is tidal at Rhuddlan, flows out at Rhyl. A fun city through and through, it provides the valuable service of being all the things that more sedate resorts dread to become. They do not have to provide funfairs and hot-dog stalls, bingo and candy-floss, and various ways of losing money, at Colwyn Bay, Llandudno and Conwy. Rhyl is only half an hour away, and you can get your fill of them there. Only half an hour up the same coast, but in a different world. Can it be existing out there all the time, while everything goes on so quietly? Surely we should hear the rumpus of its hurdy-gurdies, the blast of its juke-boxes and the rattle of a chorus of a thousand one-armed bandits? But one returns, over the bridge and down the long promenade, and finds it as rowdy as ever, quite unexhausted.

For once it would be inaccurate to say that there is nothing like it. Great Yarmouth is very like it. Blackpool is the same thing only bigger. One stumbles across them in various places in various parts of the world, landing with a bit of a shock among the endless glaring lights, the big wheel turning high above you, the sirens of the swings and roundabouts, pop music jangling, every corner of auditory space packed full of hubbub, every patch of darkness flashing with lights. If it is not everybody's idea of fun, it is clearly that of many. Jammed tight in the soggy bars they squeeze their way to a drink, the sweating barman passing pint mugs out over a sea of shoulders. They queue endlessly at the chip-shops, though there are chip-shops everywhere. They stagger in large groups to the fair, where many acres of elaborate machines whirl them round and round, up and down, in and out, the body crushed and stretched by suddenly changing or increasing gravitational fields, the extremes of physical movement themselves becoming drug which acts on the mind. Rhyl spins, side to side or upside down, in a blur of coloured light; faces flash recognizably past for a micro-second; one is aware of the boy who collects the money standing calm, unshaken and balanced in the middle of the chaotic world. The physical world has gone out of order, and is dissolving and flowing like liquid. One's centre of consciousness no longer relies on it. The disordered sensations which it receives can no longer be counted as evidence through the senses. It seems to last for ever, but then slowly begins to release its hold. The lights come on, people appear again, distinguishable against the darkness; the world reassembles itself in time for you to step shakily out into it. It rocks unsteadily, as though about to tilt and drop you. If not drunk already you would walk as if drunk. But if not drunk already you probably wouldn't be there.

It would be rash indeed to be too scornful of people's ability to play. The world is drab enough during the week and the long working year. Certainly no one would benefit if the whole coast were a line of Rhyls; in any case it would lose much of its point that way, its vital quality of intensity. One hears it spoken of in the tone reserved for other people's pleasures – that of self-righteous disapproval. But the world would be a poorer place without the chip-shops and the beer.

Afon Clwyd which flows out into the sea at Rhyl is an amalgamation of two rivers, Afon Clwyd which provides the luxuriant farming valley of the Rhuthun and Denbigh *(Dinbych)* area, and Afon Elwy, which comes from the northern Denbighshire uplands. They flow either side of the hill on which St Asaph stands, a few miles inland, where the main road from Chester crosses them. St Asaph is, in fact, called Llanelwy in Welsh.

It would be easy to overlook the fact that St Asaph is a cathedral city. A small, old country town on a hill. The church, not apparently much bigger than most, is squat and sturdy. But it has been a diocesan cathedral since the system reached Wales after the Norman conquest. It had been a bishop's see, however, since the sixth century.

Strangely it was not founded by St Asaph. A bishop called Kentigern came from Strathclyde and built a church there in AD 560. He went back to Strathclyde later, and Asaph was his successor. It was, of course, in a vulnerable position, and was destroyed with pitiless regularity. Giraldus, who visited it in

1189, called it 'the poor temple of Llanelwy'. It seems that every time anyone invaded North Wales they paused on their way to burn down St Asaph cathedral. Edward I's attempt to have the seat of the diocese moved to his town of Rhuddlan failed, although it was supported by the Bishop and canons on the grounds that its present side was so exposed to marauders that they hardly dare go near it.

Some of the Bishops of St Asaph have been prominent, both in local and national history. Geoffrey of Monmouth, whose great work *Historia Regum Britanniae* still provides, if not information, at least amusement, was ordained Bishop of St Asaph at Westminster in 1152. North Wales was at war at the time, and it is doubtful that he ever actually went to his see. It was a bishop called John Trefor, in the late fourteenth century, who warned King Henry IV of the danger which could result from Glyndŵr's quarrel with Lord Grey. Shortly afterwards Glyndŵr added his name to the list of those who burnt down St Asaph cathedral. Trefor's successor, early in the fifteenth century, carried out much of the restoration which was to bring the long-suffering building to its present general form. The beautiful and brilliant oak stalls in the chancel date from the end of that century, while the clerestory windows in the nave belong to the beginning of it.

The tall memorial in the churchyard commemorates an event with which St Asaph's connection is tenuous. The translation of the Bible into Welsh was instigated by William Salusbury, from Llansannan, the neighbouring parish, in the 1550s. It was completed by William Morgan, from Penmachno, whose complete Bible appeared in 1588. Morgan became Bishop of St Asaph in 1601. His work is the rock on which the present Welsh language is so strongly built. It marks the appearance of a cohesive standard language, Modern Welsh.

As if a thousand years of destruction and desecration had not been enough, our incredible ancestors unleashed Gilbert Scott on the cathedral in 1869. To this last onslaught we owe the removal of the stucco ceiling in the nave and aisles, the loss of

43

the rood screen, the splitting up of the great east window, now distributed through various parts of the church and replaced by a new one, and the general restoration of much of the historical building to what the confident Victorians thought was its original state.

Perhaps we should not quibble. It is still lovely, grey and evocative, particularly in the gentle autumn light.

The road and the rail converge towards Abergele, the one running still along the shore, the other through rolling, wooded country which begins to look more and more like Wales. The seaside, however, along this coast, is bleak. On the one hand the waves stretch even and featureless, mile after mile. On the other hand stretches a sea of caravans.

There is little one can say in excuse of the holiday slumland which is all too visible to people arriving in North Wales by train. In Conwy and Llandudno and Colwyn Bay they are thankful that Prestatyn, Rhyl and Abergele exist, but this is only to say that they wouldn't want them any closer. It must originally have been somebody's idea of what people wanted. They could hardly otherwise have expected to see such ugliness and monotony. We can see now that it was neither necessary nor desirable to fill acres and acres of clearly visible land with caravans packed door to door. The doubtful general economic usefulness and plain aesthetic distastefulness of these supposedly mobile yellow tin boxes has not become apparent to everyone. The best one can say is that it would not happen now. Nor, presumably, was it anybody's intention that it should take the overwhelmingly ugly form it did. It was an accident of progress, a sort of historical trend which was not checked in time. Efforts have been made to do something about it, but once the things are there it is hard either to remove or resite so many, and at the same time to provide an acceptable alternative in the form of cheap accommodation which will benefit the area without destroying it visually.

Whatever it may look from the train, Abergele is a small market town, which has little to do with the holiday camps and

44

shanty towns of the coast. Its weekly agricultural market is now closed, but once was the focus of the lives of many of the farmers of the Clwyd and the Conwy valleys. They used to gather here whether or not they had anything to sell or intended to buy anything, to exchange the thing which no farmer ever likes to be without: news. One wonders sometimes how it is that an item of information in North Wales has a velocity of circulation apparently exceeding the speed of light – so that something you were just about to do has been round and come back to you again before you have done it; and one knows who said what about whom, even if they do not yet know themselves. It is because people from all parts of the country meet each other every week at farm markets and, while waiting to see what the price of stores will be, have nothing better to do.

Visitors are often surprised to see, sprawling along the hill above the Abergele by-pass, the towers and battlements and lookout turrets, walls and wall-walks, of an enormous, ancient baronial castle. Gwrych Castle. It was built in 1815 by a Mr Hesketh.

There are some figures whom one encounters, it seems, wherever one moves, in this much-trampled area of North Wales. Here, on the otherwise unromantic road towards Colwyn Bay, that desperate pair Richard II and Henry Bolingbroke occur again. On this westerly journey their story is being told backwards. In Glyndŵr's country we saw Henry as king, Richard as a sad memory in the Welsh mind. At Flint took place their change or roles. Here, at the top of the hill, as the road turns and one looks down suddenly on Colwyn Bay, Bolingbroke's men took the crucial step of ambushing the unsuspecting king, travelling east at the time with the treacherous Earl of Northumberland. And at Conwy we shall meet them again and find out how it happened.

The writer who recorded this, among other events, on plaques near one of the entrances of Gwrych Castle, said that Richard was ambushed by 'a military band'. The image of the surprised king being suddenly surrounded by trombones and tubas – 'No more! I surrender!' – has, for me, thrown an altogether different light on the whole affair.

Perhaps Colwyn Bay's best feature is that great sweep of bay, the view which opens for a moment before one goes down into the town. The promontory of Rhos, the background of the Little Orme; and the sea. 'In conjunction with its enterprising neighbour, Rhos-on-Sea,' a guidebook claimed in 1909, 'it forms, as it were, the entrance-gate to the Paradise of North Wales.' All gates are meant to be passed through, and that into Paradise presumably faster than most.

The town came into existence after the 1860s. It was built quickly and perhaps without sufficient care during the last few decades of the century. Not very much of it now is earlier than the 1890s, and what there is of that is not magnificent. Subsequent building has done little to improve its appearance. Moreover, as a town, it falls awkwardly between a number of stools. It was never really the ideal seaside resort. Rhos-on-Sea, a suburb which retains to a large extent a separate identity, almost achieves this, being on a spit of land with a beach close to the town. Colwyn Bay is on the slope of a steep hill, and the railway separates the town from the sea. There is a thriving industrial suburb, and it seems likely that the future of the town is as an administrative and commercial centre.

Inevitably there is rivalry between such close neighbours. Llandudno aggravates this by smugly having everything that Colwyn Bay lacks. It is flat, being set between two beaches on the isthmus which joins the Great Orme to the land, and bounded on the other side by the same type of headland in miniature, the Little Orme. It is planned as a harmonious and coherent whole, architecturally consistent and dating largely from the 1850s. It has a long, sweeping façade facing directly on the promenade, a mile and a half long, and the bay. It is a comfortable distance from any through-road, and on a branch line which arrives discreetly from behind.

Before the nineteenth century this was a spit of shingle and sand. St Tudno (whose *llan* it is) founded his small settlement in the sixth century; but he did so some distance from where the town of Llandudno now is. The church which he built was probably mud and wattle, and has gone. It was high up on the Orme, where the present parish church of St Tudno still stands. This has some medieval portions (the west end of the north wall) but the bulk of it was built during the fifteenth century and around 1500.

The Orme *(Penygogarth)*, is a wild and open, untamed hill now, and it must have been wilder then. It is an anomaly in the area, a long bare outcrop of carboniferous limestone, which has withstood the battering of the weather. Perhaps because of its unclad nature (when the world was all one dangerous forest); or perhaps because it was accessible from the sea; or perhaps, again, because the stratified nature of the rock has made it terraced, convenient to live on; for one reason or another it was a favoured spot in prehistory, when no doubt exposure to the wind and rain mattered less. St Tudno and his followers were by no means the first residents. The earliest probably lived in the round huts near the Marine Drive, at the very end of the headland. Above St Tudno's church is a group of three long huts. Oldest of all is the cromlech, a burial-chamber a little way below the summit. But it is in poor condition, and there are better examples in other parts of North Wales and of this book. The remains of an Iron Age hillfort can be found on the scrub-covered hill, the cliffs of which fall to the Happy Valley gardens. Signs of cultivation, whether in Tudno's time or before or after, can clearly be seen on the slopes above his church.

Llandudno was originally a mining town. The Romans probably discovered the rich veins of copper there, and Roman coins of the third and fourth centuries AD have been found near the mines. In fact recent work by the Great Orme Exploration Society has revealed prehistoric mining dating back to 1,800 BC, which has revolutionised our knowledge of The Bronze Age, placing its start nearly a thousand years earlier than previously thought. The Great Orme Mines now, with several miles of tunnel, form one of the largest and oldest pre-historic mine-working in the world.

Copper mines were still flourishing on the Orme in the 1830s and the town of Llandudno then, a small cluster of terraces, was high up in the cleft of the hill in the neighbourhood of the route of the Orme tramway. Copper mining stopped in the 1860s, partly because sea-water had somehow managed to penetrate the shafts, but largely, one suspects, because by then there was a new industry: people.

The fortunes of the Mostyn family and of Llandudno are interdependent. Neither of them would have done so well without the other. It was originally common land, but was acquired by the Mostyns in 1843 by an enclosure order. The timing was perfect. The railway mania of the 1840s helped to bring about the habit of going to watering-places, which caught on quickly. But the Mostyns by no means plunged hurriedly into this new business, to emerge with what they could. The town was planned, with no attempt to save space, and even with provision for future growth. The plots were offered for lease in 1849, subject to strict conditions. A branch-line collaborated shortly afterwards, and within ten years Llandudno had started its role as a fashionable resort.

There is still plenty of room, still a feeling of space, still a good deal of the harmony and elegance which were built in to the original plans. It still has Mostyn Estates presiding over it. Its popularity has scarcely wavered, though it could hardly now be described as 'fashionable', and the world of parasols and trailing skirts and bathing-machines has gone. The beach is as packed with people on a fine day in the summer (and there are usually one or two) as any beach could be, though it has recently been sadly obstructed by the importation of stone to provide sea defences. Even on these acres and acres of sand there is no room for one person more: and when the tide comes in they are gradually compressed backwards, to end up sitting elbow to elbow on the steps of the promenade. There are still seaside shows, a town band, donkeys, sand-castle competitions, even a Punch and Judy box. Mallorca and the Costa Brava have a lot to compete with.

The other sea, the West Shore, though perhaps even more favoured scenically, has missed the architectural display which makes the front of the town so pleasing. It is a windier shore, catching the prevailing weather. There is no evidence that Lewis Carroll ever came to Llandudno, despite the fact that the delightful memorial by the yacht-pond asserts that it was 'on this very shore' that he was inspired to concoct the Alice books. Certainly the Liddells at one time used the large house nearby (which has since been extended and become a hotel) as a holiday home. They may or may not have brought the Reverend Charles Dodgson with them, although his letters and diaries indicate rather that they did not than that they did. Seashores occur occasionally in both the books, and it must have been some beach on which, in his imagination, the Gryphon and the Mock Turtle danced the Lobster Quadrille, and some sea on which the sun shone in the middle of the night, when the Walrus and the Carpenter, who were walking close at hand, wept like anything to see such quantities of sand. Why not imagine it to be this one? It answers the description as well as any.

> *If seven maids with seven mops*
> *Swept it for half a year,*
> *Do you suppose, the Walrus said,*
> *'That they could get it clear?'*
> *'I doubt it,' said the Carpenter,*
> *And shed a bitter tear.*

Three

DYFFRYN CONWY

Geologists say 'Before the last Ice Age' in much the way the rest of us say 'Before the last war'. And so it is hard to be precise to within a few thousand years, about just when Afon Conwy started to carve its way through a rock-fault towards the north coast. The Conwy valley *(Dyffryn Conwy)*, is not a glacial valley – although the northern glaciers certainly flowed down much of its course – and so it is thought that there was a river there before the ice, draining what was then the vast smooth dome of mountains. The glaciers deepened the valley floor, which silted eventually with riverborne alluvium to give the wide, flat, fertile bottom which it has today.

There is actually some suggestion that the river once flowed in the other direction – that is, south-east, towards Llangollen, to join the Dee *(Afon Dyfrdwy)* – since some of the tributary streams in the upper reaches have what are known as 'reversed junctions': they point upstream instead of down, as if they had been led to expect that they would be going the other way.

At the point of outflow the Conwy's course is once more controversial. An ever-popular local legend holds that 'at one time' it flowed out along the course of the little stream called Afon Ganol, to reach the sea at Penrhyn Bay. It looks so probable: the low, U-shaped valley is a straight continuation of the one that Afon Conwy runs in. The evidence put forward for this theory is rather indirect, however. It is that the salmon still try to enter the river from the north coast, at Rhos; and since this is so plainly the wrong way, it is claimed that at one time it must have been the right way. But if Afon Conwy ever ran that way it was before the Ice Age, since signs of terminal moraine have been identified at Deganwy and the Conwy Morfa, so that we know that the melting ice at any rate went in that direction. If Afon Conwy had originally flowed towards Rhos, its course might well have been impeded there by the banking up of 'Irish Sea ice' (large bulks which had broken away and flowed south from Scotland) and, unable to get out, it could well have built up backwards and broken through the other way. But the salmon can scarcely be an argument in favour of this speculation; I find it easier to believe that they are misled by the fresh water which trickles from Afon Ganol, rather than that they have a race-memory extending back to pre-glacial times, considerably more than twelve thousand years.

Afon Conwy starts its eventful journey from a shallow lake in a moor, and flows for its first stretches through a different world, and a different chapter. It is not until it reaches 'Conwy Falls' that it makes the breakthrough: turns north, having scented the sea, and begins to make its determined descent. There the Conwy valley starts.

'This,' George Borrow announces triumphantly, 'was the Dyffryn Conway, the celebrated Vale of Conway, to which in the summer-time fashionable gentry from all parts of Britain resort for shade and relaxation'. You will find them bumper to bumper on a Sunday afternoon, or peering down at you from their vast shiny, cream-coloured coaches. Fortunately they seek their shade and relaxation in one or two selected places.

First there are the beauty spots. The Falls itself, and a little lower down the Fairy Glen. Certainly the effect of the latter is spectacular, and one should obviously be grateful for the swirl of water through a deep chasm, the interplay of currents and eddies, the feeling of mass and force which the river, forced through a narrow gorge overhung with an arch of trees, conveys. But to me it is a little too blatantly pretty, too clearly assured of its incontestable position in the hierarchy of scenery.

Below the Fairy Glen the river is joined, from a valley running west, by Afon Lledr, and the new, larger river becomes calm for a moment as it flows, under the Dolwyddelan road, into a large, still, deep hollow called Beaver Pool. This misleading name is a translation of the Welsh Llyn-yr-Afanc, and although *afanc* does in fact mean 'beaver', it is also used as the name of a particular type of water-monster, considerably larger than the beaver and more troublesome. In this case it should have the latter sense, since the pool takes its name from the monster which once lived in it. It was apparently responsible at one time for the flooding which still troubles the Conwy valley farmers during the winter. (The cause is now attributed to other monsters, such as the River Authority or the Forestry Commission.) The locals eventually decided that they had had enough, and could no longer afford to support a monster in their midst. They dragged it from its home in the pool. It was taken across the mountains, pulled on an iron chain by two oxen (one of which, in its exertions, lost an eye on the western slope of Moel Siabod) and deposited in Glaslyn, a lake near the summit of Snowdon. Here, it was felt, any flooding it caused would affect valleys other than the Conwy. It does not seem to have done much damage from then on, however, and as far as is known it is still living there peacefully.

There is, though, some suggestion that the connection with beavers is not just a philological error. Dafydd ap Gwilym, in the fourteenth century, apparently saw beavers in South Wales. They still existed in parts of Wales in the time of Giraldus Cambrensis, although (a somewhat negative point) he found that they had gone from North Wales when he paid his visit in the late twelfth century. Thus it is possible that the word *afanc* has lingered in the Conwy valley rather longer than its original subject.

To the west the valleys run towards the Snowdonia mountains. To the east the bank rises regularly upwards to the uplands of Denbighshire, a maze of disorientating lanes, dotted with lost villages, leading eventually down again to the Clwyd valley (*Dyffryn Clwyd*), Denbigh (*Dinbych*), Rhuthun and St Asaph. Without venturing too far into this hinterland, one can loop right from the main A5 road before it drops towards the Conwy Falls, to pass through Capel Garmon. It is worth the detour, since Capel Garmon has a fine example of a megalithic chamber tomb.

This lonely, exposed construction, perched on the valley's edge, is one of the few things left by one of those first waves of invaders, the Neolithic people of the third millennium BC. Sometime between 2500 and 2000 BC they reached Wales from the sea, probably arriving in small groups, and bringing with them agriculture, which was to remain the country's way of life for the next few thousand years. They were our first farmers.

Farming is still pre-eminently the local occupation in this area, and the town of Llanrwst, a little further on, is characterized by agriculture in much the way that Conwy, at the end of the valley, is characterized by fishing. Llanrwst is the market town of the Conwy valley *(Dyffryn Conwy)*. It always has been, and it is easy to believe that it always will be. It serves not only the large farming community of the valley itself, but the farming uplands all around. It often seems as if everyone there is occupied in one way or another with the farming industry. Large and sturdy with pink faces and muddy gumboots. In the pubs at night (and like all old-established towns with a strong settled community it has pubs everywhere) they sit in the corners with their caps on and talk (in Welsh) about farming.

Perhaps to understand the solid historical basis of the town one has to stop at Gwydir on the way. It is a stately Elizabethan house, close to the road on the western side of the river. Once the focus of coach-trip commercialism, Gwydir now remains open to the public in a more subdued and sedate way, conveying an air of gentle venerability. Lovingly restored to its authentic character, it has greatly benefited from the discovery of a whole room, the panelling, door, window shutters, chimney-piece, patterned leather frieze and magnificent heavy portico surround to the doorway, with ornate curling columns. The room's woodwork and trappings had been sold-off in a sale in 1921, bought and shipped to America by William Randolph Hearst, remaining unused and still in their packing-cases to be re-bought and returned to Gwydir in 1995. The building is of historic interest in itself; the gardens contain some magnificent cedars said to have been planted to commemorate the marriage of Charles I; but the real significance of it is that it was the seat of the Wynn family, who, with one or two other families to whom they became, of course, closely related, have reigned uncrowned over North Wales from the early sixteenth century to the present day.

The Wynns and their kinsmen the Mostyns (the two families intermarried so frequently that it is sometimes difficult to tell which was which) between them occupied most of the great houses of North Wales until quite recently. The Wynns came from south Caernarfonshire, and moved from there in the second half of the fifteenth century because the feuds in that area became too dangerous. They moved to the Lledr valley, where they had only to deal with outlaws and brigands, and settled the empty country around Dolwyddelan and Penmachno. From there they moved down to the comparative civilization of the Gwydir estate. The most notable of them, Sir John (1553-1627), wrote the family's history. One after the other they held the posts of Deputy-Lieutenants, Sheriffs, Justices of the Peace, Members of Parliament, even the Archdeacons of Bangor. During the seventeenth century they became prominent at the Court in London, and one baronet, Sir Richard, was made Groom of the Bedchamber, and subsequently Treasurer to the Queen's Household. It was not insignificant that the marriage of Charles was celebrated by the planting of a tree at Gwydir: it was Sir Richard, then the Wynn heir, who went with Prince Charles and the Duke of Buckingham to Spain, to woo Princess Henrietta Maria, the future Queen. News of this affair came to Gwydir every few days of April and May, 1623, from various Wynns in the city. 'The marriage with Spain goes forward'. Sir Richard had arrived safely, and was staying 'with other of the Prince's servants at a town called Burgus, within two days' journey of Madrid'. Finally he is returned, reports his brother, 'and says he will travel no more to Spain, for there is such plenty of victuals there that it breeds a loathing, so that both Sir Richard and his man look as lean as "shotten-herrings".' Evidently Spanish cooking did not agree with them. Sir Richard was glad to be home. 'Castile and Aragon together are not worth one of the worst counties in Wales.'

The Wynns survived the Civil War, and emerged again in true form at the Restoration. Letters continue to come to Gwydir from the great world. In 1665: 'The plague is in all towns and villages near London. Last week's bill of mortality was 8,252, and there is now no shutting off of infected houses.' And in 1666: 'It began Sunday morning last near London Bridge. The wind was easterly and very strong . . . Two-thirds of the city and suburbs lie buried in ashes.'

It was Sir Richard who built, in 1636, the little hump-backed bridge over the Conwy. Its sides rise so steeply that a vehicle coming up one side would be unable to see a vehicle coming up from the other. For this reason it became, over the years, a local pastime, for those who happened to have nothing better to do, to stand on the top and make warning signals, like an amused set of traffic-lights. In spite of (perhaps because of) its modern impracticality, the old bridge is very nice to look at. Legend says, and refuses to be silenced, that it was designed by Inigo Jones. There is no evidence for this, and equally none against it. Certainly the Queen's Treasurer and the great architect would have known each other. Inigo Jones did some work for Henrietta Maria at Greenwich. It is suggested, moreover, that Inigo's father was a native of the area; but precise information about this family seems to be scarce.

Also attributed to Inigo Jones, and with even more apparent probability, is the small and charming chapel stuck incongruously on the side of the old Parish Church. Incongruously, because the church is solid and simple, whereas the little chapel is decorated and pretty. It was built, again by Sir Richard, in 1634, and is a treasure-house of masterpieces. Possibly Inigo Jones did sketches for Sir Richard of both the bridge and the chapel; certainly they are both delightful architecturally, and in their setting, peacefully by the fast-flowing river, have an air of aptness and taste about them. But the hand of the master is perhaps irrelevant to the contents of the chapel.

There are fine engraved brass portraits of members of the Wynn family (one of them being the Great Sir John) on the wall; a beautifully carved wooden screen; a monument of some rather Gothic splendour, skull and crossbones and other symbols of life, time, war and death; a wooden rail with heads carved in a strangely primitive, un-European style; a vast slab over the tomb of the sons of John Wynn, bearing the mysterious, ominous words 'FUNUS, FUMUS, FUIMUS, ECCE'. By the door is the bottom part of a large stone coffin. It was the coffin of Llywelyn the Great, and was brought to Llanrwst from the Abbey of Aberconwy (which the Prince founded, and where he was buried in 1240) when the monasteries were dissolved. Near the coffin is a stone effigy of a knight in fourteenth-century armour, a tall and magnificent man, a lion lying like a pet at his feet. It is Hywel Goch, natural son of Dafydd, Prince of Wales, who fought at the battle of Poitiers. It was from his family that the Wynns acquired the Gwydir estate.

Across the valley from Llanrwst, under the western slope, is the village of Trefriw. It was a spa when spas were what people wanted, and occupations such as gathering in the Pump-room and taking the waters held some special place in the social drama. It was, and is, a centre of the woollen business, and judging by the solidity of the mill, enlarged during the 1960s, it is expected to remain so.

According to Leland, Llywelyn the Great had a residence at Trefriw. Certainly Llywelyn is closely associated with the area, and it is claimed that he built the Trefriw parish church. It is now greatly restored, and none of the present building is earlier than the fifteenth century. If the tradition is true, the structure which Llywelyn founded has disappeared.

Before the church in the village was built, Llywelyn and his wife Joan (the daughter of King John) used, legend says, to walk up to the old church of Llanrhychwyn to worship. He had the lower church built to save his wife the walk.

The little church of Llanrhychwyn is in a different world. It is in Llywelyn's world, the world of medieval ideals, the world of such pure and unambiguous concepts as God and man, peasant and nobility, church and state. You come to it out of the wooded, tamed valley, suddenly emerging in hill country, open horizons, and enormous sky; a plateau of exposed marginal farmland opens out around, to the ridges of foothills in the distance, beyond which are the mountains. Stunted clumps of indigenous birch, oak and hazel dot the landscape, emphasizing rather than masking its width, size and exposure. Earth and sky is the dichotomy, and we crawl insignificantly between, bent through having to walk in this small space between the high land and the low sky.

The little church sits solidly in the fields, ancient yew trees protectively smothering it, themselves appropriately traditional symbols of timelessness. It is small and squat under its wide roof, so low that you have to stoop to go in. The part of the present structure around the doorway, and the wall immediately on the left as one enters, is of medieval date. The remainder of this half of the church is from the fifteenth century (with one or two eighteenth-century repairs), and the north aisle was added in the sixteenth. The font (a rough, square, tapering sandstone bowl) is very ancient, probably twelfth century.

Above Trefriw, beyond Llanrhychwyn, are the lakes. The choice between Crafnant and Geirionnydd is rather like that between claret and burgundy, Mozart and Beethoven, and so on. Crafnant is prettier, gentler, well-proportioned in its theatrical setting of skyline and slope. Geirionnydd is nobler, more imposing, more the image of a mountain lake. Both are approached by lanes which run through the quick succession of types of scenery which is the special advantage of North Wales.

Suddenly you are in forest land, and look for the bears. Then, gripped between high hedges, a domesticated summer country of trees and streams. A hanging valley opens out, stretching into the immense distance with nothing in it but an isolated farm. The lake appears suddenly, probably in its favourite pose: the infallible mirror-trick, which never fails to raise an 'Ah'. The trees, slopes, crags and mountains stand precariously on their heads, every detail of them, every leaf and stone, inverting the natural world so that we can see it with a new perception.

The sixth-century poet Taliesin (whose appearance at the court of Maelgwn, King of Gwynedd, is a story which concerns Deganwy, on the estuary) is said (by legend again) to have lived for a time on the shores of Geirionnydd. And a stone monument at the end of the lake commemorates him.

When Llywelyn lived at Trefriw, the Abbey of Aberconwy was still at the mouth of the river. Forty-three years after his death, it became incompatible with the garrison town which Edward I was building there, and the king moved the Cistercians to Maenan, in the valley. He did it in the least high-handed way imaginable, going through the proper channels. A bull from the Pope, 'on the part of our dearest son in Christ, Edward,' explained to the monks, 'that your Monastery for many reasonable causes could not remain conveniently in the place where it then was'; and the king took care to renew all the rights which Llywelyn had given in his original charter. The fortunate monks at Maenan were not only to be free from every tax one could think of: 'scot and geld . . . hidage, carucage, danegeld, hornegeld, and scutages, tallages, lastages, stallages,' etc., etc., but were also entitled to collect 'sok and sak, tol and team, infangenetheof and outfangenetheof, namesok, gridbruigh, Bolwyk, ffythwyth, fferewyth, hengith, leirwyth, . . . hordel, and horest, within time and without time, and in all places, and with all causes which are and can be'.

There is nothing to be seen now of the old abbey, which was well and truly dissolved. The present building bearing the name was built in 1848.

A little below Maenan is the point at which the Romans crossed the Afon Conwy, building at Caerhun, on the western side, a fort to guard the ford. There is little to be seen of this now, only a few remnants of wall among the tree roots, and the outline of foundations in the form of mounds and banks under the grass. One can see from a few stones lying about that they imported Cheshire sandstone to build it. In spite of its virtual disappearance, it was obviously a large and substantial fort, and possibly the explanation for its size is the value of the Conwy pearl industry. Suetonius records that Julius Caesar was impressed by the size of British pearls.

The Conwy pearl fishery, which is no longer practised, was a fresh-water industry; taking place mainly above Trefriw. Sir Richard Wynn (a later one than the bridge-builder) presented a Conwy pearl to the Queen of Charles II, which is thought to be still among the crown jewels. It was Camden who made the association between the pearl fishery here and the Romans, but there is no evidence that it was this which increased their interest in Conwy. We do know, however, that the pearl industry was still flourishing in the early nineteenth century.

The pearls grow in the large 'horse-mussels', which according to some reports may still be found in the river in the Trefriw area.

In post-Roman times the river was crossed by ferry, lower down at Tal-y-cafn. From at least as early as 1301 until the bridge there was opened, in 1897, a ferry operated at this spot. Travellers wanting to avoid the hazards of the coast road would cross here and take the route of the Roman road through a pass across the mountains. It was a safer crossing than at Conwy, and although it involved a rather steep ascent, it seems that the route was used by many until the opening of Conwy bridge.

It is probable, in fact, that even when the legionaries first came, they found a road already there. When, in AD 61, the soldiers, mercenaries and cavalry commanded by Suetonius Paulinus crossed the hills west of the Conwy, they were hardly moving into undiscovered country. It had been inhabited for

59

centuries. In places the Roman road runs within yards of hut settlements, burial chambers, and compounds, and in its first section up the slopes from the river it is overlooked by the impressive hill-fort of Pen-y-gaer.

This Iron Age stronghold must have been of considerable importance. It consists of two concentric ramparts (heavier on the side of least slope, and absent, because not needed, on the steep side), one of stone and one of earth, possibly representing two periods of occupation: a new invader, for instance, refortifying the hilltop they had conquered. Within the large circle enclosed by the ramparts are, here and there, the signs of hut circles. There was certainly room for a lot of people to live here safely, looking out, from up in the sky, on the whole country around. From the steeper edge the view is almost that of an aerial photograph, the Conwy valley, patchwork fields and woodland, spread out for inspection.

The thing of most significance about Pen-y-gaer is its *chevaux de frise*, an area of slender upright stones spread out on the western slope to block approach from the ridge. Although far less spectacular than the ones with which the great forts of the Aran Isles are surrounded, the existence of this primitive equivalent of a tank trap makes Pen-y-gaer unique in Wales and England.

The Roman road actually rises from the valley, within this wonderful view, a mile to the north, in the vicinity of the village of Rowen. It passes along the contour of the long, amorphous mountain called Tal-y-fan, passing close to a burial chamber known as Maen y Bardd. This, which is of the same period as the one at Capel Garmon, is of simpler form, being a single cell, a number of large stones set on edge with a massive capstone over the top. It stands impressively, defiantly, on the rocky slope, unmarked, unattended, untampered-with. With its lofty position, its isolation, and its broad view of the valley, it is quite my favourite burial chamber.

The road follows the slope round the mountain, and enters the pass. Today the pylon lines from the nuclear power stations take the same route, dwarfing everything. They even dwarf the massive prehistoric stones which stand beside the road – marking, one speculates, the line of the ancient trackway. The two largest of these stones give the pass its name: Bwlch y Ddeufaen, the pass of the two stones. Here the route of the Roman road is still clear, running through what is now empty moorland. Scrape away a little of the turf, and you can see the jig-saw of small flat paving-stones underneath.

The traditional explanation for the presence of the two upright stones, and of a large heap of smaller stones nearby, suggests that the route across the hills to Anglesey *(Ynys Môn)*, was in use even before the time of the ancient Britons, in the days when the island of Britain was inhabited by giants. A giant and a giantess were on their way across the hills, intending to build a house for themselves in Anglesey *(Ynys Môn)*. He was carrying, for the purpose, the two huge slabs; she had her apron full of smaller boulders. They met a man who misinformed them about the distance to their destination, and, disheartened by the news, they threw down their burdens. There they still stand, as they were thrown.

The road across the mountains continued to be used; a ruin with trees growing in it on the slopes of Pen-y-gaer is still marked on the map as 'The White Hart'. Apparently enough people came this way to Anglesey *(Ynys Môn)*, to justify the existence of a travellers' inn. An anonymous writer in 1770 reported that 'Such as travel from Chester to Holyhead, sometimes go by a place called Bwlch-y-ddau-fain, therby avoiding Conwy and Penmaenmawr.' As late as 1813, Richard Fenton wrote in his *Tours in Wales* that, having failed to cross the Conwy Ferry, he was obliged 'to go all round to Tal-y-Cafn; and then, through a most tempestuous night over Bwlch-y-Ddwyfaen to Aber.'

This alternative route had already been officially recognized when, in 1777, the Caernarvon Turnpike Trust obtained an act providing for the construction of a road from Aber over Bwlch y Ddeufaen to Tal-y-cafn. Communications in North Wales would have been radically different if this scheme had been carried through, but for some reason the funds never appeared. Even then, when the first of the Parliamentary Committees sat to consider the problem of the route to Anglesey *(Ynys Môn)*, in 1810, the Bwlch y Ddeufaen and Tal-y-cafn route was one which it considered. A select committee in 1815 expressed its opinion that the coastal route was utterly unsuitable for the mail coach traffic. But in the meantime, in 1811, Telford had submitted a design for Conwy Bridge. The various committees then spent ten years making up their minds, and eventually in 1821 the bridge was approved.

Below Tal-y-cafn the valley widens quickly, the river becoming more and more an estuary. On the slope at the curve of the river, but set back in a private valley of their own, are Bodnant Gardens, a horticultural Mecca, laid out in 1875 and now probably in their prime. It is almost too much: the giant cedars, the stately terraces, the tropical growth everywhere, magnolias the size of trees, engulfing camellia walks, the air choked with the smell of azaleas, the vast extent of it all, pitching you down the slope with your senses overburdened with stimuli. At holidaytime to all this is added the feeling of being part of the largest coach-party in the world.

When, beyond Bodnant, the valley opens out, the coastal plain is in sight, industrialized, residential, thoroughly settled. Glan Conwy, a roadside, riverside village, was, until Telford's fateful causeway changed the flow of the river, a flourishing small port. Vessels of more than forty tons met the carters from the valley and the uplands bringing agricultural produce and wood for shipment to Liverpool, Lancaster and Chester. Only the presence of two old pubs and, on the river side of the road, the last remaining of the large warehouses, testify to the solidity of its past. The future approaches from the other direction. Glan Conwy is a frontier post between the rural valley and the urban coast. Beyond this point it is the twenty-first century, and we are in Western Europe.

Four

ABER CONWY

The future will win, of course. The past is troublesome in taking so long to die. It will win surely and inevitably; why should we try to stop it? It will not be us under the sulphur-coated sky. It will be those to whom it belongs. Who, never having known of the alternative, will not regret its not having taken place. What is the thought like: that by the year whatever-it-is, with the growth rate at its present level, the whole world will look like Llandudno-Junction?

Well, Llandudno-Junction is not so bad. A cheerful, friendly, populated place. It has two chip-shops and pubs, shops and services, a car-wash, a café. And above all its industrial estates provide employment, which is money. Not just for the ones with the wage-packets, but, filtering through the network of shops and garages and betting-shops and bard, multiplying itself as it spreads and spreads, money for the whole of north-west Wales. And the only expense to the community is the intrusion of Llandudno-Junction into the view.

Moreover it is a place which is easy to escape. The RSPB's bird sanctuary and nature reserve lies right alongside. Such urbanisation would be different if, coming to the end of the street, one did not look out suddenly on to the high tide and the opposite wooded bank and the long, spacious stretch of the mountains: but on to another Llandudno-Junction, and beyond that another one . . . The question is too big: it is the quality of life question; it is that of evaluating between the supposedly greater pleasures of the few, and the lesser pleasures of the many.

Llandudno-Junction is one of the three parts of the Community Council area of Conwy. The other two stand opposite to each other at the mouth of the river. Deganwy on the eastern side, and Conwy across the water. Their physical location is a good image of the opposition of viewpoints which they tend to represent. They have only the river in common.

Few rivers of its size have given so much trouble. The crossing of the Conwy is still a point which arouses dispute, and has been, presumably, since Ostorius and the tenth legion were encamped at Caerhun, and probably long before.

It formed the barrier, through the Middle Ages, between the low-lying area between there and the Dee *(Afon Dyfrdwy)* (accessible to the English), and the inner sanctuary of the mountains of Snowdonia *(Eryri)*. Afon Conwy was the limiting point of the raids and counter-raids which swept across the Marches. Mutual irritation reached its flashpoint in the time of Llywelyn the Great, whose success in plundering the lands of the Earl of Chester attracted the attention of London; and in 1211 the king brought a large army into North Wales. They reached the river Conwy without much difficulty, but there they came to a halt; and for some months King John looked across it from the hill at Deganwy, until his starving troops were reduced to eating their horses, and he was forced to turn back to England.

The first large-scale invasion of Wales, by John's son Henry III, also reached the castle on the hill above Deganwy. Henry found himself marooned there in 1245, his army underclad and suffering from the cold. One of his men wrote, in a letter home from Deganwy: 'This arm of the sea lies between us and Snowdon, where the Welsh quarter themselves, and is, at high tide, about a crossbow-shot wide.' This small frontier proved too much for them. The Welsh defended the other bank with the fierceness of people with their backs to the wall, and some months later the invaders retreated hastily, without waiting to bury their dead.

Henry gave Deganwy Castle, among other possessions, to his son, and in 1256 the young Prince came to visit it. It was then that the future Edward I looked across the Conwy for the first time, and perhaps conceived the crucial ambition to cross and plant a fortress on the further shore. King Henry came to Deganwy for the second and last time in 1258, and again retreated from there with difficulty. By 1263 Llywelyn ap Gruffudd reached the conclusion that the castle at Deganwy was so useful to the English that it had become a danger to the Welsh. He entirely demolished it in that year. When Edward came again, as king, he left the ruins at Deganwy unrepaired. With that decision began the English invasion of Wales west of Afon Conwy.

Because of this there is little to see now of what once was Deganwy Castle, crowning the round hill which looks down over the narrows where the river Conwy meets the sea. For this reason, perhaps, it is easy to overlook the fact that the settlement at Deganwy was older, when the fortified town of Conwy was first built, than Conwy is today.

Deganwy now is a small and pleasant Victorian seaside town, set on the mouth of the river and facing the mountains, Conwy Bay, Anglesey *(Ynys Môn)* and the sunset. Its role is yachting. A curve of the shoreline gives a pool for the moorings of Conwy-One-Designs. Any fine weekend in its long season the foreshore is all oilskins and outboard motors, marine activity of every grade making the water as fully used as the land ever is. The tide churns in or out through the narrows with frightening force, and boats struggle out or in against it. On fine days of swollen new-moon tides craft sit perched on the brimming river. At low water an endless beach stretches away out to the mussel beds, the sea out of sight over the wet sand.

The entrance to the Conwy river from the sea is, even in a part of the world so profuse with scenery, something which never loses its impact. It is the tilt of the slope on which Deganwy is set, the Vardre, a round, prominent hill, rising out of the wooded slope. The view of the Vardre is perhaps only rivalled by the view from it.

From on top one looks down at the river, the tree-covered headland of Bodlondeb on the opposite bank sheltering Conwy harbour, and out along the coast, the mountains sloping sheer to the sea. And north to Llandudno with the Great Orme rising over it. And past Conwy to the entrance to the valley, where the sheet of water turns to disappear into a cleft between the high land of the eastern side and the steep western bank.

A few fragments of medieval walling on this hill scarcely give an idea of what it has been. Excavations on the summit in the early 1960s revealed successive ages of habitation, including Roman coins of the third and fourth centuries. A dry-stone wall was discovered, which, it was thought, might even be as early as the second century. Pieces of Mediterranean amphorae from the fifth or six centuries indicated the existence of a prosperous court on the hill during the Dark Ages.

These are the archaeological facts, and what little we know of the history of that long and obscure period helps to explain them.

The arrival of invading Saxons was not the only result of the Roman withdrawal. For the Brythonic Celts of the fourth century an equally serious threat came from the people of the same race on the other side of the Irish Sea. Towards the end of that century the Irish raids on western Wales had become so intense that their inroads extended as far as Chester. Tradition, supported by the ninth-century historian Nennius, associates their final expulsion from Wales with the arrival of Cunedda and his sons, which must have taken place towards the turn of the fourth and fifth centuries. This colonization by the northern tribe – which is what it amounts to – presumably in answer to a plea for help, is of great importance to the course of Welsh history. From Cunedda are descended many of the royal lines of Britain.

That it was on the hill above Deganwy that Cunedda built his castle – and that some of the fourth or fifth-century finds there may be attributable to him – cannot be proved. We may only say that this would be a likely place, considering his purpose: to defend the coast of Wales against the Irish. It was certainly here, at any rate, that his great-grandson, Maelgwn, ruled in such splendour. The luxurious court indicated by the sixth-century finds was presumably Maelgwn's.

The private life of Maelgwyn Gwynedd, who established here what must have amounted to a palace and small town, is surprisingly well known to us. Much of it comes to us from a contemporary, a rare survival of dark-age literature, the pamphleteer Gildas, who wrote in the mid-sixth century. Because Gildas's diatribe was intended (as he admitted) as no more than a complaint about the state of the times, we cannot take its description of Maelgwn at face value. But reading Gildas one sees nevertheless a hazy outline of the real king of Gwynedd looming between the lines. An impulsive, bad-tempered, egocentric man, with many good qualities obscured by wilfulness and strength of character. 'Exceeding many in power and at the same time in malice, more liberal in giving, more excessive in sin, strong in arms, but stronger in what destroys thy soul . . . Why showest thou thyself to Him, the King of all kings, who made thee superior to almost all the kings of Britain, both in kingdom and in the form of thy stature, not better than the rest in morality, but on the contrary worse?' A picture begins to build up of an extravagant man, surrounding himself with flatterers, allowing a taste for poetry and music to degenerate into the maintenance of sycophants.

The best stories about Maelgwn come not from Gildas, nor from other authentic sources such as the *Annales Cambriae* (in which his death is recorded in 547), but from medieval and later manuscripts. It is said of him, for instance, that he held the first eisteddfod, either here on the Vardre or across the river on Conwy Mountain. On one occasion when the eisteddfod was across the river, Maelgwn, who wanted his beloved bards to out-do the musicians, removed the boats. Competitors had to swim across, and as a result the harpists found their strings ruined; the bards were refreshed by the dip.

Perhaps the best-known story about Maelgwn is the visit paid by his nephew, Elffin. Elffin came from the south of North Wales, and the flooding of his inheritance by the sea is the subject of Peacock's story *The Misfortunes of Elphin*. He came to visit his uncle at Deganwy at Christmas-time, somewhere around the year 540. Perhaps his big mistake was bringing with him his bard, the great Taliesin. A clash between this genuine poet and Maelgwn's hired flatterers was inevitable. It seems that Elffin was not, in any case, a very tactful person, and he took insufficient account of Maelgwn's famous temper. The result was that the nephew was confined in a cell cut out of the rock under the castle. If one turns away from the view for a moment, it is there: a large square pit cut into the hill's summit.

Taliesin, to rescue his patron, composed a riddle, in the form of a poem, still extant and rather long and obscure. This had the effect of spell-binding the bards – perhaps Taliesin had the power of hypnosis – so that they were struck dumb. All they could say, the story specifies, was 'blerwm blerwm'. According to some versions they did this by rubbing their fingers over their lips, like children. The poem which had this remarkable effect has caused scholars to say 'blerwm blerwm' at great length ever since.

To have one's voluble bards suddenly reduced to saying 'blerwm blerwm' is an unnerving experience, and Elffin was quickly released from his pit, at which the spell was duly lifted.

It was Taliesin also who foretold Maelgwn's death: a creature would come out of Morfa Rhianedd, to punish the dishonesty of Maelgwn Gwynedd. 'Its hair and its teeth and its eyes are yellow; and this makes an end of Maelgwn Gwynedd.'

The king, terrified, tried repenting. He locked himself in the little church of Llanrhos, nearby; the yellow monster would never get him there. But, unable to resist his curiosity, he looked out through the keyhole and saw it waiting. That was enough for him, and he died. According to some accounts he was buried at Llanrhos, and to others the monks from the monastery which he had reputedly founded on Puffin Island (Ynys Seiriol), off Anglesey (Ynys Môn), rowed him out and buried him there.

The yellow monster was very probably the yellow plague,

which swept Europe in the mid-sixth century. The king had presumably contracted it when he retreated to the church. It was recorded that it travelled on the wind, and to get a smell of it was enough; one fell dead without delay.

Another story relates how Maelgwn achieved his eminence among his contemporary petty kings. He held a competition on the sands of Aber Dyfi. The trick was to stay there longest when the tide came in; the one who could withstand the tide would be the High King. Maelgwn was more successful than Cnut under the same circumstance, having had a special throne made of wax and goose-quills, which floated. One imagines that there were a lot of kings that day with red faces and wet feet.

Unfortunately, for all their charm, these stories have little claim to authenticity. The best that can be said for them is that some of the material may be medieval. Their existence testifies, however, to the impact which the man made. And indeed it is hardly surprising that his image has survived so long, in view of his prominence at a turning point of British history. Had he been a different man he might have seen his opportunity, as one of the most powerful kings in Britain, to organize the revival of Celtic Britain in time to check the spread of the Saxon colonists.

In spite of his failure the dynasty which Maelgwn set up at Deganwy continued, and indeed still survives. Both the houses of York and Lancaster, and hence the English royal family and most of the royal families of Europe, may trace their descent back to Maelgwn Gwynedd. Among his earlier descendants are such well-known names in Wales as Cadwaladr, Rhodri Mawr, Hywel Dda, Gruffudd ap Cynan, and of course the two Llywelyns.

Once Edward had crossed Afon Conwy, the importance of Deganwy diminished, and that of Conwy town began. Previously there had only been Llywelyn's abbey there. Once it became a crossing-place, its destiny was fixed. It was to have people travelling through it for the next seven hundred years.

Edward built Conwy Castle and town walls in four years –

less time than it would take now, with our advanced technology and administration, to make the decision. He gave the order to start it early in 1283, and came to Conwy himself in March, staying there until May. Over the next few years it cost him £15,000. About a million and a half by present standards. A labour force of some one thousand five hundred men was drawn from all over Britain. Twenty carpenters came from Northamptonshire, and another twenty from Oxfordshire and Berkshire. One hundred and fifty men were drawn from Yorkshire, seventy from Buckinghamshire and Bedfordshire, and so on. By 1287 the work was largely finished.

One remarkable thing about this achievement is that Harlech and Caernarfon castles were being built at the same time. The man who was responsible for all this, an architect who deserves more fame than history has given him (overawed perhaps by the shadow of his master, Edward), came from France. Master James of St George, the Master of the King's Works in Wales. He took his name from a castle near Lyon, Saint-Georges d'Espéranche.

Although the sudden appearance of this fortress must have been the medieval military equivalent of the atom bomb, it was evidently not James St George's opinion that because a thing was useful there was no need for it also to be beautiful. A glance at it from Castle Square tells us this: the symmetry and proportion and satisfactory roundness of the towers. It might have worked as well without looking so lovely.

A closer look tells more. To begin with, the whole castle, when it was finished, was painted white. Traces of the white plastering or limewash can be seen on the south side, and particularly clearly on the small tower of the eastern barbican, on the road side near the suspension bridge, where the line of the whitening shows the route taken, curving round the tower, by the staircase which once rose from the water-gate.

In order, apparently, to give the building an elegance which it might, being so massive, have lacked, Master James added to the merlons of the battlements small pointed stones (known as finials), many of which still remain. Since they can have had no conceivable use, the purpose of these must have been purely the aesthetic one of giving the building an air of lightness.

By a closer inspection of its walls we can also see how the castle was built. Rows of small holes slant upwards, and twist round the towers. These are called putlog holes, and were a French style of building. They provided a ramp up which material for the current level of building could be wheeled.

Many of the lower windows are just slits, but the larger ones, higher up, were protected with iron bars: the holes in the surrounding stone are visible. Another interesting feature of the castle's defence is that even the chutes from the latrines had protecting walls. One can be seen against the tower above the present entrance.

The arrow-slits on the battlements are arranged at alternating heights, not, apparently for aesthetic reasons, but in order to give two ranges of cover: archers in the high ones covering the distance, and in the lower ones the foreground.

Being built on a rock, the castle has had to fit itself to its position. It is not in fact as regular a shape as it appears. The south side is bent to fit the rock, with the result that the Great Hall is curved. The well in the middle of the castle is sunk into the rock to over 90 feet; it is remarkable that they were able to find fresh water at all, in such a site.

Originally there were only three gates to the town. These are clearly distinct from the later ones, being flanked by sturdy round towers. The Upper Gate, in the south-west wall, the Lower Gate, opening on to the Quay, and the Mill Gate, now happily forming a pedestrian entrance to the town from the main visitor car-park. All other entrances to Conwy are later additions.

Between the Mill Gate and railway arch are a row of twelve latrines. One can see them quite distinctly jutting from the wall. It seems odd that they should have wanted twelve latrines in a row.

The castle itself is in two halves. The four eastern towers are topped by turrets, watchmen's lookout towers, and this was the half of greater security. To enter it even from within the castle, one had to pass through a second gateway. This was the part of the castle which housed the king and queen. Conwy was a royal residence as well as a military station.

Edward and Eleanor were probably in Conwy for Easter 1284, not long before their son, to become Edward II, was born at Caernarfon. When the king came again, in the winter of 1294, he had arrived hastily to put down the rebellion of Madog ap Llywelyn, and attempted to push his retaliating attack on as far as Bangor. He overlooked a Welsh force gathered on Penmaenmawr, with the result that he lost his baggage train, and had to retreat with indignity to Conwy. The strong walls turned out to be useful. He was trapped there for a bit, and spent a bitter January looking out over the river. It was in flood when he arrived, and cut off his communications. Provisions grew scarce during the January weeks. There was a cask of wine left, but, with a democratic gesture surprising in a Plantagenet, Edward refused to touch it. Instead he drank water mixed with honey. The flooded river eventually fell, the supplies of his attackers were cut off, and, according to one report, the king celebrated a late Christmas.

The original garrison of the castle consisted of thirty men: half of them bowmen, the remainder watchmen and other workmen. The town Edward aimed to fill with English burgesses, although it seems that fewer than he hoped were willing to undertake the adventure. He offered considerable incentives in the form of tax relief.

All that remains of this medieval town is the street pattern. But that to a large extent has determined the character of the present Conwy. One fine, sturdy, overhanging house on the corner of High Street and Castle Street remains, and as it dates from probably not much later than the castle it gives some idea of what the early town might have been like.

Once into history Conwy stayed there. Such a large and

secure building could hardly fail to have its uses in a nasty moments. Such was the return of Richard II from Ireland, where he had foolishly been while Bolingbroke was raising a support. His army began to dwindle when he reached Wales, and, evidently starting to panic, he tried first Conwy, then Beaumaris, then Caernarfon, then Conwy again a week later.

Bolingbroke by this time was in Chester. He sent the Earl of Northumberland to Conwy, with instructions that if he could not bring the King to Bolingbroke by peaceful means he was to bring him by force. 'Under the rough and lofty cliffs of a rock' (writes the chronicler), he concealed, as we have seen, the bulk of his men: at Penmaenrhos, east of Colwyn Bay. Coming to Conwy with only a few attendants, he was admitted to the castle.

Northumberland told Richard that Bolingbroke wanted peace. 'Duke Henry wishes for nothing but his land, and that which appertaineth to him; neither would he have anything that is yours, for you are his immediate rightful king . . . ' He offered to swear to the truth of this.

The King agreed to think about it, and Northumberland retired. When he had left the room Richard said to his advisers that he thought that all was lost, and there was nothing left to do but to agree. But whatever he agreed to now, 'if I can ever get him to my advantage, I will cause him to be foully put to death, just as he hath deserved.' It was hardly a straightforward agreement.

Northumberland was called back. Perhaps they then went together to the chapel, in the north-east tower. We read in the annals what happened next.

Masse being celebrated, the Earl of Northumberland sworne upon the hoaste that the Duke should hold all that he had told the king. The Earle haster the king forward to horse-backs, but the king prayed the Earle to goe before into Rutland [Rhuddlan], there to prepare dinner. The Earl roade apace untill hee came where he might see his people under the mountains, whom he much commended for observing his commandment. The king passing the water rode a foure miles before hee came to the rocks; when he saw the ambushe he was sore abashed, knowing well he was betrayed by the Earle, for he was in such a place as hee could not escape. The sea beating on the one side and the rocke keeping him on the other, and if he should have fled backe, they would have caught him, ere he could have come to Conway, for hee hadde not past three and twenty of all his company.

They went on to Flint, where Bolingbroke met them the next day. Shakespeare rolled these two days into one scene, and linked the message of Northumberland with the confrontation with Bolingbroke, placing them both in Flint castle, and so not mentioning Conwy.

Conwy changed hands, subsequently, several times during the Wars of the Roses. But to a large extent the use of gunpowder had taken from the castle some of its glory. It was no longer unassailable. It was no longer the ultimate weapon, the flowering of medieval technology. It was out of date.

The castle was not in a good state when war broke out between Parliament and the King, in the 1640s. Conwy came back into the front line for a reason which owes more to chance than to history. It happened to be the birthplace of a certain John Williams.

Having become Dean of Westminster and then Bishop of Lincoln, Williams was Archbishop of York when the war broke out. He was one of the king's most important supporters, and found himself, at York, the vulnerable target of a Parliamentary advance. He fled by night, and made for Conwy. Once there he set about making it the Royalist headquarters of North Wales. He repaired and garrisoned the castle at his own expense. Not unreasonably he then demanded to be made governor, in place of the existing one, whom he disliked.

I have repaired, victualed, and supplied it with ammunition at mine own charges, and I am more likely to give his Majesty a good account for it than this gentleman is, who without my costs and charges was never able to repair the town as now it is, nor hath he any arms but what I lent him to defend it.

The Archbishop was in virtual command of Conwy for a time, since the governor, Sir John Owen, was absent; but when Owen returned he seized the goods which rightly belonged to Williams, and seems to have treated him as badly as he could. John Williams left Conwy and retreated to his house at Penrhyn, outside Bangor. It turned out to be a critical mistake on Owen's part.

By this time General Mytton and the Parliamentary army had taken Chester. They pushed on west into Wales, and we find the Wynns accommodating Mytton himself at Gwydir. The Parliamentarians attacked Conwy in August 1646, and by that time Archbishop Williams had changed sides. Although then aged 64, he took part in the assault on Conwy to the extent of being slightly wounded. They took the town by scaling the south wall; there then remained the castle, which Owen was determined to hold. Mytton besieged it, and while the siege was on the ex-Archbishop preached in Conwy church. The text which the fiery old man chose for that morning's sermon was Psalm 144, verse 1: 'Blessed be the Lord my strength, which teacheth my hands to war, and my fingers to fight.'

The castle surrendered in November, and it was Conwy's last battle. The castle was in so bad a state that it would not have been economically feasible to repair it. Nor was there any reason to. They must have known that it would never be used again. In 1665, the owner of it, Lord Conway, decided to remove the lead and timber. We are told that the local people were 'misgreeved att the taking of it downe'. The wood was rotten, but the lead and iron he shipped to Ireland. Perhaps it is the desire for poetic justice which has added to the story the conclusion that the ships sank on the way.

It is often said that the town walls of Conwy are complete, and have never been breached. In fact they were breached in the nineteenth century by those two arch-vandals, Thomas Telford and Robert Stephenson.

For many years Conwy had both benefited and suffered from the traffic. In 1774 Wyndham wrote: 'We were now in the great Irish road; the article of eating was doubled in our bills, and the door of our Inn was crowded with beggars.' John Byng, in 1784, was even more forthright: 'Conway is a poor mean place and only subsists on the travell thro' the town.' The ferry was unpopular: it caused delay and was dangerous. The ferrymen were accused of 'wilful delays' and 'gross and barefaced impositions.' William Bingley recorded at the turn of the century: 'I have my self known them with the most impudent assurance possible, charge half a guinea for ferrying over a gig, and after receiving that, importune in addition for liquor.'

Consequently it was proposed, at the beginning of the nineteenth century, that a causeway and bridge should be built. It was probably largely due to the necessity for providing as quickly as possible a route by which the mail could reach Holyhead from Liverpool that the Select Committee of 1820 recommended Telford's bridge, instead of the previously favoured route over Bwlch y Ddeufaen. The building of the bridge began in 1822, and in 1826 it was opened. In the same year the Mail packets began to run from Liverpool, removing this factor from the argument a little too late. The Mail, for which it was built, crossed the bridge for only two months.

Telford altered one of the wall-towers to make what is now the Bangor Arch. Stephenson, using Telford's causeway to bring his railway along the coast, in the 1840s, again had to construct a new archway in the south wall. The castle was then bracketed by two main lines of communication. In the process it lost its river entrance, which was removed to make way for Telford's road.

It would not be allowed today. The castle and walls (now in

the more enlightened care of the Welsh Office's ancient monuments branch, Cadw) were guarded by their previous custodians, the Ministry of Works, with a single-mindedness which was sometimes a little frightening. In places they carried out what amounted rather to rebuilding than restoration. In places the structure was in danger of becoming no longer a ruin, no longer part of history. Certainly we must recognize the debt we owe to the Ministry of Works for caring for our ancient buildings. And that some repairs are necessary to prevent their deterioration; and some reconstruction necessary to make them safe and accessible. But the castle which we have here now is smart and respectable, and no longer the eloquent remains of the structure which Edward and Eleanor walked in. The chapel looks new, which it largely is, and imagination has to be forcibly exerted to picture it as the shell of the room which surrounded Richard II and Northumberland.

Ironically the damage to the town and castle which Telford had initiated by driving a main trunk route through the town's heart was perpetuated by the Ministry of Transport, which, belatedly putting into practice an outdated plan, built yet another bridge in the same place in 1956. It was obvious immediately that this was the wrong place for the road, and that a proper by-pass of Conwy would eventually have to be constructed. However, we have had to wait a further thirty years for this, since the construction of the tunnel crossing of Afon Conwy which was finally to provide the town with such a by-pass, did not start until the autumn of 1986.

Fortunately Conwy is many things besides its castle, and even on a sightseeing level the town is full of interest. The enormous house in the High Street, 'Plas Mawr', was the town house of the Wynns, the counterpart and contemporary of Gwydir, and is now meticulously restored by CADW to an authentic period state.

The parish church stands firmly in the middle of the medieval town, which circulates around it like a wheel; the still point of the turning world. It is built on the site of the Abbey of Aberconwy, established there in the 1190s and moved from there in 1283. When the church became the parish church for the new borough, its present structure took shape. The lower parts of the easternmost end, however, either side of the altar, and the western wall of the Tower, with its three lancet windows, are the remains of the Cistercian Abbey Church. The remainder of the Tower and the Chancel, together with the nave, are of the period of the church's new role, and date from 1300. The south transept is early fourteenth century.

Although it was probably not in this very churchyard that Wordsworth wrote the poem 'We Are Seven,' there is a seven-crossed grave to mark the spot where he did.

'Sisters and brothers, little Maid,
How many may you be?'
'How many? Seven in all,' she said,
And wondering looked at me.

'And where are they? I pray you tell.'
She answered, 'Seven are we;
And two of us at Conway dwell,
And two are gone to sea.

'Two of us in the church-yard lie,
My sister and my brother;
And, in the church-yard cottage, I
Dwell near them with my mother.'

'You say that two at Conway dwell,
And two are gone to sea,
Yet ye are seven! I pray you tell,
Sweet Maid, how this may be.'

And so their doggerel conversation went on.

In spite of its appearance of being composed almost entirely of history, Conwy is not, and never will be, a museum piece. It is rather more something of a living survival. A town in which people live and work, which happens to have evolved in the same place, with the same street pattern, during the course of some seven hundred years. A community which is tightly interlinked, resistant to interference, enclosed and separated from the rest of the area by a metaphoric wall as solid as its physical one. The tourists are an added bonus, but Conwy survives when they have left.

It survives from its own resources, and in particular from its waterfront, which is the focal point of the town. The mussel-gathering in the winter occupies several families, and in the summer the same people tend to become fishers of men. The same men, and in some cases the same boats, which worked the tide at the necessary hour (within the limits of daylight) and in almost any weather, are back on the foreshore when the season starts, advertising trips upriver and out into the bay.

Conwy moreover has a small fleet of trawlers. And anyone who thinks that the town's only attraction is its medieval wall, should look to see which way the visitors' cameras are pointing on the quay. The fishing-boats have a visual drawing-power with which even the castle cannot compete.

It seems at first a little mysterious. What is it about this way of life that makes people reach for their cameras? There is a touch of envy in it, an attempt to exorcize a vague longing. Perhaps the root of it is this: that pre-industrial occupations are growing rare enough – herding, ploughing, chopping trees – and stir in us a recognition of our remarkable continuity as a species. A longing for lost times and ways of life, safe to long for because they are, for most people, safely lost. We shall not have to work cold and wet, be short of sleep and suffer long hours and bad conditions. Since this is so we are free to see the glamour of it, the healthy outdoor unencumbered unpolluted life. And so, like all remnants of things becoming rare, aspects of pre-industrial life are treasured.

But this activity is even pre-agricultural. Fishing is hunting: we do not yet grow or herd our deep-sea fish. It is as if four or five men went out into the hills for a few days with a net to see how many sheep they could catch – nobody knowing for certain how many it would be. Consequently it provides us with a direct contact with the point at which we started, and also with an emblem of the changelessness running through all those periods of change. It takes us back at one leap past all the other periods of the past, the Tudor gentry in their great houses, the Plantagenet invaders, past Llywelyn's ordered medieval world, Maelgwn's perilous court, the Roman legions, the Iron Age tribes, beyond even those remote and unknown megalith builders, whose arrival brought the first technological innovation, farming.

Except when (as has happened in the 1990s) the fishing industry in general is in recession, the presence of working boats has been a factor in the character of Conwy. Now although (temporarily, we must hope) the trawlers have gone, the mussel fishery continues to thrive, maintaining Conwy's pre-industrial base.

The Great Orme Head, Llandudno.

Llanddwyn, the sanctuary of St Dwynwen
on the western coast of Anglesey.

Capel Garmon chamber tomb.

Tre'r Ceiri, an Iron Age fort in Llŷn.

Din Lligwy, Anglesey.

Moel Arthur, in the Clwydian range.

Fflint castle

The castle at Beaumaris

Cromlech Dyffryn Ardudwy

Deganwy castle remains.

Dinas Brân, above Llangollen.

Eglwys Llangar, near Corwen.

Caernarfon castle

Dolbadarn castle

Rhuddlan castle

Penmon priory

Yr Wyddfa and Crib Goch in the high Snowdonia range.

Dolgellau

Tu hwnt i bont, Llanrwst.

Conwy harbour

Llandudno, from the Great Orme.

Llyn Tegid, near Bala.

The HSS ferry leaving Holyhead harbour.

Menai Suspension bridge

Britannia bridge over Menai.

Porthdinllaen, Llŷn

The Rhinog mountain range in Meirionnydd.

Trefriw Spa

Wrecsam

Part Two

The Inner Sanctuary

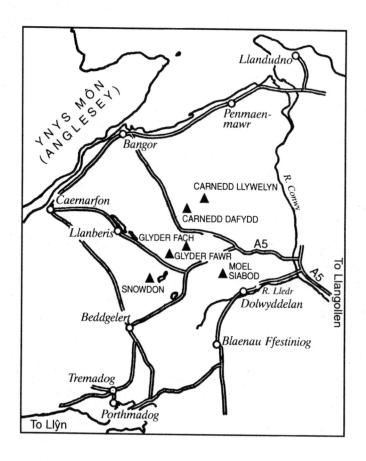

Five

BETWEEN THE HILLS AND THE SEA

The coastline is best seen from the sea. From out in the bay one can properly grasp its proportions, its rise from the long beaches of its shoreline to the bracken slopes and heather patches of its steep sides, and then to the round grassed summits above. A spectacular and tempting coast, characterized mainly by variation, but almost always soft and green. In spite of its steepness and proportions, there is nothing harsh about it.

The coastline is always changing, never being twice the same, as the light and the season never exactly combine in the same way twice, and the direction of the wind critically affects the cloudscape in this area on the fringe of Atlantic weather. It changes within itself as one follows the channel out, from the bracken and hill-grass of Conwy Mountain *(Mynydd y Dref)*, past the rougher prominence of Penmaenbach, the perfectly rounded, bilberry and heatherclothed Moel Lus, further to the long even ridge which rises to Penmaenmawr's at one time craggy headland.

Two roads lead out of Conwy. One, the obvious one, follows the coast. The other, from the top of the town, goes the other side of Conwy Mountain, the 'Town Mountain' which stretches its ridge down almost into residential Conwy. From the top of this area can be seen laid out like a relief model: the bay, the Orme, the distant shipping lanes, Anglesey *(Ynys Môn)*, the estuary, the various parts of the Borough, even a stretch of the valley. Towards the western end of the mountain is a stone ring-fort, smaller and less impressive, however, than Pen-y-gaer.

This road passes through a miniature Alpine Pass, the Sychnant Pass – the name, meaning paradoxically 'dry stream', accurately describes the extraordinary deep, riverless valley on one's right hand as one descends.

There is an inundation story connected with Conwy Bay, the only definite sign of which is the name of a small hill which this inland road passes, on the left-hand side shortly before one reaches Penmaenmawr. Twyn-y-Wylfa: the hill of weeping. It was on to this hill that the surviving inhabitants of the broad and fertile plain which stretched where the sea now is, between Puffin Island *(Ynys Seiriol)*, and the Great Orme's Head *(Penygogarth)*, climbed out of reach of the waves which had swallowed their homes: and looked back. It is said, without proved foundation, that the ruins of the palace of their leader, Helig, can be seen at very low tides, a group of rocks near the Conwy channel about a mile from the headland of Penmaenbach. Certainly when the tide sinks and the miles of sandbanks rise, it is easy to see this whole area as dry land.

When people complain that progress is destroying the landscape, all that is normally happening is that its appearance is being changed. In the case of Penmaenmawr they are actually taking it away. The process has been going on for so long now that we have come to accept it. But if it were proposed today that a once-beautiful mountain should be removed, day by day, cube by cube, in order to provide the world with granite chippings, the under-taking would probably be considered unthinkable.

Penmaenmawr has always been a quarry. In fact this particular type of igneous rock was, relatively-speaking, in even more demand when stone was the primary material of production. That is, during the Stone Age. There seems to have been a thriving business here about five thousand years ago. The distinctive axe-heads and other implements which came from Penmaenmawr during the Neolithic period have been found at places as far away as Bournemouth, Scotland, Cornwall and Northern Ireland.

This old quarry has been swept away by the newer one. Penmaenmawr granite quarries started operation in the 1830s.

By 1905 (when the quarry already boasted ten miles (16 km) of tramway) Penmaenmawr stone was being used in sixteen UK counties for the building of roads. It was then shipped from the jetty at up to a thousand tons a day. In 1911 two companies merged to form one large quarry. Stone is now shipped to Liverpool, South Wales, Northern Ireland and Glasgow. Moreover, by an arrangement with a German company, Penmaenmawr started in the 1960s to go direct to Hamburg, for the making of German roads. There it has recently formed part of the western Hamburg by-pass and the construction road for the building of the Elbe tunnel. It is the durability of Penmaenmawr stone (technically not granite, but a mixture known as pyroxene granophyre) which makes it still universally popular. This durability is due to the uniform distribution of its various constituents: the crystals of augite, enstatite, felspar and quartz (along with a few others) which are interlocked to form a hard and beautiful stone. Besides its long-standing and continuing use in macadam, Penmaenmawr chippings have become widely used for the making of concrete, and through this medium the mountain which was once there now finds itself forming, among other things, the walls of the Mersey Tunnel. Wallasey Sea Wall, the air-strip at Bristol, and the bathing-pool at New Brighton.

The mountain was once 1,553 feet (473 m) high. It would be rash to attribute a height to it today, since it is still being systematically taken away.

With its easy access to both sea and hills, and its envied possession of a long and sandy beach, Penmaenmawr has had a career as a resort less successful than it deserves. Perhaps being under the mountain makes it a little gloomy. Certainly there is (compared to Llandudno and other spots) a shortage of sun, and this presumably would account for its lesser popularity now than in Victorian days, when sunshine was to be avoided – it made your skin go dark, like that of the lower orders. Gladstone was fond of it; he called it 'Dear old Penmaenmawr'.

It is said that Elgar, who was also an habitue, composed one of his oratorios there. Those were the days.

Ironically Penmaenmawr's prospects seem to be improving as its scenic attraction diminishes. They say there that now the mountain has grown lower the town gets longer hours of sunshine.

Llanfairfechan, on the other side of the headland, is unaffected by the gargantuan excavations, and has been able to continue its life at a steady pace. It is by nature a well-situated, small, peaceful seaside town, not in any way remarkable, and probably quite glad of that. It has (like Penmaenmawr) a good beach and a selection of ways into the hills. It also shares the view, of Anglesey *(Ynys Môn)*, and, from the beach, the Great Orme's Head *(Penygogarth)*, enclosing between them the bay.

The little village of Aber, further along the coast, seems from the road to be of even less remarkable interest. Not so. From the sea at a certain point the gorge into the hills opens out, and one looks beyond Aber landwards to see, quite clear even at such a distance, the long white vertical streak of its waterfall. Afon Goch comes over the cliff and drops spectacularly about two hundred feet (61 m).

But impressive and absorbing as this famous sight is, it would be less worth going to see if it were not for the walk up the valley. Indigenous deciduous groves fringe the river, clumps of oak, thorn, birch, rowan and hazel. In summer these little woods are scented with wild garlic. In autumn they smell of moss and damp humus. The well-trodden path winds up through the enclosed valley, more than a touch of the idyllic around it. Arcadia was once like this.

Again a warning must be sounded. In spring and late autumn, and preferably during the week, one can walk undisturbed. But even the Garden of Eden would be unbearable on a British Bank Holiday.

Although Aber is, rightly, best known for its falls, it was at one time of considerable importance. It was one of the main homes of Llywelyn the Great and his wife, Joan.

Llywelyn's palace has now disappeared. Possibly it stood on the round mound between the lane and the stream, not far from the main road. This was certainly the motte part of a motte-and-bailey castle, and was probably constructed in the eleventh century. Another contender for the court's site is the old house, Pen y Bryn, nearby, which itself dates from about 1600. Older foundations of buildings lie under its drive and yard, though the date and nature of these have not yet been positively identified.

In front of Aber, when the tide is out, stretch Traeth Lafan. In the time of Llywelyn, and up to the early nineteenth century, a road to Anglesey *(Ynys Môn)*, ran across them. The channel between the sands and the island is quite narrow, and a ferry operated there. It was a risky business when the tide was coming in, since one was at the mercy of the ferrymen, who were far from reliable. One pair of travellers in 1631 left it a bit late. Puzzled at first as to why some other travellers had started galloping, they quickly understood the situation. 'Finding the water grow deeper, . . . we suspected the sea might be comeinge in, as it was.' They came at last to

> *the place where they were expecting the ferrie boat, which was at Beaumaris, and the ferrimen drinkinge. Wee all made as loud a call as we could . . . askt my father if he could swim; he sayd when ye was younge he could . . . At last the ferrimen sett out, and came to us, telling us we were in noe danger, but by such tyme as we and our horses were on board a ship might haue rode between us and the shoare behind us, and all was couered with water where wee stood longe before wee gott to Beaumaris.*

The road was marked by posts stuck in the sand, and was about four miles long. In foggy weather, a writer records in 1798, 'the large bell of Aber is rung constantly . . . to direct those coming from the island.'

Between Aber and Bangor the bulk of Penrhyn Castle, rising above its surrounding woodlands, begins to become prominent in the view. One reaches its great gates at Llandygái. Originally the home of the Lords Penrhyn (perhaps the most prominent among the quarry-owning families), it now belongs to the National Trust. The Penrhyn family was the first to start slate-quarrying on a large scale, at Bethesda, at the end of the eighteenth century. The present building was begun in 1827, the architect being Thomas Hopper, and stands on the site of the previous family seat. It now includes various museums and an exhibition of old railway engines. The structure itself is a vast, grotesque monument in stone to the unwisdom of building Norman castles six centuries after their time.

On one side the wooded slopes of that world-famous waterway, the Menai Straits. On the other the wide ranges of the Snowdonia mountains. A fishing-port nearby, and yachts moored within view of the town. A pier, a boatyard. University town and cathedral city. It is very hard to understand why Bangor is such a failure.

Architecture has a lot to do with it. The cathedral is in no way exalted. The main college block is heavy and formidable. The new university buildings are for the most part soulless and imposed, as new university buildings always seem to be. The town itself (with the notable exception of the fine terrace of Menai View in Upper Bangor) is mostly grey and drab, the streets unostentatious, even unobtrusive, as if afraid to be thought to be enjoying themselves.

Socially too Bangor lacks cohesion. The University is the main focus, involving about two hundred staff, and has a cultural and social life of its own, which hardly seems to affect the town.

Bangor Cathedral suffered, like St Asaph, a long succession of destructions. It seems the Normans somehow managed to destroy it as early as 1071. Glyndŵr wrecked it in 1404. It was rebuilt between 1496 and 1532, and then remained more or less intact until the arrival of Gilbert Scott in 1869. He claimed to have restored the transept to its design 'as erected in the days of Edward I . . . and that, too, without destroying any old features of subsequent date, except the very wretched windows which had been made up in place of those of the original transepts.' The oak ceiling in the nave was constructed in 1880, and the rood screen was added in 1908.

The east extremity (apart from the modern vestry) is early thirteenth century. The two transepts are from about 1300, rebuilt by Scott. The aisles date from the fourteenth century, and the west tower was added in the early sixteenth. A central tower, intended to become a spire, was built by Scott in 1870.

Beyond Bangor the coastline gives a twist, and runs off into a different world. The long line of cloud which has been looming on the western horizon turns out to be an island. The Anglesey *(Ynys Môn)* bank faces the mainland across a gap in time and cultures. And as one goes down the firm wedge of the Straits towards Caernarfon, a different kind of Wales opens up.

Its presence has been felt all along, somewhere at one's back, probably obscured by billowing cloud. Borrow's term 'Wild Wales' has stuck with us. It is a handy summary. Much of Wales is tamed, but some can still accurately be called 'wild', in the sense of not yet having been completely domesticated; nature not quite subordinated to the needs of civilization. Much of it is wild in the sense in which the hill-ponies are wild: they look after themselves without our help, their natural biological cycle unbroken by human artifice, they move as they please in uninhabited areas, and if you annoy them they will probably kick you.

Borrow did not make up the fortunately alliterative phrase. It comes from a poem, probably medieval, attributed to Taliesin.

Eu nêr a volant
A'u hiaith a gadwant
Eu tir a gollant
   Ond gwyllt Walia.

(Their Lord they shall praise, and their language they shall keep; their land they shall lose, but for wild Wales.)

The thirty-mile stretch of Britain south-east of Bangor is virtually empty of roads, towns, dwellings, and (in a large part of it) people. It is mostly mountains. This fact, and the particular nature of them, is of crucial significance to the character of North Wales. It is, in essence, a mountainous country. To understand it fully one has to leave the car and put on one's boots.

Six

CENTRAL MASSIF

1. *The Mountains*

You have to be fond of weather. It changes in a moment. Rain sets in and can last for weeks. Wind on the high ridges into which you lean at forty-five degrees and are still in danger of being blown over backwards; or wind so cold that one side of the face becomes paralysed, unable to whistle or smile. Rain driving across miles of shelterless country, horizontally. Mist which gathers in globules on your eyebrows and hair, so that you seem to be decorated with glass. Frost which feathers the rocks with elaborate growths, like birds' wings, pointing in the direction of the wind. Snow which isolates you in a white void, closing over your footsteps behind to leave you walking in a world deprived of all the four dimensions.

Very few people (I am selfishly glad to say) live within an hour or two of the summits, and are in a position to be able to desert their desks for those sparkling, hand-made days when to work at all is a form of blasphemy. With limited time if one wants to see the mountains one must be prepared to get wet. It is the wettest rain in the world and however waterproof you are it will find its way down your neck. But some precaution can be taken, and it is essential, even in what appears to be a long fine spell, to be wearing the right clothes. You have to be well-equipped.

The mountains are of human proportions and look hospitable, so that it is difficult to be scared of them. Perhaps it is this factor, however, which is partly to blame for the considerable annual loss of life. It leads people to overlook the essential point that the Welsh mountains have to be approached with proper respect. Maybe one has climbed the Wildspitze in one's youth, and a mere 3,000-footer consequently looks like a stroll. But this is no reason for not taking proper precautions. To those who bear this in mind, of course, they are safe enough.

The element of danger resides very largely in the fickle weather. The mist can come down suddenly and change a country which was recognizable and full of landmarks into a yard or two of rock surrounded by grey blankets. It is therefore important to have a map and a compass, and some idea about how to use them. A watch is also important, both to give a guide of how far one has come, and to keep a necessary eye on the approach of darkness. In rain and mist, too, the rocks are slippery; wearing adequate boots is some safeguard, but probably a better one is going carefully. Spare clothing and food additional to normal requirements should always be carried. People do not die of broken legs, but they do die of exposure. Even in summer the temperature drops very sharply at night on high ground.

April and September are the best months for walking. October can be as good, but is less reliable. March and May come next in order of likely fine weather. By the middle of June it is growing too hot, and after that there is scarcely standing room on the main peaks. You have to step aside to let twenty schoolgirls go past, only to be halted at the next corner by a party of boy-scouts. The weather is never reliable, of course, and perhaps these generalizations are rash. But we have come to recognize, over the years, that one thing is certain: it rains for the whole of August. The holiday-makers trudge around the seaside towns in their plastic macs. Walking in the winter can be exhilarating and exciting, but is more hazardous, and the days are much too short. By the end of March the snow has started to melt and the season starts again.

There are fourteen peaks of over 3,000 feet in North Wales, and more than fifty over 2,000 feet (609 m). They lie in three main ranges, with some extensions. The Carneddau (the Welsh plural of Carnedd, meaning cairn), in the north, occupy the most space. The area in which they lie is one of the largest land-masses of such a height in Britain. Next, going south, and separated from the Carneddau by only a narrow valley, is the Glyder group. These in their turn look over a valley to the Snowdon range. Two main roads occupy these two parallel valleys, and a third one runs in the same direction on the other side of Snowdon.

The three ranges are completely different in character. The Carneddau are massive and broad, extravagantly unconcerned about the wide-stretching acres which a single flank or cwm of them takes up on the earth's surface. They are rounded, clothed, whalebacked, with long gentle slopes. The Glyderau on the other hand are mostly steep, craggy, everywhere visibly made of rock. They are black and fierce as Mordor, inspiring perhaps, but quite uncompromising. Snowdon is, as everybody knows, a set piece. Formally perfect, its thin ridge and pointed peaks being exactly what a mountain should be. Accessible, approachable, the most comprehensible mountain, probably the essence of mountain-ness, the Platonic ideal of which all other mountains are gross exaggerations or feeble imitations, lacking its precisely correct proportions, and its acceptable size.

2. *The Carneddau*

To me the summit of Carnedd Llywelyn is one of the most beautiful places in the world. The first and simplest reason for this is that there is no one there.

There are twenty-five thousand people to the square mile in Central London. England is the second most densely populated country in the world. North-west England is the most highly populated part of Europe. Yet Carnedd Llywelyn is surrounded by an uninhabited area of 30 square miles (48 km^2), and on most days over most of it there is no one at all. Within a hundred miles of this open, empty dome, that feels like the top of the world which one is too rarely on, lie Liverpool, Manchester, Bradford, Stoke-on-Trent, Sheffield, Nottingham, Wolverhampton, Stafford and Birmingham. Several of these, and their satellites, are considerably closer. Extend the radius only a few miles and it takes in Coventry and Leeds. Yet here, on the stony flat top of the mountain, the world seems an ecological vacuum. If the sheep penetrate to the bald plateau they walk over the flat stones without affecting them at all. Nothing happens. Nothing changes. What became of the pollution, the overcrowding, the consumption of resources?

Two other things, besides the solitude, are remarkable about this isolated, inaccessible place. One is that in the view from Carnedd Llywelyn there is nothing ugly. There is, indeed, nothing evident within eyesight but the peaks of mountains. All man-made objects in the view are so reduced by distance that they form no significant part of it. Even the surrounding mountains are, from this height and distance, crests and ridges only, small disturbances of the landscape of giant-land. One can in fact see Llandudno, but it is a patch of tiny dots which might, through a microscope, reveal itself to be an organism. Even the factory at Llandudno-Junction is scaled to these new proportions. It is a small blur, a minute dull white splash like the piece of lichen which, if one looks carefully and closely, one can see growing on a nearby rock. Cut down to size like this it could no longer look unattractive or out of place. Nothing obtrudes. Nothing can obtrude. Everything is filtered through the lens of distance.

The second thing which is so unusual as to make this a place of special significance, is the silence. On a still day, if you listen, you can hear it. The sound of nothing. Other mountains are within traffic-sound, or the rumble of the Penrhyn Quarries, or have their mountain streams close enough for their steady roar to be heard. Here if there is a wind you can hear it whistle over the stones, the sound of a passage of air. If there is none, there is silence. It is not the silence of covering your ears, or of under the sea, because then you can hear the rushing blood in your head. It is a positive, definite thing, received through the ears. The equivalent of deep, velvet darkness, which is the total absence of light.

Four ridges stretch down from the top of Carnedd Llywelyn. That to the north extends away for ten miles towards Conwy, a line of five mountains broken only by the pass through which the Roman road runs; on the east of it the glacial valleys drain to the Conwy valley; on the west the land levels out to a plateau of moorland above Penmaenmawr; and above Aber two distinct deep valleys, both full of character, lead Afon Anafon and Afon Goch towards the coast.

The glacial valleys lie mostly in the north-eastern sector of the four divisions formed by the four arms of Carnedd Llywelyn, the top of the range. This is because it was facing that direction, the aspect of least sunlight, that the ice held longest. The cwms, the hollows eaten by the ice deep into the mountains, almost all face between north and east; it is one way of getting one's bearings. Each of these valleys now contains a lake, making this side of the mountains a plentiful water-supply for the coastal towns.

To the south-east a shorter and sharper ridge forms the limit of this area, the watershed between the Conwy and the Llugwy valleys. It encloses the enormous empty extent of Cwm Eigiau, down which flows a stream so beautiful that it is almost impossible not to plunge and wallow in its deep pools.

The north-western ridge is short, sheer-sided, ending abruptly in the peak of Yr Elen. Under Yr Elen's steep sides a long slope runs down to the village of Bethesda, a quarrying village owing its origin to the Penrhyn Quarries which loom above it; a small, grey, squat town, dominated by enormous chapels, which contrast strongly with the tiny terraced houses. A strange assessment of priorities, it may seem to us now, to spend so much money and exert so much pride and sense of grandeur on a building to be used once a week; and so little of all these things on the humble, or humiliating, dwellings. But the place of chapels in Welsh village life is a big subject, and it will recur.

Between Yr Elen and Carnedd Llywelyn's northern spur lies a small lake. It is almost entirely enclosed in its cwm, under the two bulky mountains. Ffynnon Caseg, the mare's well. It is, by old tradition, where the wild ponies come in the spring to give birth. However quaint this may seem, one can go there in the spring and see them.

So the range is not quite uninhabited. How many wild ponies there are it is impossible to say, since they roam around in the thirty or so square miles of upland, and one comes across them everywhere from Carnedd Llywelyn to Conwy, Aber to Eigiau. They are sturdy, alert, nicely-proportioned creatures. They seem to live in extended family groups, a small herd together, grazing or lying in the heather. They get up, watchful, if anyone approaches, and move away suddenly if you go too near. For most of the time the hills are theirs, undisturbed. Even in the height of summer one can walk over much of the large area north of Carnedd Llywelyn without seeing a single person.

Apart from the ponies there is little wild life. A few foxes, hares, grouse, and plenty of larks. And of course the sheep. The *ffrith*, the rough pasture of upland grassland, is an essential part of Welsh farming. Wherever possible the sheep are taken down from the mountain in the winter, kept below the mountain wall, or farmed out in the valleys. Even where it is not possible to take them all off the mountain, they are brought down to the lower fields to lamb; and not until the lambs are big enough do they return. You see the flocks flowing in late spring, like water in reverse, winding up from the main valley and thinning and spreading on the mountain. The farmer and his shepherd and their dogs, glad also, almost certainly, to get the mountain air again, flank the tail of the flock. An occupation almost as old as farming. The seasonal transhumance of pastoral people.

Men stopped living in the hills some time ago, but at one time the upland area was highly populated. Bronze Age cairns and barrows are thickly clustered there, more than seventy of them lying in this triangle bounded by Afon Llugwy, Afon Conwy, and the coast. Nine Iron Age forts also lie in the northern uplands. Long huts, round huts, hut enclosures, groups of huts, are too numerous to count, and are probably spread, in their origins, over a long period of time. These are sometimes found as high as 1,700 feet (520 m), and are most common between 600 and 1,000 feet (183-305 m). The tree-line, which during the Bronze Age had made almost all the land below 2000 feet (610 m) impenetrable forest, had, by about 700 BC, begun to move downwards. A drier climate (the 'Sub-Boreal' period) together with the influence of man, had by then brought about the deforestation of the mountains. Man cleared the trees for fuel and for settlement space; and his grazing animals prevented their return. And the existence of peat (which has provided evidence of birch, hazel and oak) at heights where trees now would not grow, indicates clearly that at one time (up to at least 2000 BC) the mountain tops were as mild as the valleys are today.

The upper valleys (Eigiau and Cowlyd) were farmed from those pre-Roman times until the middle of the nineteenth century. The number of deserted farmsteads, now mostly in ruins, make one realize how intensively they must have been farmed. The disappearance of the hill-farm, however much regretted, is a continuing trend. Larger units than those which once required, apparently, at least six farmhouses between Cwm Eigiau and the Conwy valley *(Dyffryn Conwy)*, are now not only possible but desirable. The mountains are farmed from the valleys, and often in conjunction with a valley farm.

Slate was quarried in Cwm Eigiau from early in the nineteenth century until the 1870s, and the derelict buildings and workings can be seen in the otherwise quite empty valley.

Turning now towards the south, the fourth ridge leads to the neighbouring mountain, Carnedd Dafydd. Llywelyn and Dafydd face each other across an abysmal black hollow, down into which one looks vertiginously. Second only to the two peaks of Snowdon, Carnedd Llywelyn is the highest mountain in Wales and England, and Carnedd Dafydd the next highest. (The two Glyder come next, then the last mountain of the Carneddau range, Pen yr Ole Wen; and only then comes

Scafell.) It is not certain which Princes of Wales are being commemorated by these two appropriate peaks. Both Llywelyns were succeeded by a Dafydd. Consequently this might be Llywelyn ap Iorwerth (the Great) and his successor, his only son by his lawful wife, Joan. It might also be Llywelyn ap Gruffudd and his brother Dafydd, the two unfortunate last princes, who both had to retreat at times into the mountains. Another permutation is indeed possible. It might be Llywelyn the Great's son, and his nephew and successor Llywelyn ap Gruffudd.

The summit cairns on these two mountains, and others on their slopes, are of Bronze Age type, and were very probably the burial places of important chieftains. Since no Bronze Age habitations have been identified, it is a matter of speculation whether the people who built these cairns lived at this considerable height, or only sited their burials there.

Pen yr Ole Wen forms a suitably definite end to the range. It comes to a sudden stop. Between the summit and the Ogwen valley lies one of the steepest slopes of all. From there to the lake the land drops 2,200 feet in a horizontal equivalent of less than a mile.

It makes a fine lookout on to the next range. The reptile back of Tryfan, a hunched and dangerous-looking prehistoric monster. The two rocky humps of the Glyderau. The lakes: little Bochlwyd in its high cwm; the peaceful, secluded expanse of Idwal. The cliffs: the scar of the Devil's Kitchen, the crags above the Idwal slabs. Y Garn, another 3,000-footer, a finely-carved, demonstration mountain – this is a *hanging valley*, these are *arêtes*. They are all spread out ahead.

3. *The Glyderau*

The ice that flowed down the Ogwen valley (*Dyffryn Ogwen*) and Nant Ffrancon gathered on the northern faces of the Glyderau. Receding, it cut back into the mountains, leaving the row of north-facing cwms which characterize the range now. Bedrock thus exposed at the back of them give us the cliffs and crags of the Glyderau. The two glacial valleys on to which one looks down, Llyn Ogwen lying between them, have the even, smooth shape (their projecting spurs cut off by the ice-flow), which makes such post-glacial scenery as this so satisfying.

The ice-age is so patently with us everywhere here, that it is hard to believe that at one time the idea that there had ever been one was considered highly controversial. It was not generally accepted until the 1840s. Charles Darwin and Adam Sedgewick were in Cwm Idwal in 1831, examining the rocks for fossils. 'Neither of us saw a trace of the wonderful glacial phenomena all around us,' Darwin admits:

We did not notice the plainly scored rocks, the perched boulders, the lateral and terminal moraines. Yet these phenomena are so conspicuous that a house burnt down by fire did not tell its story more plainly than did this valley.

The episode illustrates nicely the extraordinary extent to which human observation is limited by intention. You see what you are looking for.

Cwm Idwal is a nature reserve: that is, it is the object of attention and study by the Countryside Council for Wales, a body particularly active in North Wales – though it is wholly owned by the National Trust, and also has the benefit of the assistance of the Snowdonia National Park Authority. Do not pick the flowers. Some of them too have glacial connections, since in the 'hanging gardens' of the Devil's Kitchen grow Alpine flora not found in other parts of Britain. An attractive, but not proved, theory explaining this says that they followed the retreating ice to its last refuge, and then found that, on the upper northern cliffs of the Glyderau and one or two spots on Snowdon, it was cold enough to stay. On Glyder Fawr there is even an Alpine spider; but whether this too is supposed to have crawled up after the glaciers I am not quite clear.

The Devil's Kitchen, a tall black chimney cut in the cliffs above Llyn Idwal, is of interest to the climber and the botanist, and to anyone who likes being over-awed by rock and size. The name derives from the boiling water which foams and gurgles in it, as the unsuspecting stream which trickled across a moorland plateau suddenly falls hundreds of feet through gulleys and boulders. Twll Du, black hole, its Welsh name, perhaps describes it even better.

The cliffs of the Devil's Kitchen are so unclimbable as to make them highly thought of among climbers. They are wet, over-hanging, and crumble in your hand. Just the thing they were all looking for. Approached from below, the narrowing gorge closes claustrophobically around you. The overhangs tower and drip, gloomily. If one goes round by the cliff path and comes down the stream to look over the top, vertigo replaces claustrophobia. It is a thousand feet down to Llyn Idwal, and there seems to be nothing in between.

The path which rises to the Devil's Kitchen passes the Idwal slabs, a rock-climber's training ground, which, on practically any day, has a number of flies stuck on it, joined by their rope. Coming back, four hours or so later, one seems to find them in much the same position, perhaps a few feet further on. Rock-climbing is an absorbing, obsessive pastime, like fishing, and the object of concern, the cliff, drains attention from all other considerations, such as time or coldness, or alternative occupations.

This path, passing the bottom of the Devil's Kitchen and doubling back, is an example of an exercise in the control of a most disturbing thing that is happening to the mountains. They are being eroded; not this time by ice or wind and rain, but by boots. On a steep slope such as this the loose shale and soil falls away, water starts to flow down a new bed, and the path becomes a bare, slippery scar, with no firm ground, unpleasant to walk on at any time and in frost quite dangerous. The Devil's Kitchen case shows that the use of several techniques –

revetments underpinning the path, drainage channels removing water-flows from it, lengths of fence channelling walkers away from adjoining scree, which can then recover its vegetation – can restore a path and prevent its spread. This will need to be repeated in several areas of Snowdonia to combat this serious problem (so conspicuous on the over-used tracks of the Lake District).

Reaching the top of the cliff this path suddenly tips you out into a different world. The ice-carved rock of the north side seems to have no relation to the peat moors, grass-tufted and flat, of the south. The two Glyders have summit cones made entirely of rock, but their southern flanks are long and gentle, thick with heather in the lower parts and grassed higher up. By Llyn y Cŵn (lake of the dogs), from which the stream flows towards the Devil's Kitchen, one can sit as though in rolling lowland country.

Welsh hill-farming and the Welsh mountains have never been so well described as by Thomas Firbank, in his highly readable, and still popular, book *I Bought a Mountain*. It was this southern side of the Glyderau that he bought.

The word Glyder is thought to come from a word meaning heap, or pile. And the tops themselves make this seem likely, being a great heap of large stones. Although the two peaks seem roughly the same height, Glyder Fawr, in the west, is slightly the higher. Glyder Fach is the stranger of the two, a weird, spiky, moonscaped mountain, quite unlike any other part of the earth, unlike even anything one could imagine. Between the two stands an outcrop of rock much appreciated by photographers, called Castell-y-Gwynt, castle of the wind. From this shoulder the view of Snowdon dominates even the extraordinary rock-built surroundings.

Llyn Bochlwyd, under Glyder Fach, lies in a perfect cwm, sunk into the face of the mountain, enclosed, secluded, very much on its own. Scrambling over the lip, through the boulders of its moraine, one comes on the lake in its hollow with an inevitable surprise, every time. It sits so perfectly and calmly there, walled in by black crags. The ridge enclosing it on the east leads up to Tryfan, an isolated peak standing slightly apart from the Glyderau, bony and bare. It is steep-sided, and more of a scramble than a walk. The famous rock-climbs are on the buttresses of the east side, and all but experienced climbers should keep clear of them. The peak can be climbed fairly easily up its ridge, on the Glyder Fach side, and, inevitably in such an elevated and central spot, rewards the effort with a fine view. The two people who can be seen from the road, standing permanently alone on its summit, in all weather, year in year out, are called Adam and Eve. They are a bulky stone couple, about ten feet high.

To the south, the other side of Glyder Fach, the land flattens again, with another moorland lake, and slopes endlessly down towards the Mymbyr valley *(Dyffryn Mymbyr)* and Capel Curig.

4. *Betws and Capel*

Tourism is a strange thing. It operates on a plane remote from reality, a vicious circle of its own contrivance, a self-perpetuating system dedicated to fulfilling a demand which it creates. The travellers originally come to a place because it is different, to make a contrast to their normal lives. Its particular characteristics, the aspects of it and its people which make it unlike other places, are what draws them to it. The inhabitants then present their image of the visitors' image of them: the olde Welshe hat, woollen shawl, arty-crafty vision, which nobody had even seen in its natural state, because it never existed. They then pad this out with the standard fittings of the tourist business, the cosy cafes, antiques, trinkets and souvenirs, now, in places, giving way to Local Arts. Pottery and paper-knives, wooden bowls, stones, slippers, tea-towels, walking-sticks and woolly hats. One might, with only slight changes of emphasis, be in Killarney or Stratford. Everybody is happy: money changes hands, the visitors have presents to take home. But it

117

was not Wales they went to, but Touristland.

Betws-y-coed is as near as Wales has so far come to being on the great international tourist route. It lacks the romantic associations of, for instance, Tintagel, and so has to rely entirely on its natural features. The visitors come in coaches to look at the Swallow Falls *(Rhaeadr Ewynnol)*, and who can blame them for wanting to see such a quantity of tumbling water. The roar and spray of it would be worth a stronger recommendation if they were not slightly dimmed by the incongruity of having to pay at the gate to get in, and the chance of having to share them with a few hundred other people. The English name, incidentally, is a mistake, seemingly derived from Borrow's *Wild Wales*. When George Borrow visited, a woman told him that the falls were called 'Rhaeadr y Wennol', the 'Fall of the Swallow'. In fact 'Ewynnol' means frothy, or foaming. The village of Betws-y-coed itself has only its setting to draw people to its shops. It is picturesque.

It is indeed. A river gushes through it over rapids, under a bridge. Trees grow down to the boulders of the waterside. Above the gorge oaks cling by their roots to the crags, smoke rises from cottage chimneys against wooded slopes. It has the feeling of a mountain village, without the harshness. Nobody would say that the wilder parts of the mountains are pretty. Nobody could say that Betws-y-coed isn't.

The road, the A5 (which crossed Afon Conwy above Betws-y-coed by means of Telford's ornate cast-iron 'Waterloo' bridge), now rising, passes the Swallow Falls (coaches welcome) and up through the gradually thinning forests of the river valley. The indigenous trees which bravely compete with the planted conifers make this a highly-coloured place in the autumn. Somewhere at a turn of the road between Betws and Capel Curig, Moel Siabod comes into sight; and over its shoulder one catches a glimpse of Snowdon *(Yr Wyddfa)*. At Capel Curig one becomes suddenly amongst the mountains. The Glyderau ahead obscured by their long lower shoulder; the

Carneddau stretching away to the right, and down a long valley to the left the view of the Snowdon range laid out with perfect form and balance, perhaps the most depicted scene anywhere in the country.

Capel Curig is very small, a church and a few shops, and a catchment area of outlying hotels. The A5 turns away from Snowdon to run up the valley which the Afon Llugwy comes down, flowing from a lake below Carnedd Llywelyn to run on down through Betws-y-coed towards Conwy. With the Carneddau on one side and Tryfan, the Glyderau and Y Garn on the other, the road runs flatly along the valley bottom, passing right under the towering ridge, along Llyn Ogwen, tipping down into the Nant Ffrancon Pass towards Bethesda and the land of slate quarries.

In making this journey through the mountains, one is of course travelling through the Snowdonia National Park. This, an area of 850 square miles (1370 km^2), stretches far to the south – in fact, as far as the boundary, for present purposes, of 'North Wales'. The use of the word 'National' has, over the years, led people to think that all this in some way belongs to Us. And therefore, the conclusion follows, it is ours to treat as we like. This is an unfortunate impression, and all along too little attention has been given to the problem of providing people who visit it with information about the real nature of the situation.

The mountains are all owned and farmed. They are private land. They represent somebody's capital investment and somebody's livelihood. They are not a national playground. If this were always fully understood much might be done to avoid fanning the smouldering ill-feeling between those who resent finding a family playing cricket in their hay, and those who begin to feel that 'Why can't you keep your dog on a lead?' is a customary Welsh greeting. More people, fortunately, now realize that a gate left open, a fence damaged, a wall broken down, represent animals strayed on to other people's land, and hours, perhaps days, of work finding them and putting them back. It all costs money, and this unnecessary work and worry caused to the involuntary hosts can easily be avoided by crossing a wall or a fence, wherever possible, at a gate (and closing it religiously) or a stile.

One point which has perhaps proved hardest to bring towards consensus is the question of dogs. Attitudes polarize with formidable determination. He needs the exercise, he loves the open spaces, romping about through the heather. He never chases sheep; or if he does, it certainly isn't to do them any harm. We keep him on a lead (within sight of the farmhouse). A walk is less enjoyable without a dog.

Sheep run at the sight of a dog. This may seem another instance of their foolishness, but after all they are not to know, at a hundred yards, whether it is a sheep-killing dog or not. Nor is there any certainty on this point. When the sheep run they often unleash a savage and vicious hunting streak in even the most domesticated dog. The ewe will run until exhausted, or cornered, when the dog, by then apparently transformed by an obsessive inner ferocity, frequently sets about tearing at it with its teeth. This is not a rare or freakish occurrence. It happens often, and with dogs which have always seemed to their owners to be mild and obedient. They results can be appalling.

In any case at certain times of the year – when they are carrying lambs, or with small lambs at foot – the dangers involved in making sheep run are obvious. What is not obvious is the length of time for which this applies. At any time during the five-month period between tupping and lambing a ewe may be caused to shed her foetus. And after lambing it is again a long time before the lambs are weaned, during which they are in danger if separated from their mothers. The fact remains more-over that farmers do not like having their sheep made to run at any time. It is not good for them, and if they were your sheep or mine neither would we.

5. *Siabod and the Lledr Valley*

Although only 2,860 feet (872 m) high, Siabod looks, and is, a big mountain. It occupies, on its own, a block of land between two valleys as big as that occupied by the Glyder range. It seems to stand more prominently and be visible from greater distance, than any of the other mountains. It is, in fact, the end of a long and widening range, but the other mountains of this lie far outside the area of the central peaks and so are seldom visited. They appeal less, also, because they are not so high. Siabod, however, almost ranks with its neighbours, the 3,000-footers.

Siabod is not difficult to climb, but because of its bulk it tends to be slow. It is a long sweat on a hot day, and a wet walk on other ones. The main feature of the top is perhaps the view of Snowdon: but one does look out the other way onto yet more open, empty country: the uplands the other side of the deep Lledr valley, forest country rising towards the moorland hills above Llyn Conwy.

Skirting the fat flanks of the mountain, the Lledr valley branches off Dyffryn Conwy, and runs parallel to the Betws-y-coed/Capel Curig valley, Moel Siabod being between them. It is tempting to be definite here, in full knowledge of the claims of the vales of Conwy, Gwynant and Ffestiniog, and say categorically that the Lledr valley is the loveliest in Wales. It outsparkles them all in surprises and scenic virtuosity.

What the valley has, in intense form, is the particular characteristic of the scenery of North Wales. Every stretch of it is different, so that one can hardly compare one bit with another. In some places one goes beside a flowing brown river licking over rounded stones. In others a cream stream gushes through a gorge. Waterfalls and pools spout and gurgle. The river slides over smooth slabs, or suddenly lies dead, mill-pond still. Salmon and trout leap to mind. The banks too display the same versatility. You are plunged into a few yards of Bavarian forest, and imagination populates it at once with men in leather trousers, feathers in their hats, trudging down from the hills with bucks slung across their backs. Out again into the air: Disneyland crags, each of which should be topped by a towering castle, rear over the road. As the valley rises the terrain changes again. Scrub birch in waterside thickets becomes then mountain ash. The land grows wild, heather and scree slopes sliding down to the road.

Wales, I suppose like everywhere else, is all too often oblivious of its greatest treasures. The small diesel train which runs from Llandudno-Junction up the Conwy valley to Betws-y-coed and then up the Lledr valley to Dolwyddelan, finally passing through a mountain to reach the end of the line, the end of the world, at Blaenau Ffestiniog, goes on its trip practically empty. It is unknown, unthought-of. It is kept alive by a large subsidy because it provides a vital link for the people of the upper valleys with the towns of the coast. Yet it should be one of the major tourist attractions of Wales. Even at a moderate estimate this must be one of the dozen most beautiful journeys in the world.

This train gains what the road lacks, since it runs by water most of the way. Squarely on the valley bottom (until the Lledr valley becomes too narrow and forces it on to the slope) it gives open views both of the river and the slopes. The difficulty of wanting to be on both sides of the carriage at once is overcome by taking the return trip. Few people, in any case, would want to spend the rest of their lives in Blaenau Ffestiniog.

The strange thing is that far from being world-famous among connoisseurs of scenery, this little line is constantly in danger of closing through lack of trade. At the very point at which tourism could do good, and no harm, the potential is almost completely ignored.

Dolwyddelan is the only town in the valley. Once a quarrying community, it now, like several upland towns which have lost their use, has its problems. One ancient monument is not enough to keep a town alive. Dolwyddelan Castle stands just beyond the village and out in mountain country. High on its crag, grey and tall and austere in its uncompromising starkness, it stands embattled against the weather, a mountain castle matching the hard grey clouds. It is one of the few remaining native castle, built by the Welsh princes for their own protection long before the wars with England. The father of Llywelyn the Great built it, in 1170, and it is therefore possible that Llywelyn was born there, it was certainly his father's home during his early childhood.

Llywelyn's grandson, Llywelyn ap Gruffudd, made the castle (by then extended by a curtain wall and a west tower) his headquarters during the last phases of the war with Edward. The English captured it in January 1283, and this was perhaps the critical event which gave them victory. Edward refortified it and from there controlled the upper valleys. It was this which enabled him to move down the western bank of Afon Conwy, and to build the castle at Conwy on the Welsh side of the river. Once Dolwyddelan had fallen, Edward was able to control the inner sanctuary.

In 1488 Maredydd ap Ifan moved to Dolwyddelan from his home in the south-west of Caernarfonshire. He bought the castle, which he then made his home, enlarging the keep by another floor. This was the ancestor of the Wynn family of Gwydir, which Maredydd's grandson built. His great-grandson, Sir John recorded that when he went to church in Dolwyddelan (then in the middle of a land of outlaws) it was necessary for him to be accompanied by twenty armed men, with a lookout posted on the rocks above.

The remains of the castle now relate to its successive stages of inhabitation. The base of the substantial keep (though restored on the outside) is of the original period, late twelfth century. Maredydd's second floor has gone from the inside, leaving only the shell of the keep. The curtain wall which Llywelyn ap Gruffudd added in the thirteenth century is clearly visible in places, but largely derelict. Ruins of the north-west tower, also of this period, remain.

Maredydd ap Ifan built Dolwyddelan church, about 1500, to replace a former one, which, being in a thicket (again according to Sir John), was too dangerous for him to approach. One wonders why it did not occur to him that it would be easier to cut down the thicket.

Dolwyddelan is in a valley, but the land rises all round, and as soon as you leave the village you are in mountain country. The road climbs, winding, finally to come up into moorland, a 1,000-foot (300 m) crossing of the ridge, known as the Crimea Pass. On the one hand stretches yet another view of the mountains: the Snowdon group spread out in an unusual pose. On the other side, as one gains height, the rolling land which was once covered with reed and mountain fescue, heather, bracken, mat grass and bilberry bushes, has now become a forest. Another overwhelming issue obtrudes into the view.

The Forestry Commission is a glutton for land. Its policy seems to be to acquire all it can, presumably because somebody worked out that at some point it will begin to reverse its considerable annual loss. It uses marginal land, land which previously supported only one sheep to several acres. It employs local people, and indeed there are areas of North Wales which would be badly off if the Commission stopped work. With the double influence of better machines and stronger economic pressure, however, it employs fewer and fewer of them. It may be argued that the hill-farm is going anyway, that it has been on the way for years, and its eventual disappearance is as much a consequence of the change in Britain's economy from an agricultural to an industrial one as to any policy regarding the use of land. The case for the forests is that they are a crop growing on land which would otherwise be under-used.

There are two main groups of apprehensions which can be expressed against this view, one the aesthetic doubt about the changing landscape, the other the social question of the change of land-use.

'When planting or replanting,' says their leaflet, 'the Forestry Commission pays careful regard to the incomparable scenery of the Welsh vales and hillsides.' The fact remains that the over-whelming proportion of the trees they planted for decades were Sitka Spruce. This was inevitable, since it grows fast and suits the ground. That the policy has now changed, and replanting is mainly done with native species, shows that this could have been the case from the start, that the prime responsibilities are ecological and long-term.

One cannot be dogmatic about an aesthetic issue. Some people love Sitka Spruce. Some people feel more at home with coniferous forests than with open mountain, prefer to see the hillsides clothed than bare. The Black Forest and other wooded parts of Central Europe have their attractions for many. The Welsh uplands might to them seem bleak and horrible.

The fact is, however, that these heavy coniferous coverings do three things to the countryside. They rendered it one perpetual colour. Previously, and naturally, the hillsides (which were far from bare) changed continuously in both the dimensions of space and time. Bracken: light green, dark green, yellow, brown, russet, red. Grass: fawn in winter, rich green in the spring, light brown in the summer, yellowish in the autumn. Reeds followed a similar spectrum. Heather, adding dark patches in places, provided, at times, acres of purple ground, always startling where the eye expects ground to be green. Indigenous scrub oak, silver birch, mountain ash, all different colours, varied from yellow-green to red-gold through the year. There was always change, marking variations in the land and in the season. Sitka Spruce never changes.

One further loss involved in this was the loss of perspective. The light combines with the colour to give a feeling of distance and size to the rolling slopes of hill. The green of spruce seen against the green of spruce gives no idea of the contours and wrinkles of the land, at least, replanted with broad-leaf it will one day have texture again.

The second way in which widespread planting of coniferous trees affects the countryside is this ecological one of dominating the other natural elements of the land. Under a Sitka forest nothing will grow. No leaf-mould feeds the ground, no light flickers through the branches. It is all black and dead. Where there is no undergrowth there is a corresponding lack of birds, small animals and insects. The whole cycle has been broken, and it is hard to believe that it can ever be set in motion again.

The third thing they do is quite simply block the view. This, of course, is more objectionable in some places than in others. Where planting takes place on high land, previously a look-out on to surrounding mountains, such as the moorland around Llyn Crafnant, after a few years the view is effectively screened, and, walking through the woods, one might be almost anywhere in the world. One of the great features of Welsh walking used to be the outlook.

Certainly people's visual habits vary, and the loss of a view is of more profound importance to one person than another. But it would be rash for anyone to make the implicit assumption, without at least giving it some thought, that, because it is not visibly bought or sold for cash, a view has no value, no assessable worth which can be set against some putative fractional diminution of our timber imports or a statistical increase in the economic return from mountain land.

The most anomalous thing of all about afforestation, particularly within the National Park, is that, for all these years, it has (being a 'crop' and not a 'change of use') been free from planning control. Thus while the individual has had to struggle to get permission to put up a garage or a garden shed, any party with the money (and there are others less responsible than the Forestry Commission) could cover thousands of acres with any tree it liked, quite without asking.

The effect of afforestation on the visual environment is perhaps a matter of opinion. The effect on the social environment is not. The farming community is being gradually displaced. If (as may be the case) hill-farming is not necessarily a dying occupation, but could continue to thrive in many areas of North Wales, the high prices paid by forestry concerns for marginal land would make its disappearance inevitable. Farmers cannot compete. They can only farm the mountains if land is cheap enough for them to be able to acquire a large enough amount.

The Crimea Pass tilts down the other side, steeply, into what might easily be mistaken for the entrance to the Underworld. The earth has been turned inside out, the normally hidden inside of it lying everywhere in massive heaps. It is too impressive to be ugly. It is monstrous, horrible, almost unbelievable; but so black and big as to be in some way fascinating. Out of this turmoil the town of Blaenau Ffestiniog grows.

Slate quarrying and Blaenau Ffestiniog were always, until quite recently, practically the same thing. The town was caused and sustained by slate. Even the fences bounding its fields are made of slate. It now faces the bleak problem of all single-industry economies: what happens when its *raison d'être* fades away?

At their peak the Blaenau Ffestiniog quarries employed more than a thousand people. Now there are only jobs for little more than a hundred. This means not only relatively high unemployment, but the possible gradual dying of a town. By 1971 the population had shrunk to less than half its former size. Blaenau Ffestiniog is not well placed for any alternative use.

There is nothing unique about Blaenau Ffestiniog's problem; it is simply isolated in this case and therefore seen in an intensified form. Unemployment and depopulation are, and have been, the characteristic features of much of the mountainous rural area of North Wales. Tourism is a major industry, but it has several flaws. It is notoriously fickle; in a bad period the visitors may come but not spend. And it is seasonal. It leaves us with the long hard winter.

The dilemma then arises, in such places as the Lledr valley:

how can jobs be provided to retain the population, without damaging the scenery? To some people this is not a problem. The bread-or-beauty question is seen as an either-or, and the answer must be 'bread first'. The plea that scenery is the raw material of the tourist industry, and that its destruction would therefore be economically harmful, is overborne by the contention that the tourist industry is unsatisfactory and cannot, in any case, maintain everybody. As long as any social problems exist and anyone is out of work, underpaid, under-privileged, then romantic and unrealistic considerations such as the need to conserve wild country must be sacrificed for material advantages. Power-stations, dams, mineral working, anything. We are entitled not only to things like cheap electricity, but to the money which is injected by the process of providing them. It may be only in the short-term that, for instance, a large undertaking such as a dam provides jobs. But short-term work and wealth is better than none; and when the problem comes of replacing these sources of work we shall meet it in the same way. It may be that ultimately only a few local people would be employed by, for instance, a power station. But a few local people in work is a few families fed, and the multiplier effect benefits the whole community. Who are we, what right have we got, to deny people immediate prosperity for the sake of some vague benefits in an uncertain future? An area which is losing its population is, in any case, losing an important part of its character. Why conserve the scenery and not the community? If there is a conflict between the two, it is people that must take priority. Land is a valuable resource, and in this overcrowded island it would be economic madness not to use it to the full. In any case the mountains are not in a natural state; they have been exploited for centuries, by quarry-owners and farmers; sheep keep down their undergrowth, and indeed have done so for millennia; walls, pens, cairns, cromlechs mar their slopes; bogs have been drained, peat dug, trees felled, rivers dammed, fields cleared of stones for centuries; we are only proposing to continue an age-old process.

Nor is it felt that a replacement population is any solution; the Midlands families which now inhabit the farmhouses and cottages at the weekends and for a month or so in the summer are no substitute for the settled community. The principle that the most appropriate people to inhabit a place are those whose ancestors have been there longest, has much to recommend it. A long process of adaptation, perhaps, enables them best to conform to the terrain – in Auden's memorable phrase:

Adjusted to the local needs of valleys
Where everything can be touched or reached by walking

and the continuity of the population gives the place its strength of identity. We worry about the disappearance of leopards and gorillas. Why should the Welsh uplander be given the choice between poverty and extinction?

Yet (says the swinging pendulum of opinion) the loss of natural beauty is irreversible, and there is little enough wild country left in Britain. Perhaps the nation needs fresh air as much as economic growth. Perhaps the service provided by National Parks is as essential as cheap electricity, copper, lead; they, at any rate, can be had elsewhere, whereas Snowdonia cannot. If even now the urban pressure has made the open spaces of such great value, how much more will this be so in fifty years. Space and scenery are not to be lightly relinquished. We have, in any case, a duty to posterity. How can we say which resources the future will value greater, wilderness or power, mountains or minerals? It is easily lost, and, as William Morris put it (though about Oxford) as long ago as 1883, 'it was a possession which did not belong to us, but which we were trustees of for all posterity.'

The question of what exactly is our debt to the future is perplexing. But it is clear at any rate that the present has to be taken into account as well, whatever we consider will or should happen when we are no longer here. We have to face the fact that many aspects of the rural life have already gone. The small industries: saddlers, blacksmiths, bakers, tailors, and most small shops; they no longer support the large work-force which they once did. Today a weekly shopping trip will get it all in the nearest town. Because of mechanization many fewer people are needed on the farms. All this has, in some way, to be replaced. It is never going to be the same sort of rural life; but there must quite simply be a way of keeping people living in the country, if the country itself is to live.

The problem varies in its details from area to area in North Wales, and will have to be solved on a local level. Permanent light industry of a scale and type which will not interfere with its surroundings must be introduced where it is needed, and to the degree to which it is needed, avoiding as far as possible the more sensitive areas. This (they will say reproachfully) is easier said than done. It evidently is, since it has been said often enough. Now it must be done.

Seven

SNOWDON

It was easy for the writers of the Romantic Revival. They could use terms like 'the magic', 'the enchantment', 'the spirit' of Snowdon. The words had not then been devalued by over-supply. They meant something. I find it hard to describe by a current equivalent the sensation which it sometimes causes, which is something like a smell, the sort of once-familiar smell which evokes a sudden mood. I suppose that what it is, in fact, is that the mountain builds up cumulative associations, which it is then able, by a turn in the path revealing a sudden view of a lake, to release. Much in the same way one's favourite city has the knack of re-creating a past mood: as, for instance, for some people a corner or a stretch of Paris recalls a certain day in early spring, and for others Dublin's mellow October evokes a former self.

Theodore Watts-Dunton (whose *Aylwin* is perhaps the epitome of Victorian romantic novels, and one of the best to feature Snowdon), perhaps describes such feelings, though in different words: 'Then I felt coming over me strange influences which afterwards became familiar to me – influences which I can only call the spells of Snowdon.'

It is even tempting to attribute to magic the way in which it tricks the eye. It has the appearance of a full-grown alp, five times as high as it is. The story in which an alpine mountaineer or a Sherpa is asked, standing outside the Penygwryd Hotel, to estimate how long it will take him to climb it, has grown into something like a local folk-tale. They screw up their eyes and give it a knowing look, like a farmer weighing a heifer. Pointing to the slope of Cwm Glaslyn, they say, 'We should be able to bivouac there on the first night.'

Far from the estimate of 'about three days' which the character in this story sometimes gives, it in fact takes about three hours to reach Yr Wyddfa at the most sedate pace possible. This, the summit peak, is really only one peak of a long ridge. 'Snowdon' is a term used vaguely. It can mean either the whole range, or the single highest peak. The Welsh name 'Eryri' is not much clearer, meaning something more equivalent to 'Snowdonia' – the Snowdon mountains and the other mountains around them. Literally 'the place of eagles', the eyrie; but it is some time since there were eagles in these mountains. (Giraldus mentioned them, and in 1639 a naturalist, Thomas Johnson, was prevented from exploring the cliffs of Carnedd Llywelyn because his guide was scared of the eagles which nested there. There are, however, no certain records of eagles, only the name.) The word 'Snowdonia' is not, as some suppose, modern. It was coined by Pennant in the eighteenth century. The mountain had, apparently, been called Snowdon since long before that. (The earliest recorded use of it, in the form 'Snawdun', seems to be 1095.) The name, of course, means Snowhill, the 'don' part of it coming from the Saxon word which gave us 'dune' and 'down'.

There are basically five ways up Yr Wyddfa, one approaching from the west, two in the south, one from the north, and one again from the east. The southern routes have to cross long slopes, and although the views of the mountain ahead are always good, the going is a little tedious for the early part of the walk. Moreover, of these, the Watkin Path makes what I consider to be the great mistake of approaching the mountain up a valley instead of along a ridge. The bulk of it hangs over you, pressing you down, and, quite apart from the steep slope, the effect is demoralizing. The Snowdon Ranger Path, from Llyn Cwellyn, is a good, short, interesting climb. The path from Llanberis in the north is long but easy, and difficult to mistake since it follows the railway almost all the way. The approach from the east is really two paths, the Pyg Track (a name spelt thus because of its traditional association with Penygwryd, often known as P.Y.G.; but probably originally referring to the shoulder, Bwlch Moch, 'pig pass', which it crosses), and the Copper Mine Track, which starts from the same place at the top of the Llanberis Pass.

Of all these possibilities there is no doubt that the last is the most attractive. That peaked, lofty view of Snowdon which is so well known comes into sight after the first few bends of the path, and stays there for the rest of the walk. Water and lakes break the possible monotony of hillsides. Tiny Llyn Teyrn is under you almost at once. The track (at this point really a road) rises slowly and easily to Llyn Llydaw. On the left the black face of Lliwedd, the outlying peak of the chain, shelters the long lake. By the time one has reached the causeway across Llyn Llydaw one is right amongst the mountains.

The shoulder which dips slightly between Lliwedd and Yr Wyddfa is called Bwlch y Saethau, the Pass of the Arrows. Legend states categorically that it was there that King Arthur received his fatal wound. In a cave on the face of Lliwedd his knights are asleep, waiting for his second coming. Like so many sleeping knights in so many caves of European folklore, they were once disturbed by a shepherd; but the cave has never been discovered since.

It is certainly not hard to picture Llyn Llydaw, curving off into the mist, as being the 'great water' by which the events which the myth described took place. Tennyson's versification of Malory comes closest to the mood of the place: 'the water lapping on the crag, and the long ripple washing in the reeds'. The cliffs on which Sir Bedivere, 'clothed with his breath,' looked 'larger than human on the frozen hills' –

The bare black cliff clang'd round him,
as he based
His feet on juts of slippery crag that rang
Sharp-smitten with the dint of armed heels –
And on a sudden, lo! the level lake,
And the long glories of the winter moon.

The solitude of the scene is slightly disturbed now by the presence of the ruins of mine-workings. Copper has been mined above Glaslyn and Llyn Llydaw since early times, however, and was probably mined there in King Arthur's time. The mountain is very rich in minerals, and occasionally one can break open a stone to find it seamed with rich red dust. Others when banged together clang like metal. The workings which can now be seen were in operation from the middle of the eighteenth century until 1915. The miners lived during the week in the row of rather primitive cottages which lie by the edge of Llyn Teyrn, and at the weekend crossed the mountains to their homes in neighbouring villages. The ruins of the workings at Llyn Llydaw now stand like a pantomime palace on the lake's shore.

The path rises steeply from Llyn Llydaw to the lip of the cwm from which a roaring white stream pours out of Glaslyn. This still lake under the cliffs which drop straight from the mountain's summit peak is both bottomless and haunted. Moreover it is here that the water-monster resides which once plagued the Conwy valley (*Dyffryn Conwy*). Perhaps it is because the lake is bottomless that the water-monster is never seen. We presumably share it with a similar location in Australia.

What Glaslyn is haunted by is never specified, but whatever it is its influence is very strong. The lake has an air of unreality about it, of not being part of the natural order. It is set apart by its height, its withdrawn seclusion, and by the dominance of the mountain. What is more it is a colour which nothing else is. The Welsh word *glas* describes it quite accurately, since it means both blue and green. Glaslyn: blue-green lake. It is that deep colour which is arguably either, but can only adequately be described as both at once. The particular colour of Glaslyn, a deeper blue-green than any other lake, is undoubtedly due to the copper which must be continually flowing into it.

At first sight there seems to be no way out of Cwm Glaslyn. In fact the path rises on the other side through the rocks, and develops in due course into the zig-zags. It runs over chasms and gulleys where the mines once were. About halfway to the ridge it is joined by the Pyg Track, which has run along the contour most of the way from the other end of Llydaw. Above hangs the crest of Y Grib Goch and the rocks below the summit of Crib y Ddysgl, the other two peaks in the Snowdon chain. One last precipitous slope, and over the top on to the ridge. A different country and a different climate are blown up the west slopes into your face.

Perhaps inevitably, after such a long approach, the summit of Snowdon is likely to be an anticlimax. Not only is there a railway and a few hundred people, but, just below the summit rock, an obscenely inappropriate air-raid shelter made of concrete, which is known as 'the hotel'. Inside, it is not much better; a large and echoing canteen steamy with damp and tea. The summit of Snowdon has always been a ridiculously busy place. The Victorians used to come to it up the Llanberis path on ponies, and a photograph of it taken in the 1870s shows a sort of shanty town of huts, rather like old changing sheds at a decrepit seaside. The railway was built in 1896.

From the summit one can appreciate the shape of the range. Two horns of it stretch out each side: on the one hand Crib y Ddysgl (the next highest peak) and the long knife-edge ridge of Y Grib Goch, and on the other the two humps of Lliwedd. The circuit of the range, known as the Horseshoe, is well known to be the finest ridge-walk in Britain.

On a fine day there is of course the view. The structure of North Wales lies revealed, and foothills fade away to England. More probably much of it will be under cloud, the woolly plain which one looks down on from the air, with, in this case, the black points of the larger mountains sticking out. The cloud slides over their ridges and licks around their summits, shifting but remaining, a heavy sea under which the world suffers its gloomy weather.

In an equivalent position to Glaslyn but on the other side of Crib y Ddysgl is another haunted lake. Llyn Du'r Arddu, an ominous enough name which even so hardly does it justice.

Hidden by defensive mounds of moraine, it lies low in its cwm, looking small and insignificant until one realizes how long and steep is the slope down to it. Black indeed, and surrounded by blackness. Besides the fairy which haunts it, it has one other extranatural quality: a triple echo. Stand by the water, face the cliff, and shout; three people will answer. Sometimes a faint fourth, buried deep in the evil-looking crags, adds his weak voice. A number of notes sung come back merging as a chord, reverberating on into a prolonged diminuendo around the echo-chamber of the mountain.

The cliffs to which one thus talks, standing by the lake, are perhaps the most famous climbing-grounds in Britain. Clogwyn Du'r Addu, or Cloggy to its friends, is more or less the birthplace of modern rock-climbing.

Climbing originated not as a sport but as a necessary part of the study of botany. A botanist called William Bingley recorded a climb on Clogwyn Du'r Arddu as early as 1798. But rock-climbing hardly became a recognized activity in its own right until the middle of the nineteenth century. It happened in close connection with the rise in popularity of the Penygwryd Hotel, which began to take its rightful place among mountain inns during the 1850s. The Alps had already been discovered as a source of adventure, and it was quickly recognized that the Welsh mountains were, though smaller, every bit as alpine. But at that stage it was still the mountains, not the cliffs, with which they were concerned.

The separation of the two concepts began, according to Geoffrey Winthrop Young, who had personal experience of these early days, when people started to climb the cliffs of Lliwedd during the 1880s. But it was surely not until Clogwyn Du'r Arddu became the common climbing ground, in the years after the first world war, that the divorce was really apparent. Cloggy is not the way up a mountain. At the top of it you have got nowhere. The Snowdon Ranger path reaches the same point at a comparatively early stage of its ascent, and with great ease.

This is simply the most precipitous and vertical of cliffs.

The East Buttress of Clogwyn Du'r Arddu (now, in the days of Joe Brown, no longer the image of the impossible), formed, for a long time, a test of greatness. And it was Piggott's successful conquest of it in 1927 which provided the psychological breakthrough leading to the fast development of climbing during the 1930s. The emphasis was shifting more and more towards technique. It was now the climber not the cliff to which attention was given. This second change was part of the progress towards the next inevitable step, the use of artificial aids.

It was said at one time that the man who could hammer a piton into British rock would be capable of shooting a fox. The values behind this attitude may strike us as strange, and certainly the heat has long ago gone out of the debate. The change is part of the greater one, of the shift from élitist activities to the participation of anyone who wishes. The amount of people climbing, as, it seems, the amount of people doing anything, has simply grown with an accelerating rate of increase. Fox-shooters to a man, they have perhaps ousted an old activity and replaced it with a new technique. We see the change coming in the old photographs. Tweed, plus-fours, caps and pipes give way to sweaters and corduroys. At one time, Young wrote, his climbing companions included those of whom 'three earned the Order of Merit, four had the Nobel Prize, five became Cabinet ministers, seven were made peers and one a life peer, fifteen were knighted . . . ' Now we are in the days of the tent and the Youth Hostel, the crags swarm with roped youths, and there is hardly a Cabinet minister to be seen.

From the Penygwryd Hotel (still, deservedly, highly favoured by climbers and others, and the base from which the Everest team carried out their pre-expedition training) two roads fork to take the two side of Snowdon. The one to the right rise before dropping, and reaches the 1,000-foot contour at the pass, the start of the Copper Mine and Pyg Tracks. From there, right under the sharp sides of Y Grib Goch, it descends steeply into the glacier-smoothed valley of Nant Peris. Llanberis, with its two lakes – it must be surely by now have been called the Interlaken of Wales – has managed to overcome the disadvantages of being a quarry town. The Dinorwig Quarries, growing like a giant sculpture out of the slopes opposite the town (in much the way that Penrhyn Quarries overhang Bethesda) have for some time been growing less and less active, fading to complete closure, (with Penrhyn by the end of the 1990s' down to less than 200 men) and are now finding a new purpose in connection with the Country Park for which this setting is so suitable. A quarry railway line now carries sightseers along the shores of Llyn Padarn and the repair and maintenance works of the Dinorwig Quarries have now become 'The Welsh Slate Museum', an evocative display of the process of producing slate which is worth a visit if only for its awe-inspiring giant working water-wheel. Providing recreation and tourist facilities in the Llanberis area will, one hopes, do much to relieve the pressure on the vulnerable open area of Snowdonia. Llanberis certainly settles naturally into its new identity: a sort of Tyrolean or Bavarian mountain town, with Welsh scenery.

In the meantime Llanberis's major claim to fame could quite easily be missed. Here, across the lake, is a major engineering project which is practically invisible, being largely inside a hollowed-out mountain. In the late 1970s three million tons of stone were extracted from Elidir Fach to form a cavern now containing Europe's largest pumped storage hydro-electric power station. It is strange, to the layman, to think that this vast undertaking is for emergency use only, and is not intended to be put into general operation. If the power drops in the National Grid, either through very exceptional demand or through the failure of two main generators at once, then Dinorwig can open up and restore the balance within a mere ten seconds. A surge shaft would then open to allow water from Marchlyn Mawr on top of the mountain to fall to the turbines and emerge on the shore of Llyn Peris 1,640 feet

(500 m) below. Off-peak power would then be used to pump it all back up to Marchlyn Mawr.

The castle at the lower end of the first, and smaller lake, as one descends the long straight valley, is (like Dolwyddelan) one of the native Welsh castles. It was built in the early thirteenth century, and originally comprised (as well as the tower which now survives) a courtyard, hall, and small west tower, extending along the outcrop of rock on which it stands. Leland (in the sixteenth century) records that it was here, at Dolbadarn Castle, that Llywelyn ap Gruffudd imprisoned his brother Owen in 1255. (The habit seems to have run in the family. Sixteen years earlier Llywelyn's father was imprisoned by his brother in the castle at Cricieth.) Probably the castle was erected by Llywelyn's grandfather (the Great) sometime before his death in 1240. Tradition also says that it was at Dolbadarn, in 1401, that Owain Glyndŵr imprisoned his conquered enemy, Lord Grey.

The southern route from Penygwryd also descends into a beautiful valley with two lakes. Between these lakes is the starting point of the Watkin path, called after Sir Edward Watkin, a railway king who, in the late nineteenth century, made his home in this glen on the lower slopes of Snowdon. It was Watkin who (over a hundred years ago) founded a Channel Tunnel company, and actually got as far as starting excavations at either end. Mr Gladstone was a friend of his, and formally opened the Watkin path in 1892, standing on a rock higher in the cwm to do so, in spite of the fact that he was then 84 years old. The place from which the venerable politician harangued his Welsh audience of about 2,000 people, duly marked with a plaque, is now known (and named on the map) as The Gladstone Rock.

Just below the foot of the lower lake is a spot less celebrated but perhaps of rather more importance, Dinas Emrys. It is, as far as one can see, nothing but a small, round, wooded hill, overlooking the road at the lower end of the valley, Nant

Gwynant. Legend connects it with both one of the most influential events of British history and one of the most striking episodes of British mythology.

Excavations carried out during the mid-1950s throw some light on the background to its reputation. Signs of occupation from pre-Roman, Iron Age times onwards were revealed; and in particular articles showing that the hill was occupied by a settlement of luxury and wealth towards the close of the fifth century AD. The ruins of a twelfth-century keep (about which nothing is known) are clearly visible.

Largely overgrown now with scrub oak, the hill is craggy and steep to climb. There is no sign to indicate its significance, and only a rough sheep track winds around it. In the trees are the low remnants of stone ramparts, and through the uppermost of these walls one comes out on to the bare, level top of the round hill. In the centre of this summit is a deep hollow, almost a glade, boggy and mossy-floored with clumps of reed. In this miniature marshy valley is a square depression, waterlogged and choked with weed, which, during the excavations, was found to be a man-made pool, a cistern, probably cut during the early Roman period occupation of the hill. On the banks of this pool, and over an area of the pool where it had silted, a paved stone platform was discovered, thought to belong to the Dark Age period. Further on, the base of the square medieval tower is conspicuous on the highest part of the summit clearing.

The name of the hill associates it immediately with Ambrosius, a historical post-Roman general whose Welsh name is Emrys. Legend however goes one step further, and connects the spot not only with Ambrosius (*Emrys*), but also with the earlier high-king Vortigern (*Gwrtheyrn*), ruler of Britain during the middle of the fifth century, immediately after the Roman withdrawal. Strangely enough the historical facts, or the nearest one can get to them, as well as the archaeological findings, are not inconsistent with this claim.

The later version of the legend as compiled by Geoffrey of

Monmouth introduces the impressive figure of Merlin, whose confrontation with Vortigern *(Gwrtheyrn)*, has become one of the best-known stories of Welsh myth. In concocting the figure of Merlin, which he made central to his story, Geoffrey seems to have had in mind the sixth-century north Brythonic poet and prophesier, Myrddin ap Morfryn. It happens, however, that he was writing in Latin, and the correct transliteration of Myrddin would have been Merdinus. It is by no means certain that Geoffrey of Monmouth had a sense of humour. But if he had he must have smiled at the thought that he had nearly trapped himself into calling his hero something like 'Shitty'. He changed the 'd' into an 'l'. And thus, by a philological accident, the wizard Merlin was born.

Merlin was invented by Geoffrey, but nevertheless became quickly accepted into the national imagination; and this vantage point over the Nant Gwynant pass is an apt place for him to make his entry into British culture.

The story arose out of a historical, and in fact crucial event. By an improbable chance we know a little of the political background. Vortigern's *(Gwrtheyrn's)* immigration policy and its results received the furious and bitter condemnation of the sixth-century ecclesiastic Gildas, the Enoch Powell of his day, who foretold in no uncertain terms that if something were not done to halt the influx and spread of Saxons, whole areas of the island of Britain would become dominated by them. 'Those wild Saxons, of accursed name, hated by God and men.' Here at least was one cleric who could tell Angles from angels. Vortigern *(Gwrtheyrn)*, he said, allowed the foreigners in 'like wolves into folds, in order to repel the northern nations. Nothing more hurtful, certainly, nothing more bitter, happened to the island than this'. The Saxons, of course, lost no time in complaining 'that their monthly supplies were not copiously contributed to them, intentionally colouring their opportunities,' and shortly made this the excuse to break the treaty. The fire of their onslaught 'blazed from sea to sea . . .

until it burnt nearly the whole surface of the island, and licked the western ocean with its red and savage tongue'.

Vortigern *(Gwrtheyrn)*, was then in worse trouble than before. The ninth-century historian Nennius give us the sequel to this story. The king called together his wise men, who advised him to retire to the 'remote boundaries' of his kingdom, and there build a citadel. Vortigern took this advice and retreated to North Wales, where he found a suitable hill in Snowdonia. But the citadel he tried to build there failed, literally, to get off the ground. Whatever was built during the day disappeared at night. After the third time this had happened, the king called together his wise men again. They were not at a loss for an answer, and directed that before the castle could be built the king must sacrifice on the site a boy born without a father. The themes of the advising magicians and the intended human sacrifice indicate, if they have any validity, that Vortigern *(Gwrtheyrn)*, was not a Christian.

Messengers were sent out. They found, fortunately for them, a boy of whom it was claimed that he had no father, who was duly brought to the hilltop near Snowdon. The boy quite reasonably demanded to know what was going on, and asked to see the wise men responsible. He then questioned them: did they know what was hidden under the paving on the hilltop? They admitted ignorance, and he told them. There was a pool there. They dug, and found the pool. He asked them then what was in it, and again was able to inform them. In the pool were two vases. Step by step the questions and the search revealed, in the vases, a tent; in the tent two serpents, one white and one red. On his instructions they unfolded the tent, and watched. The serpents began to fight, the white one winning and then the red one recovering and driving out the white. The boy explained all this to the astonished king. The pool symbolizes the world, the tent his kingdom, the two serpents being the dragons of two nations. The red one is the native dragon, the white that of invaders 'who occupy several provinces and districts of Britain, even almost from sea to sea; at length, however, our people shall rise and drive away the Saxon race from beyond the sea, whence they originally came.' Vortigern, he said, was to leave that hilltop; it was his. The high-king asked the name of this extraordinary child. 'Ambros,' he said.

Ambrosius Aurelianus (as he appears in Gildas) almost certainly existed. 'A man of unassuming character,' Gildas records, 'who, almost alone of the Roman race, chanced to survive in the shock of such a storm.' Probably Ambrosius *(Emrys)*, did in fact succeed Vortigern *(Gwrtheyrn)*, as leader of the British resistance. A likely date for his rise to power would be about 475, which tallies satisfactorily with the late fifth-century finds on the hill which bears his name. Moreover Gildas speaks of him as rallying the terrified Britons, many of whom had fled 'to high hills, over-hanging, precipitous, and fortified'. Dinas Emrys would be a suitable base from which to launch a counter-attack.

The discovery during the 1950s excavations that the post-Roman platform was built partly over the earlier and partially silted pool, is a curious echo of the details of this tale. It would not be too fanciful, under the circumstances, to wonder if this paving, adjacent to and over the edge of the pool, was all that remained after the earlier excavations carried out by Vortigern's *(Gwrtheyrn's)* magicians under the direction of Ambrosius *(Emrys)*.

Geoffrey of Monmouth, repeating the story in the twelfth century, attributed it all to his invented character, Merlin. A phrase, 'Merlin, who was also called Ambrosius,' was probably added later by someone who thought he knew better. In fact Geoffrey was familiar with Ambrosius *(Emrys)*, who plays quite a large part in his history. His purpose here seems to be to provide an entry for Merlin and a setting for his prophecies.

A story in the *Mabinogion* (the great collection of Welsh traditional tales) explains how the dragons came to be there. In the form in which we have it, it dates from the late fourteenth century, but probably, as with much of the *Mabinogion*, it was drawn from earlier material. It tells how Lludd, king of Britain, found that his kingdom was suffering from a disturbance which was explained to him as two dragons fighting. The beasts had to be lulled to sleep, wrapped in a covering, enclosed in a stone chest, and buried. 'And so long as they are in that strong place no plague shall come to the Island from elsewhere.' He acts accordingly, 'and in the safest place he found in Eryri he hid them in a stone coffer. The form by which that place was known thereafter was Dinas Emreis.' Although this is the first time the hill is named, it at least indicates that from an early date Dinas Emrys has been associated with the buried dragons, and hence with the Vortigern *(Gwrtheyrn)* story.

Whatever the truth as to dates and sources, it is clear that what we have is a sort or symbolized history. What occurred at Dinas Emrys was that Ambrosius *(Emrys)*, unearthing the dragons, set them fighting. This might be interpreted as recording that it was Ambrosius *(Emrys)*, taking over command from the ineffective Vortigern *(Gwrtheyrn)*, who made the decision that the Saxon invasion must be resisted. As propaganda the image of the dragons is effective, as it probably was if Ambrosius *(Emrys)* first used it trying desperately to stir the cowed British into resisting the spreading invasion. Glyndŵr used it to arouse national feeling during his briefly successful revolt. And in effect the prophecy at last came true (as well-known prophecies are likely to) when Henry Tudor defeated the army of Richard III on the field of Bosworth under the standard of the Red Dragon.

By then, however, the repatriation of the Saxons as suggested by Ambrosius *(Emrys)* in the Nennius story, had become impracticable.

Arthur does not figure in these early tales, although Nennius mentions him in other connections, and he only became associated with the already strongly-developed story cycles of the 'Merlin' figure and of the Grail at a later date. His role is so similar to that of Ambrosius *(Emrys)*, that some people have tried to identify him with that better-documented leader. But the evidence, slight as it is, indicates that he would more likely have been the successor who continued Ambrosius's *(Emrys's)* policy. The Anglo-Saxon Chronicle shows that there were no further advances during the years 514 to 547. Chroniclers speak of Angles emigrating from Britain to France in 531. Since these dates coincide with the date given for him by the *Annales Cambriae* (a mid tenth-century work), in which he is said to have died in 537, and since the earliest mention of him (by Nennius, working in the early ninth century but possibly using earlier material), states explicitly that he was fighting the Saxons, it is reasonable to ascribe his active life to that period. This would have made him a contemporary of Gildas, who wrote his diatribe in about 546. And the fact that Gildas never mentions his name is often brought forward as a reason for supposing that Arthur never existed. He mentions the battle of Mount Badon, in which, according to Nennius, Arthur distinguished himself, and which, according to the *Annales Cambriae*, took place in 516. But in view of Gildas's stated purpose, not 'to relate the deeds of her brave soldiers in a cruel war, but rather those of her degenerate sons' (a purpose which he fully pursues), it would have been odd indeed if he had mentioned Arthur. There was no reason for him to do so, and it would certainly not have suited his purpose. Far from having to say why Gildas is silent on this subject, we should have to ask why if he were not.

The valley turns, below Dinas Emrys, beginning to turn away from the mountains to run south. At the bend in the landscape is the town of Beddgelert.

Beddgelert is an old-established settlement, a monastic cell in the time of the two Llywelyn, and in fact probably originating in the sixth century. It was certainly thought of as being the oldest religious house in Wales. Giraldus describes it, in the late twelfth century, and about 1200, lands in the area were granted to Aberconwy Abbey. The present church contains some thirteenth-century portions, and parts are perhaps older.

The name means 'the grave of Celert', who was presumably an early saint. Somewhere towards the end of the eighteenth century, however, the saint turned into a dog. The achievement of this remarkable metamorphosis is usually attributed to Mr David Pritchard, a man of South Wales with a flair for publicity. The was the landlord of the Goat Hotel at Beddgelert at the time, and erected, for the benefit of his sentimental customers, a mount and a stone in a field, which became known as Gelert's Grave. Generations of travellers then trooped to it to shed a few tears over the faithful hound. 'Though the legend is known to most people' (as George Borrow put it), 'I shall take the liberty of relating it.'

Llywelyn the Great had a dog called Gelert, and also an infant son. He left the latter in the custody of the former, and went out hunting. In those days there were wolves in Wales (asserts the legend). One of these found its way into Llywelyn's tent, and took a fancy to the tasty-looking babe. It reckoned, however, without our canine hero, our faithful friend. Bold Gelert, despatched the wolf. The tent was in such confusion by this time, however, that returning, Llywelyn failed to notice the dead wolf and living child. What he saw was the signs of turmoil and his dog's mouth stained with blood. Not surprisingly he formed the false conclusion that the dog had eaten the child. 'Llewelyn' (Borrow continues) 'in a paroxysm of natural indignation' (to put it mildly) 'forthwith transfixed the faithful creature with his spear. Scarcely, however, had he done so when his ears were startled by the cry of a child from beneath the fallen tent, and hastily removing the canvas he found the child in its cradle, quite uninjured, and the body of an enormous wolf frightfully torn and mangled lying near.' He was, of course, in an ambivalent emotional state: glad of the child's survival, sorry to have killed his dog. Not satisfied with this heart-rending ending, some particularly poignant versions of the story add that Gelert, faithful to the end, licked his master's hand as he died. The moral of the story is perhaps that campers with small children should be careful in wolf-ridden country.

This story was not invented, of course, in eighteenth-century Wales, by David Pritchard or anybody else. It is a universal folk-tale of respectable antiquity and dispersion. It is thought to be of Oriental origin, and has been found as far away as Tibet. By a chain of translations collections of Indian tales made their way, through Arabic, into Europe, over the course of six or seven centuries during the early Middle Ages. The Gelert story (according to Professor Kenneth Jackson) did not reach Wales until the fourteenth century. Although it seems not to have been known in Beddgelert until the eighteenth, its modern survival there is a striking instance of the great strength of the international popular tale.

The craggy mountain over Beddgelert, Moel Hebog, shelters on its northern side an association with another less legendary, hero. The cave which distinguishes these cliffs was traditionally a hide-out used by Owain Glyndŵr, and this is very credible. It lies, still, in a wild, unfrequented part of Wales, all the more so perhaps now that the Forestry Commission has blocked off the approach up the slopes from the valley.

Beddgelert at one time, almost unbelievably, was near the sea. Ships could sail up to the gorge through which Afon Glaslyn so spectacularly rushes, up the creek of an estuary among the mountains. Land reclamation had been considered, and, on a small scale, practised, for centuries – one of the first to suggest it was Sir John Wynn of Gwydir – but it was finally undertaken extensively in the early nineteenth century by a Mr W.A. Madocks.

Madocks started slowly. He had moved from Denbighshire to the banks of what was then a gulf of the sea, near Tremadog – which, like Porthmadog, was called after him. He founded there a water-powered woollen mill, the remains of which, now part of a laundry on the main road, can still be seen. By 1800 he had started to reclaim land near his home, and, by farming it, proved the usefulness of doing so. It then occurred to him that transport, as well as agriculture, would benefit from a causeway right across the bay. In 1807 he started on what would have seemed to anyone less self-confident to be a foolhardy enterprise. But Madocks appears to have been unshakeable in his belief in anything he once set out to do; and by 1811 the embankment was completed. It suffered a temporary setback when a storm breached it shortly afterwards, but the local people, who had somehow come to believe in the affair, raised funds and helped to repair it. The poet Shelley, who was living at Tremadog at the time, made a speech to raise support, and, such was the fervour which had been aroused by Madocks's work, travelled the country seeking funds.

Madocks had built Tremadog on reclaimed sand on the shores of the estuary, and the model eighteenth-century style he used (with a decent hierarchy of buildings, and spaciously wide streets) says something for his taste and the mood of the period. The loss of the tidal water, however, was to be regretted at once (among others, by Shelley's wife); and the gain in land (which is of a rather poor quality) and in communications across what was once dangerous sand, have probably not justified the effort.

The harbour, which was to become Porthmadog, was built by the same amazing man, completed in 1824, and at once began to serve the quarries and mines of the mountains. In 1836 it was linked to the Ffestiniog slate quarries by a narrow-gauge railway, now a popular tourist trip. The harbour of Porthmadog could take larger boats than the estuary, and copper and slate were soon on their way from there, by schooner, across the world.

Seagoing and shipbuilding are now so deeply built into the social background of the area, that it is hard to believe that the whole thing came into existence suddenly during the middle of the nineteenth century. The ocean-going schooner in which Porthmadog specialized remained the main trading vessel until it was eclipsed by steam in the first two decades of the twentieth century.

When, by the beginning of the First World War, Porthmadog's role changed from that of trading port, its new identity as a resort was already established. But the schoonermen had, in their short period of dominance over the sea-routes, between Newfoundland, Rio, New York, Boston, South Carolina, and Wales, implanted a new tradition in the blood of the North Wales people. 'Great in this,' R.S. Thomas puts it in his poem, 'Schoonermen,' 'they made small ships do big things . . . '

> *From long years*
> *In a salt school, caned by brine,*
> *They came landward*
> *With the eyes of boys,*
> *The Welsh accent*
> *Thick in their sails*

Part Three

Anglesey *(Ynys Môn)* and Llŷn

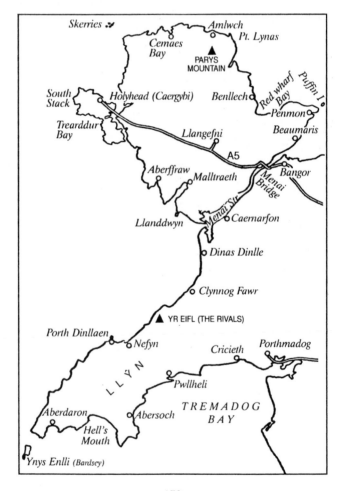

150

Eight

ANGLESEY (*YNYS MÔN*) WEST

About five thousand years ago the whole of the British Isles sank by approximately 60 feet (18 m). It is not an enormous amount, but the deep glacial valley which separated the north-west coastal plain from the Welsh uplands was so low-lying that it was enough to convert Anglesey (*Ynys Môn*) into an island. A rise in water level of another 100 feet (30 m) would make another Strait between Red Wharf Bay and Malltraeth, and turn it into two.

The whole island is, in fact, very low, particularly in the south-west. It has, in its 290 square miles (475 km^2), only nine points above 400 feet (121 m). The highest of these, Holyhead Mountain (*Mynydd Cybi*), rises to an impressive 720 feet (220 m). The rolling, smooth-contoured country which Anglesey (*Ynys Môn*) is now was formed at the end of the ice-ages by the deposit of glacial drift. This resulted in a thick layer of good soil, and made the island what it is and always has been: farming country. The fertility of the soil determined its character from an early date. Although probably wooded over much of its extent when the Romans came, the island had been deforested by the Middle Ages, when it became known as 'Môn Mam Cymru'. Mona, mother of Wales. It owed the title to its cornfields, of which it was said that Anglesey (*Ynys Môn*) could, alone, supply sufficient grain to feed the whole of Wales.

Môn is the Welsh name for the island, Mona the Roman one. The name 'Anglesey' is Norse, and probably means 'island of the strait'. Stuck out in the northern coastal sea-routes, it suffered, as we shall see, from the attentions of the Scandinavian raiders, who, ironically, have given it its English name.

The smooth surface of the land disguises, rather than reveals, its true character. Inland Ynys Môn is relatively dull:

151

rolling Midland country, all shallow valleys without corresponding hills. Seen from the sea (for instance off the south-west coast on a summer morning) it shows what it really is, an entirely coastal place. Cliffs and crags, headlands and inlets, as of a mysterious uninhabited island. The sort of rocky land with a cove-dotted coastline which one sees, on passage, from the decks of ships, and longs to stop. 'If only' (the feeling irresistibly grows), 'if only I could stop off here for a few days and explore.' Can it be the same monotonous, windswept, often depressing island?

Not that the interior, rolling acres of farmland broken by outcrops of rock and gorse, could be said to be devoid of character. For many there is even great attraction in the sight of its substantial farms, its prominent decapitated windmills, its stubble and starlings, and the tall clamour of its rookeries. It is simply that it cannot compete, for either interest or beauty, with its coast.

Although a great deal remains of the first few thousand years of Ynys Môn's history, the island only enters the records of Europe in about AD 61. At that date we get a tantalizing glimpse of the last flourish of the old religion.

The Druidic religion in Europe was one of the problems which the Romans found they had to tackle. It was, it seems, the source of nationalistic inspiration which nourished resistance to their orderly, well-run Empire. Julius Caesar recorded that Druidic customs were 'thought to have originated in Britain', and that Druids from Gaul went to Britain to learn the ritual. That Druidism survived strongly in Ynys Môn is clear from the campaigns of Suetonius Paulinus, who set out from Chester to invade it sometime between AD 59 and 61. He crossed Afon Clwyd near St Asaph, the Conwy valley at Caerhun, the mountains through the pass called Bwlch y Ddeufaen, descended to Aber and marched along the coast. The last stronghold seemed now to be beyond the Menai Straits, and many refugees had gathered there for a final stand. 'The island of Mona,' Tacitus writes, 'was feeding the native resistance.'

Suetonius had with him an army of two legions, four thousand mercenaries, other infantry, and a force of cavalry. But when they came to face the Ynys Môn shore they hesitated. Tacitus clearly reports and eye-witness account; his father-in-law. Agricola, was with this remote army at the time.

By the shore stood an opposing battle-line, thick with men and weapons, women running between them, like the Furies in their funeral clothes, their hair flowing, carrying torches; and Druids among them, pouring out frightful curses with their hands raised high to the heavens . . .

The unaccustomed sight for a moment intimidated the soldiers. But their commanders rallied them, and the army began to surge across. A flotilla of flat-bottomed boats had come round the coast from Chester, and with these the foot-soldiers were ferried over. The attack was launched at low-tide, and the horses swam. The Druids were slain where they stood, and their sacred oak-groves systematically cut down. Tacitus refers to these as being 'devoted to cruel superstitions . . . They deemed it a duty, indeed, to cover their altars with the blood of captives, and to consult their deities through human entrails.' His account of the Druid cult, however, can hardly be taken at face value.

By a historical chance the conquest of Ynys Môn was not to be carried through to its full conclusion, the garrisoning and colonization which presumably would have followed the initial pillaging and burning. As Tacitus puts it, by taking so large a force so far west Suetonius had 'exposed himself to a stab in the back'. While the felling and burning of the sacred groves was proceeding, the famous revolt of the Iceni under Boudicca was breaking out in the south. Colchester was under attack. A messenger brought the bad news all the way to Anglesey *(Ynys Môn)*, and Suetonius and his army had to leave at once and set off back on the long march south.

Agricola perhaps felt unsatisfied at having to leave this piece of work unfinished. At any rate he marched into North Wales again, having succeeded to the generalship in about AD 77. 'He decided,' Tacitus records, 'to reduce the island of Mona, from the occupation of which Paulinus had been recalled by the revolt of all Britain.' This time, it seems, the inhabitants were a little better prepared. From previous experience they expected the army to be provided with a fleet, which, apparently through the haste with which the attack was conceived, they were not. Agricola picked men 'who had experience of fords and had been trained at home to swim with arms and horses under control beside them.' He was then able to launch a surprise attack, since the Welsh were still waiting for the fleet to appear in the Straits. Outwitted, they surrendered.

In the course of these manoeuvres the Romans had succeeded in their objective. The old religion had been dealt a blow from which it never recovered. Perhaps because of this sudden disappearance very little is known about it, and we can only conjecture from archaeological finds and perhaps some strands of Welsh mythology what gods, rites, beliefs and practises were involved. But it does not seem, from the evidence of early classical authors, and from the descriptions of Caesar (who made a study of the subject) that the Druids were the kind of blood-thirsty priests that Tacitus describes. Perhaps he saw the matter through a haze of military propaganda, an invading general's view. It seems more likely that they were teachers and philosophers, whose function was to instruct the young in the oral tradition of their nation (some vestiges of which perhaps, much changed, filter through to us in the *Mabinogion* stories), and to arbitrate in disputes in the manner of elders; and who, by this means, kept alive the Celtic identity through the earlier periods of Roman domination.

One trace of the Roman arrival in Ynys Môn did perhaps come to light, when, in 1943, a large number of Iron Age finds were discovered, thrown into what had at the time been a lake.

Besides ornaments and tools in the Celtic style, there were a large number of animal bones: ox, pig, horse, dog, sheep. Since there is no indication that these were the refuse from a settlement, the conclusion follows that they were sacrificial. Posidonius, one of our earlier sources of information on the Druids, mentions the placing of votive offerings in sacred pools. He was in Gaul during the first century BC, and claims eye-witness experience of Druidic practices. The finds in the Ynys Môn lake date from the middle of the second century BC, and end in the middle of the first century AD. What one may perhaps deduce from this slight evidence is that it was animals, not humans, which the Druids were sacrificing when Suetonius arrived, and long before, and that his slaughter and attack were sufficient to bring the practices to a sudden halt in about AD 61.

For many centuries after these invasions the Straits were crossed by ferries. One (as we have seen) ran from near Beaumaris to Traeth Lafan, where a road came to the edge of the channel during low tide. Another crossed in the Bangor area. In 1725 Daniel Defoe crossed the Straits there, and reported a story to the effect that Edward I had intended to build a bridge across at Bangor. 'The king was very positive in his Design for a great while yet he was prevail'd with at last to decline it.' Knowing that determined Plantagenet, one may guess that it was (as another version of the story claims) only the war with Scotland, distracting his attention, which prevented him from carrying it out.

In 1782 serious discussions started about the possibility of building a bridge. Rennie submitted a design in 1802, and Telford added another one in 1811. But no bridge was built at that time, and it was not until Telford's successes with suspension bridges elsewhere that, in 1818, he was asked to submit a further design. He had in the meantime been building the A5, and the new road reached Bangor in 1817. It proceeded across Ynys Môn in 1822. In the intervening years Telford's bridge was being built; started in 1819 it was opened on 30th January 1826, five months before the smaller one at Conwy, which was begun in 1822.

Telford's Menai Bridge, one of his masterpieces both aesthetically and technically, is not exactly as it was when built. Between 1938 and 1941 it was adapted for increasing traffic; the old chains which suspended it were replaced by stronger ones, and the carriageway, originally double, was widened by making it into a single road.

As at Conwy, the road bridge is matched by the railway one. And as at Conwy this was a superb tubular construction by Robert Stephenson. It was built between 1846 and 1850, again concurrently with the Conwy one. The Conwy tubular bridge was, however, completed two years earlier than that at Menai.

Both road and rail traffic to Ynys Môn (and hence to Ireland) suffered from the disadvantage of being at the mercy of these two old, beautiful, but narrow crossings. There are no alternative ways on to the island. The fire which broke out in the tubular bridge in 1970 brought this fact home, stranding rolling-stock on one side and cargo on the other. At the same time it offered the opportunity to provide a much-needed alternative to the suspension bridge. For many years the inhabitants of Ynys Môn have been uncomfortably aware that the collision of two large vehicles at a critical point on Telford's bridge could leave them literally isolated. The occasion of the fire, and the necessary large-scale repairs, has provided a chance to provide a road-crossing over the top of the railway.

Stephenson's bridge has suffered a little in the process, losing its unique leanness, looking now rather like any other major bridge. Its lines are not quite altered, and rather coarsened, by the supporting arches added in 1971. Its new design also makes it no longer strictly tubular. But although all this may seem hard treatment of the fine lines and elegant balance of Stephenson's design, it certainly solves a long-standing problem.

'Menai' refers to the narrows, the stretch of water but during the Middle Ages it came to refer to the area around it on the Ynys Môn side, the commote of Menai. Now the water is known as the Menai Strait, although for some reason, incorrectly, this is almost always put in the plural. The small and pleasant town near the crossing has been called Menai Bridge for a century and a half, although Porthaethwy, the Welsh name, has been around for much longer.

Sadly the annual autumn horse-fair which gave Menai Bridge a day and night of carnival is in the past now, though a street funfair lingers on as a reminder of it. Without the horse market, which added the influx of traders and breeders it has less of an air of madness and wildness, has become like anyone else's fair. The rest of the time Menai Bridge, though less crowded, is still enjoyable. Apart from being a market town, it has strong yachting and waterside elements, and is otherwise mainly residential.

The A5, having crossed, skirts the edge of the town and turns to run for a short distance along the bank of the Straits. A magnificent view both of the suspension bridge and, if the sky is clear, of the mountains behind on the mainland, distinguishes this short stretch of road. The noble figure on a 90-foot-high (27 m) pillar which rises above the road as it turns away from the coast, is Henry Paget, first Marquess of Anglesey. Lord Anglesey was Wellington's second-in-command at Waterloo, where he lost a leg. The column was erected to commemorate his achievements, in 1816; and in 1860 the statue of the Marquess was, with some difficulty, added.

The column is open to the public – to those, at least, able to climb more than a hundred steps – and provides a quite remarkable view. One sees from there not only the two bridges and the Straits, but a strangely contrasting pair of views on the island and mainland sides. Ynys Môn stretches away, low, ancient, crouched farms and cottages among the maze of fields, villages in the folds of rolling land, unemphatic but relentless. On the other side of the coin is upland Wales: sunlight on the patched flanks of the hills, banks of cloud growing like more chains of mountains, and heaped-up slopes on which one can almost smell the warm grass and the bilberry bushes, the whole land welling up out of its foothills. All coastal Caernarfonshire is spread out there, from the Great Orme, through Penmaenmawr, the long bank of the Carneddau, through to the Snowdon ridge, and down again to the mountains of the Llŷn peninsula.

Not far from the column is the seat of the Marquesses of Anglesey, Plas Newydd – it has been called 'new' since about 1400 – a palatial and lovely house which is now in the ownership of the National Trust. The present Marquess however continues to occupy a top-floor flat. The house and garden, now open to the public during the summer, are visited by some sixty thousand people each year. Plas Newydd contains two military museums, one devoted to the Battle of Waterloo. It also has a fine mural by Rex Whistler, and much pleasing architectural detail; a house of great elegance and decency, its wide lawns sweeping down from the terrace to the Menai Straits.

The moderate-sized village nearby would perhaps never have been heard of at all if its name had always been, as it is now, Llanfairpwll. This, however, is a shortened version of the original name, Llanfair Pwllgwyngyll. As such, the-church-of-St-Mary-in-a-hollow-of-white-hazel, it is fairly long even for Ynys Môn names. And it was a bright idea of somebody's to use this substantial base to concoct the longest place-name in the British Isles, by adding to it a further descriptive phrase about whirlpools and red caves (the latter giving the satisfactory ending 'ogogoch'). Needless to say this long name has never been used, being mainly a gimmick in connection with its railway station.

Llanfairpwll is distinguished, if for anything, by its remarkable collection of overhead lines. It seems that every authority in the business of decorating our skies with wires has launched itself into the competition here, ornamenting Llanfairpwll with an unequalled assembly of pylons and poles, from the grand monumental wonders of the CEGB right down to the humble tangle of the GPO.

The road which forks from the A5 at Llanfairpwll and runs along the Marquess's imposing wall, passes not far from one of the best examples in North Wales of an early chambered tomb. Bryn-celli-ddu consists of a passage, a chamber, and a circle of stones surrounding its mound. The mound, which had largely slipped away by the nineteenth century, is now replaced as it must have been, and this enables one to see (as the bare tomb at Capel Garmon does not) to what extent the style resembles the great burial mounds of the Boyne valley in Ireland, which in turn, in the construction of their chambers, are irresistibly reminiscent of the even larger 'beehive' tombs at Mycenae in Greece.

There is no certain date for this monument, but somewhere between 2000 and 1500 BC is likely. When fully excavated in 1928, the passage was found to contain human bones, many of them burnt. A smooth stone pillar is at its centre, in the chamber, in all about 8 feet (2.4 m) high, 5½ feet (1.6 m) of it now being visible. Unusually for Welsh tombs there was also a patterned stone, now in the National Museum. A cast of this is in its original position. Signs of fire were found everywhere within and around the tomb, and the large amount of burnt bones, including one complete skeleton, suggests the practice of cremation.

A little farther into the south-west one encounters, among the formidable village names, one with a surprisingly English appearance. Newborough means what it says. It was founded in 1303 as a Welsh Borough to accommodate the population displaced by the building of the castle and garrison-town of Beaumaris, rather in the way that the abbey of Aberconwy was moved from Conwy to Maenan. The village now is small and undistinguished, and the name, to most people, means that large and empty corner of Ynys Môn between the village and Caernarfon Bay.

Newborough Warren is, probably always was, an extensive area of sand-dunes, a rolling desert which has formed between two elements, belonging neither to the sea nor the land. This large corner of Ynys Môn is now a Nature Reserve, lovingly attended to by the Nature Conservancy. Duck and geese and several rare species of water bird visit its patch of water; wild flowers grow in the sand of its banks. One can only rarely walk the long footpath through it without seeing something of interest.

Having done so one comes out on to the beach. And here, even when all the beaches of Ynys Môn are packed (as they are in the 'season') with hordes of people who have come so far west in order to get away from it all, five or six miles of white sand stretch from Malltraeth Bay to Caernarfon Bay, empty. It is a good mile's walk through Newborough Warren, and although the beach can be approached a little further on by car, the road to the Forestry Commission's car-park is small, inconspicuous and quite primitive. In any case a whole car-park full of people spread out on the wide plain of Llanddwyn Sands, is very much the same as an empty beach. The long roll of the sea washing in from Caernarfon Bay is the only sound in the air. The breadth and scale of it all is encouraging. Here at least, one feels, it will always be possible to be alone.

Saint Dwynwen thought so, and indeed time has proved her right. Few people even now make the long walk across the sands to visit her retreat. The story is that she built her oratory on this headland in the fifth century. At high tide the promontory, Llanddwyn, is an island. Most appealing of saints, she came because (says the story) she was crossed in love. Hence she became in Welsh tradition the patron saint of lovers, and her well on Llanddwyn had the power of telling whether or not one's beloved was faithful. The method is slightly complex, and involves the behaviour of the sacred eel which lives in the well. Unfortunately, or fortunately perhaps, the habit of consulting this eel seems to have fallen out of use, and the well is now neglected.

Nothing remains, of course, of Dwynwen's original church.

But pilgrims continued to come, and by the Tudor age it was evidently necessary to build a sizeable church there for them. This is now in ruins, but what is left belongs mostly to the early sixteenth century. The nave, of which the base only remains, was probably earlier. Other buildings on the headland (apart from the foundations of an old house just south of the church) were erected during the nineteenth century in connection with a pilot station which was placed there. This particular corner was always a likely place for wrecks. Two of these cottages above 'Pilot's Cove' were in fact built to house men whose sole business was to look after the wreckage.

Before the building (in the first half of the nineteenth century) of Malltraeth Cob, the long inlet of the sea known as Malltraeth Sands included the flat valley now known as Malltraeth Marsh, forming a stretch of tidal water, parallel to the Menai Straits, extending across half the island. Malltraeth Sands is a big enough bay, at high tide, as it is; and at low tide a very large expanse of sand and seashells.

The Northern headland which flanks Malltraeth Sands is occupied by Bodorgan Estate, the old-established home of the Meyrick family. Seaward, the coast juts out in cliffs, headlands and rocky coves, a fascinating, but inaccessible, piece of country. After a short stretch of these jagged indentations, the shore curves in again, becomes tamed, reverts to the rabbit-burrowed sandy slopes of an ordinary seaside, and has by then become the long low, open sweep of Aberffraw Bay.

A little mellow grey village squats by the bridge, its feet almost in the water of a small tidal river. Two pubs, a general stores, a few unremarkable new houses. How strange it seems that Llywelyn the Great should have chosen as his official title 'Prince of Aberffraw and Lord of Snowdon'.

For more than four hundred years (from the mid ninth to the late thirteenth centuries) Aberffraw was the principal seat of the Princes of Gwynedd. The royal court there (attacked by Vikings in 968) was the main residence of both Llywelyn, and remained more or less intact until 1317. It was made of wood, and was demolished in that year to provide timber for the repair of Caernarfon Castle. No sign of it now remains. That Llywelyn also had a court at Rhosyr, near Newborough, has long been known. He issued a charter from there in 1237. It was only in the 1990s, however, that the Gwynedd Archeological Trust began digging in the field locally known as Cae Llys, and sure enough uncovered extensive stone foundations, the first actual location of the site of one of the courts of the independent princes.

Presumably because of this royal connection, Aberffraw also scores a mention in the *Mabinogion*, in the sad tale of Branwen, daughter of Llŷr. Brân the Blessed (whose name occurred earlier in connection with Dinas Brân, near Llangollen), is approached by Matholwch, king of Ireland, for the hand of his sister Branwen. The match was agreed, 'and a time was set at Aberffraw, to sleep with her, and a start was made thence. And those hosts started for Aberffraw, Matholwch and his hosts in their ships, but Brân the Blessed and his hosts by land, until they came to Aberffraw. At Aberffraw they began the feast and sat them down.'

The story (which probably dates in its present form from about 1060, though of more ancient descent) does not end happily. Poor Branwen suffers in Ireland for a trick which was played on Matholwch in Wales; she is put to work in the kitchen. An embargo is imposed on all traffic with Wales, but Branwen trains a starling which carries a letter to Brân at Caernarfon. Wales and Ireland consequently go to war, with the result that only seven men and Branwen return to Wales.

And they came to land at Aber Alaw in Talebolion. And then they sat down and rested them. Then she looked on Ireland and the Island of the Mighty, what she might see of them. 'Alas, Son of God,' said she, 'woe is me that ever I was born: two good islands have been laid waste because of me!' And she heaved a great sigh, and with that broke her heart. And a four-sided grave was made for her, and she was buried there on the bank of the Alaw.

Afon Alaw flows through north-west Ynys Môn, reaching the sea on a level with Holyhead. On its bank, at a spot traditionally called 'Ynys Branwen', a burial mound undoubtedly still stands. Known as 'Branwen's Grave', it was excavated in 1813, and a middle Bronze Age urn containing cremated bones was found in the central cist. The low-lying coast looks west towards Ireland. Possibly just after the sun has set one can see the Wicklow Hills beyond the hump of Holyhead from the top of a rise nearby. Afon Alaw is small, dirty, meandering. Even if it were not the spot at which sad Branwen broke her heart, it would be a mournful sort of place.

Aberffraw now contains no buildings older than its church, of which small portions (near to the south porch) are twelfth century. Its little hump-backed bridge (now the setting for Jonah Jones's sculpture 'The Princes') was built in 1731.

Once again the enormous stretch of sand, whichever way one turns. The poor little Afon Ffraw wanders out into it and becomes lost. Headlands break the coastline to the west, crumbling clay escarpments with boulders at their feet. In the next small bay of this uninhabited stretch of coast is a strange sight. A church in the sea. Saint Cwyfan (from whom it gets the name Llangwyfan) founded a church there on what was then a rocky hump at the end of the causeway, at some time in the seventh century. The causeway has now been washed away, and at high tide the little church is about 200 yards (180 m) off-shore. The present building originated in the twelfth century, with additions in the fourteenth. It was restored at the end of the nineteenth century, and a wall built round the graveyard to keep it from falling conclusively into the waves.

The road and the coast join each other again at Cable Bay, (or otherwise Porth Trecastell), a little inlet which would be ideal for bathing if it were not for the fact that everyone else thought so too. On the headland above it stands a burial mound, known as Barclodiad y Gawres, the giantess's apronful. Presumably a story similar to that which explains the similar cairn at Bwlch y Ddeufaen, near the Roman road, gives the heap its name. It is of the same type as the one at Bryn-celli-ddu, a passage grave with a chamber, and has been artificially covered over in modern times. This makes it a little disappointing; it is hard to appreciate either its original form or the 'apronful' effect which its moundless state must have caused in the centuries between.

Rhosneigr, the only village of any size on this coastline, is a quiet and pleasant seaside place with, as might be expected, plenty of beach. Beyond Rhosneigr the railway crosses a wasteland which the roads tend to avoid, and there is, for a little, nothing. The RAF airfield, Valley, is perhaps the best use for this very flat, rather marshy area.

Road and railway cross together from one island to another. Ynys Gybi is called after the saint who founded a church there early in the sixth century. In English the island has always been known as Holy Island, and the town, Caergybi, as Holyhead.

Holyhead is also the English name of the nearby mountain, *Mynydd Cybi*, the highest point of both islands. One approaches it through a tumble-down terrace area, outside the town, a hillside hamlet full of scrap-iron and cats, and dirty-faced children. The summit is breezy with clean air from the sea, which stretches with oceanic expansiveness all around.

The hilltop is the site of a large but not especially impressive hill fort. It was occupied probably over a long period, down to Roman times. Saint Cybi, however, chose to build his church inside the late-Roman fort, where its successor still stands, an attractive, elaborate building at the centre of the town. The monastery here was sacked by the Vikings in 961. The wall of the Roman fort cuts across the west end of the church, which otherwise is largely fifteenth-century. The Roman wall extends around the churchyard, three sides of it being still intact. Only the east wall of the churchyard is medieval or modern, rather than Roman.

Holy Island seems to have been a busy place during the Iron Age. Just south-west of the hill fort, between the mountain and the coast, is a large hut settlement, a group of about twenty sizeable, well-built, but rather dull huts, set among heather-covered hillsides falling to the sea. And south of this again, on the coast, is a promontory fort, such as one finds on remote headlands in the west of Ireland. The Irish connection, which, within sight of the Wicklow Hills, would be an obvious assumption anyway, is borne out by the traditional name for these Holy Island huts and others on the main islands: Cytiau'r Gwyddelod, the Irishmen's huts.

Today it is not very highly populated. A flourishing small resort at the sheltered inlet of Trearddur Bay is perhaps the main industry of the rural part of the island. The giant smelting-plant of Anglesey Aluminium, near the outskirts of the town of Holyhead, has, since it came into operation in 1971, done a good deal to revitalize the economic life not only of Holyhead but of Ynys Môn and the mainland. More than nine hundred people were originally employed, turning alumina (the powder made from bauxite) into aluminium, but by June 2000 this was down to some five hundred and fifty. Its workforce is predominantly from Ynys Môn and the Bangor area – more than half are Welsh-speaking. The alumina (or aluminium oxide) arrives by sea from Australia and Jamaica at a specially-constructed jetty, from where it travels to the works underground in a 3,600-foot-long (1100 m) conveyor tunnel. The aluminium is then freed from its oxide, by a process of electrolysis (of course), and leaves Holyhead in cast form at the rate of about 143,000 tons a year (a 40% increase on its original design capacity). In spite of the vastness of the enterprise, it has been so well fitted into the landscape, and tempered by a positive orgy of tree-planting, that it looks almost beautiful.

The sheltered natural harbour of Holyhead has always provided a point of departure for Ireland, 57 miles (90 km) away. However it was not until the coming of roads and railways in the 1820s and 40s that the question of an official port for Ireland became important. At the time there was great debate on the subject, and it was only after several changes of opinion that Holyhead became, in 1839, the chosen destination of the railway line which was to carry the royal mail. The line from London to Holyhead was open by 1850, and during the 1880s the railway station and present inner harbour were built. The great breakwater, which is about a mile and a half (2.4 km) long, was built during the 1840s and 50s, and completed in its final form in 1873.

Apart from its traditional and present function, a port for Ireland, the town of Holyhead is hardly a notable place. Except on unusually sunny summer days it is rather grey and grim, and holds out little attraction to stop the people who pass through it, on their way to see South Stack.

The other side of Holyhead Mountain, and not far from the hut circles, South Stack Lighthouse on its island marks the end of the world. It is one of those precipitous, extreme places, overwhelming the senses; the cliffs plunge, the sea thunders, the gulls scream. Vertiginous slopes descend to the chain bridge which precariously hold the rock and its lighthouse to the end of a tenuous link with mainland Britain. An island joined to an island joined to an island joined to an island.

Anyone who has been to those capes where an ocean turns a corner, to Land's End, to Mizen Head, or under the resounding cliffs of Cape St Vincent, will recognize the roar and spray of South Stack. It is one of the corners of the ragged coastline of Britain.

Nine

ANGLESEY *(YNYS MÔN)*
NORTH AND EAST

The northern part of Anglesey *(Ynys Môn)* is swept by the wind. The thorn trees along the bare stone walls crouch, slanted. Even the grass seems to grow at an angle. The whole of the north section is exposed to wind and rain. The rain which the Irish have finished with is passed on here, and streams for remorseless days. But at those clear bright times when the whole of inland Wales is under its oppressive cloud, northern Ynys Môn comes into its own, and shines, well-lit, washed clean. An almost Atlantic light is reflected from its surrounding waves.

From Carmel Head, the north-western corner, one can look out to sea and see islands. The Skerries, true lighthouse-keeper country, are little more than a group of rough rocks. But their position in relation to shipping entering Liverpool made them of increasing importance during the nineteenth century, and by 1840 they were the only lighthouses still in private hands. Trinity House then had to pay nearly half a million pounds, in 1841, to acquire them. The lighthouse there is now automated and worked by remote control from Holyhead.

Three other islands lie off the north coast, called respectively in English the West Mouse, the Middle Mouse and the East Mouse. These and two or three bays are its only noticeable features, as it is a low-lying and therefore rather unspectacular coast. Cemlyn Bay is remarkable for having, as well as its wide, sheltered water, a sort of trapped lagoon, the home of many water-birds. Cemaes Bay narrows to enclose the little harbour and waterside village of Cemaes, which epitomizes, in its form and size, all Ynys Môn coastal villages. And between the two stand Wylfa Head.

The great nuclear power station on Wylfa is a

disappointment. No doubt a good deal of effort and imagination has been exerted in an attempt to make it appear fine, and no doubt the drab square structure which has resulted is partly dictated by the demands of its function. But when one considers how proud and magnificent the nineteenth century's architects could make a brewery, a bridge or a brickworks, a warehouse or a group of pithead buildings, that a structure the size of a cathedral set on a remote Welsh headland should turn out to look dull is surely a symptom of a spiritless age.

Amlwch, the only sizeable village in the north, owes its existence largely to the presence nearby of a rich source of copper. Its little narrow harbour was built in the late eighteenth century for the purpose of exporting copper, and at that time for a few decades Amlwch flourished. Once in existence it continued, as towns somehow do; but with the fading of its industry's importance it has been left curiously bereft of a *raison d'être*. Now a second injection of investment and activity – the ambitious and highly modern oil terminal with its nearby area of holding tanks –appears to have come and gone, being, like the copper industry, a creature of varying economic forces.

Mynydd Parys, a mile or two south, seems by some odd chance to have been made very largely of copper. One can walk now down into the 'mountain' (it is 500 feet [150 m] high, but the term is relative) through what looks exactly like a volcanic crater, and find oneself surrounded by red, ochre, yellow, and purple rock. On a sunny day its weird assortment of colours are like nothing natural to the earth's surface, in just the way the lava-cliffs inside Vesuvius or under Santorini are unearthly, out of normal experience. Such profusion of colour in the middle of monochrome Ynys Môn adds surprise to the sensation. It is a sort of visual bonus.

The Romans had a nose for copper, and Parys Mountain did not escape them. They probably found the mountain being mined when they arrived, and simply added their expertise to the process of its exploitation. It has been worked on and off since then, and in fact the surprising thing is that any of it is still left. The greatest period began in the 1760s, when a rich vein of ore was struck. By the turn of the century there were about twenty furnaces at Amlwch smelting the copper and exporting both its products and its by-products. The industry involved a fleet of forty vessels, and consumed about 1,000 tons of coal per day. The firms minted their own coins, larger and thicker than a penny, and containing copper worth their value, with which, presumably, they paid their workers. It is strange to think how much power then resided in this bleak north-east corner of Ynys Môn. Not only did the Parys mines dominate the world copper market, but the fleets of Europe and the great shipbuilding companies relied on this output for their bolts and the sheathing which they used for their ships' bottoms – an attempt at anti-fouling much used in the late days of large wooden boats.

The mines have been restarted several times since the early nineteenth century, but with increasing competition from other parts of the world became, and are now, too vulnerable to fluctuations in the price of copper ever to return to their former state of economic boom.

Amlwch itself is not a seaside town. The seaside hotels of the north are nearby, at Bull Bay. Much of the north-east corner is rather too exposed for comfort, and remains a land of hamlets and narrow lanes. Mynydd Llaneilian, in this area, has the distinction of being 600 feet (183 m) high, and consequently gives a view of most of the rest of Ynys Môn. The tower of St Eilian's little church is twelfth century, the remainder being of the late fifteenth. Eilian was yet another sixth-century saint who founded a church in a remote place. He has a cursing well, which may (with some difficulty) be seen, the remains of a square enclosure set against a rock face, about half a mile north-west from the church, which was said to have been still in use during the nineteenth century. Nobody does much cursing there today.

St Eilian (who does not seem to have been a very nice saint) is connected in legend with Caswallon, the king of Gwynedd, who was the father of Maelgwn of Deganwy. The king had misbehaved in some way, and St Eilian took the rather drastic measure of making him blind. He then cured the blindness by prayer, and the grateful (or nervous) king granted him the parish which he still has. Eilian was apparently a great curser. When a local man foolishly allowed his greyhound to kill Eilian's pet hart, the saint cursed all the inhabitants of the parish with never possessing greyhounds again. One wonders if this prohibition is still in force.

Beyond Llaneilian down those lanes is another headland and another lighthouse. Less dramatic than South Stack, Point Lynas is still an attractive promontory, and a good point of outlook on to the Welsh coastline. There has been a light on the head since the late eighteenth century, but the present lighthouse was built in 1835. Coming from America to Liverpool many ships get their first real sight of Britain when they round Lynas; and at this point the great liners used to take on their Liverpool pilots. One can see the pilot boat sheltering further down the coast, in rough weather in the bay at Moelfre, on finer days in the more open water below Lynas. A constant stream of wiry, slightly wrinkled men with small leather cases flows back again on the Liverpool trains to Ynys Môn.

Another little island lies off the coast near Dulas, and yet another off Moelfre head. They take their names from these two places, and have no function but the scenic one of decorating the sea. At Dulas Bay one finds unexpectedly an inland extension of almost trapped water, a sudden patch of softer landscape intruding into the austerity of the north part of the island. And by the time one has gone down through Moelfre village to the little creek, sheltered by its headland, something about the cliffs and slopes belongs to less bleak country.

Just inland from Moelfre there is what can only be described a remarkable area for ancient stones. The burial chamber at Lligwy is a good example of the basic type, although it lacks its mound. When it was excavated in 1908 it was found to contain human and animal bones and fragments of pottery of Neolithic and Early Bronze Age type.

The little chapel not far to the north of the burial chamber dates from the twelfth century. The walls from about four feet high were rebuilt in the fourteenth, and the south wing was added in the sixteenth. It is now simply, without its roof, and, though suitably romantic, looking its age.

But undoubtedly the most surprising thing of all in this small area is this fourth-century town of Din Lligwy. It is surprising in many ways. Firstly it is visibly soundly-built and orderly, its massive limestone wall-foundations quite unlike any other Welsh remains. It looks at first sight, irresistibly, a misplaced part of some more ancient culture. A part of Delphi or Delos, Olympia or Ephesus. One looks around, wondering where the amphitheatre is. Then with a jolt returning to a cooler and damper climate, without gods and temples and the Mediterranean light, one faces the incongruity of finding such a town in a corner of damp Ynys Môn. Because the second surprising thing about this well-built and well-preserved site is that it is on its own. Similar villages have been found in Cornwall, but nothing so distinctive in Wales. It comes as the only relic of a black period.

What were we doing during the fourth century? Britain was under attack at the time on all sides. In the east the Saxons became a severe problem in about 365. The Picts were a constant threat around the Roman wall. By the last decade of the century the Irish raiders had begun to overrun the west. Rome had started to withdraw, and in 383 the usurping emperor Maximus drained Britain of its troops. The Celtic temple at Lydney indicated that the return to barbarism was accompanied by a revival of paganism, at just the time when Rome had officially adopted Christianity. It was before the monastic foundations, before, for instance, the founding of Glastonbury. It was before the time of historical figures – before Cunedda, the ancestor of Maelgwn, moved down from Strathclyde to impose some sort of order on North Wales.

Before Vortigern's reign and the recognition of the Saxons. Long before Ambrosius, Arthur, or Mount Badon.

How, one wonders, could anyone build a place like this at such a time? Although not large by classical standards (though it clearly covered more area than its central remains indicate) it is yet quite obviously the place of a settled and prosperous community. Its date is confidently conjectured from coins and pottery finds, which indicate its main period of occupation; but no one knows how or when it was originally built. In form it is the natural development of the Bronze Age compounds and Iron Age hill-forts: a walled area enclosing several round and square huts. It is simply so much better structurally. The Royal Commission on Ancient Monuments hazards a rare speculation: 'the monumental character of the masonry and the well-arranged plan alike suggest a palace rather than a village.' It is the most one can say.

The parish into which one moves, south of the bays of Moelfre and Traeth Bychan, is a hot contender for the longest-name record. In fact, if one forgets the spurious fourteen syllables, it out-letters even Llanfair Pwllgwyngyll. Llanfair Mathafarn Eithaf however never had a railway station, and so one supposes nobody thought it worth while to lengthen it any further.

The small resorts along this coast have always been popular family-holiday, seaside-cottage places, of which Benllech is typical. The coastline has the advantage of possessing both spacious sandy beaches and some scenic excitement with them. The cliffs are rough and craggy, and enclose occasional coves. Benllech beach extends for miles, eventually turning a corner of the land to become Red Wharf Bay (*Traeth Coch*). And this enormous extent of sheltered sea and sand, loved by curlews and oyster-catchers, visited by yachtsmen, its cottages and walls recorded by so many weekend landscape-artists, its sands the subject of childhood memories and holiday snaps, must surely be to most people the idea of what Ynys Môn is. Largely unspoilt, relatively quiet, sandy and clean in the white light. Red Wharf Bay *(Traeth Coch)*.

Red Wharf Bay *(Traeth Coch)* is the counterpart of the other deep inlet, Malltraeth, in the west; and a low-lying marshy valley runs across the island at this narrow point. Halfway across it is Llangefni, the islands' main town, a market town and shopping centre, busy (particularly on market days) but nevertheless quite definitely small. Its new residential estates and outlying industries seem to have left its nature unaltered: a small country town. Ynys Môn people tend to gravitate to Bangor for their shopping. The island's two main roads go to Amlwch and Holyhead *(Caergybi)*, and Llangefni is left rather out on its own.

A large piece of Ynys Môn sticks out to the east, forming the western end of Conwy Bay. Although perhaps everybody has their favourite areas of Ynys Môn, I think one could venture to say, objectively, that this eastern triangle is the most attractive. It has the southern shore of Red Wharf Bay *(Traeth Coch)*, the beautiful and gentle headland of Penmon, and the long wooded slopes of the Menai Straits.

Penmon Head, and Puffin Island *(Ynys Seiriol)*, its extension, are, like the Great Orme and the Little Orme which bound Llandudno bay, weathered outcrops of carboniferous limestone. There is something lovely about all limestone hills, the terraced, grassed pattern they adopt, the pitted vertical cliffs, the blunted, rounded foreheads. Penmon and Puffin *(Ynys Seiriol)* are small examples of this type.

Puffin Island *(Ynys Seiriol)* has been known by many names, and the latest seems to be little more than nickname. Priestholm is its official English title, now never used; it was in any case never English, but, as the 'holm' part would suggest, Norse. The Vikings were presumably impressed by the monastic colony there. The proper Welsh name, Ynys Seiriol, comes from the saint whose monasteries dignified both the island and the headland.

Seiriol was (as by now one might well be able to guess) a saint of the sixth century. He lived in the time and area of Maelgwn Gwynedd, to whom in fact he was said to be related. His settlement was probably around the middle of the island, where the ruins of a twelfth-century church now stand. Apart from the tower of the church there is little to see, but the walls of an early monastic settlement can be found encircling the church. According to Giraldus Cambrensis it was, at the end of the twelfth century, a sort of Mouth Athos.

The island is inhabited by hermits, living by the labour of their hands and serving God . . . many bodies of saints are deposited there, and no woman is allowed to enter the island.

Giraldus goes on to describe how whenever discord ('the temptations of human weakness') arose among these servants of God, their food was devoured 'by a species of small mice, with which the island abounds,' and when the discord ceased they were bothered by mice no longer. 'Faith,' he comments, 'is increased by tribulations.'

The island was certainly occupied by holy men throughout the Middle Ages. Now it is inhabited only by gulls, cormorants, guillemots, puffins, rabbits and rats.

One thinks of rats as being dirty and vicious, and indeed city rats probably are. But this particular colony is so isolated from humanity that they are like any other wild creature. The island swarms with them, the ground positively crumbling with rat holes.

Puffin Island *(Ynys Seiriol)* entered history briefly but significantly in AD 632. Cadwallon, King of Gwynedd and a descendant of Maelgwn, was besieged on the island in that year by Edwin, King of Northumbria. The significance of this is that, at so early a date, the Anglo-Saxon kingdoms should have started their penetration into the very heart of Wales.

Besides the ruined church there is only one building on the

island, the remains of the nineteenth-century semaphore station. The chain of signalling stations which then extended all along the coast from Holyhead *(Caergybi)* to Liverpool was established in connection with the important port which Liverpool had then become. Links in the chain were at Point Lynas, on the Great Orme, above Colwyn Bay, and at various other prominent spots. The signal was transmitted in the form of numbers, presumably a numerical code, by means of masts with movable arms. By this means it was possible to inform Liverpool of the sighting of a ship off Holyhead *(Caergybi)* within the amazingly short period of a minute.

On the mainland, Penmon Priory, an Augustinian house which flourished during the late Middle Ages, was, like the foundation on Puffin Island, associated with Seiriol. Undoubtedly he was one of the foremost saints of the island, sharing this distinction perhaps with Cybi of Holyhead *(Caergybi)*, his counterpart in the extreme west. There is a story to the effect that these two contemporaries used to meet each week near Llannerchymedd, in the central north of Ynys Môn. There they had two wells, Cybi's and Seiriol's. Because of the direction of their walk to and from this meeting place one (Cybi) always had his face in sunshine, and became known as Cybi the Dark; the other, the sun at his back, remained pale, and became known as Seiriol the Fair. Somehow Matthew Arnold got hold of this story, but rather absurdly understood it the wrong way round. He seems to have assumed that the saints met at sunset, and were called dark and fair through being, respectively, in shade and light, rather than through being sunburnt and pale.

One came from Penmon westward, and a glow
Whiten'd his face from the sun's fronting ray;
Eastward the other, from the dying day,
And he with unsunn'd face did always go.

Seiriol the Bright, Kybi the Dark! men said.
The seer from the East was then in light,
The seer from the West was then in shade.

Arnold then goes on to make an analogy (the title of his poem being 'East and West') the deep significance of which quite escapes me.

Seiriol's priory church at Penmon, as it stands now, dates from the twelfth century onwards. (The roofs are modern, and the adjoining Priory House was restored and modernized in 1923.) Among many other items of interest inside the church (a rich store of fine carved stones) is a pre-Norman cross, dated at about 1000. It bears on its sides, distinctly carved, the much-travelled and long-living ornamentation known as the Greek key pattern. A similar cross stands in a field about a quarter of a mile (400 m) west-north-west of the church.

The remains of a cloister and a fine thirteenth-century refectory stand grouped around the Priory on the south side. The beautiful and sturdy dovecote nearby, with its stone vaulted roof, dates from about 1600.

These fine remains are only the later signs of Penmon's history. The headland is everywhere covered in hut-groups and cultivation terraces, largely obscured now by a forest of sturdy bracken. But the attraction of this most easterly point of Ynys Môn is not historic. It is the sea at the foot of the gentle slopes, the rush and stream of the current through the narrows, the island, humped and solid, rising calmly from the powerful water, the view of the varied coastline which forms the other shores of Conwy Bay. A tall black-and-white automatic lighthouse adds a dramatic touch to the dangerous Sound. And, fitting the mood of this remote and wistful place, a mournful bell tolls over the water, for ever. Bong . . . It evokes the eternal, extra-temporal rhythm of oceans, the 'time not our time' of Eliot's 'Dry Salvages,' or Dylan Thomas's 'lost cathedral chimes of the rocked buoys.' The effect has just faded, allowing soft Penmon, the scream of gulls, the sun on the water and the sails of boats out in the bay all to return to our consciousness, when: Bong . . . It evokes it all again.

From Druid times on, Ynys Môn seems to have been a great place for religion; and one more monastic house stood once near this eastern end of the island, the Franciscan monastery of Llanfaes. Llywelyn the Great founded it to be a burial place for his wife, Joan, who died in 1237. Sadly nothing remains of it to be seen, the site being occupied now by a large house called Friars, near the water. A town grew up in the area, and although the castle and garrison town which Edward I built did not actually occupy the same area as the town of Llanfaes, it was nevertheless apparently necessary to move the inhabitants wholesale to Newborough (previously a harmless village called Rhosyr) in 1303.

Beaumaris was the last of Edward's castles. He started it in 1295, on level ground which had previously been a marsh. Its name has always caused confusion, being apparently both French and Latin, and perversely pronounced '"B" morris'. But it is thought that perhaps it derives from the name of the ground, Beau Marais, beautiful marsh.

On this low-lying site it was clearly never going to be possible to produce a fortress as impressive as Conwy, Harlech or Cricieth. In fact the castle looks too docile, too purely ornamental, to be effective. It was never finished. The North Gate of the curtain wall remains incomplete, and the town wall (now almost entirely disappeared) was only added a hundred years later. Edward stopped building it in 1298, leaving the upper parts of the towers and much of the two gatehouses in an unfinished state. Perhaps he grew bored with it. Even Caernarfon, so much grander, has unfinished parts.

Beaumaris Castle has not played the dramatic historic role of several of its rivals. The Bulkeleys, Ynys Môn's leading family, held it for the king during the Civil War, but surrendered to General Mytton in 1646. The castle is of interest chiefly because, unlike the others, it is a typical late medieval concentric castle. That is, it is formed in two parts, an outer curtain wall immediately encircling an inner castle. This form had, by the end of the thirteenth century, replaced the less concentrated, less refined structure, the keep and bailey, which itself had developed from the simple figure-of-eight motte-and-bailey form. Beaumaris's defences were at each point double-checked. The outer gates were set at an angle to the more massive inner gates, so that when you had broken through one line you were little better off, having then to find a way of approaching the next. The large drum towers of the inner castle complement the smaller but more numerous ones of the outer wall. The towers on both walls are three-quarters projected, to give the greatest possible covering fire both to each other and to the vulnerable base of the wall.

The town of Beaumaris is old, and English in character. Old buildings abound everywhere. One house in the main street dates (originally) from about 1400 – the hall at the back and a part of the south wing are of that date. Buildings dating from the sixteenth and seventeenth centuries are common, and it is easy to picture a prosperous town of merchants benefiting by its proximity to navigable water. Many of the gravestones in St Mary's churchyard (the church itself is early fourteenth-century) are of the seventeenth and eighteenth, when Beaumaris was busy with a shipbuilding industry. The stone coffin just inside the porch looking rather as if it has been left there by mistake, is that of Princess Joan, recovered from Llanfaes at the dissolution of the monasteries; she who found the walk up from Trefriw to Llanrhychwyn tiring; the natural daughter of King John; beloved wife of Llywelyn the Great.

A splendid alabaster couple rest recumbent in a corner of the church. They are Rowland Bulkeley and his wife Alice. He died in 1537, but the effigies are apparently earlier and so presumably were sculpted from life. Beaumaris is to the Bulkeleys what Llanrwst is to the Wynns. They ruled Ynys Môn from their seat there for centuries.

Baron Hill, the Bulkeley home just above Beaumaris, was unfortunately rebuilt at the beginning of the last century. The early seventeenth-century house which preceded it has gone. The Bulkeleys live there no longer, and now their magnificent grounds, no more open to the public, stretch in a rather sad state of over-maturity beside the road which tilts down into the town.

The pillar on top of a nearby hill, The Bulkeley Memorial, was erected in the late nineteenth century to the memory of a previous popular baronet. Although he had not quite managed to lose a leg at the battle of Waterloo, the family perhaps felt that they were not going to be outdone by their neighbours. The current baronet still lives near Beaumaris, and the ramifications of the lineage extend throughout Ynys Môn and indeed North Wales.

Somewhere in the fields inland from Beaumaris, in a line between Menai Bridge and Llangefni, one can find an old, substantial house: part farm, part manor-house, built in a jumble of styles. Plas Penmynydd. It stands inconspicuously at the end of a long, rough farm road, an old house peacefully wrapped in the privacy of its clump of trees, its tall chimneys rising among the branches. Although the structure there now is a late sixteenth-century house partly rebuilt in the mid-seventeenth, its name and the place where it stands are those of the home of a family which inherited it from Llewelyn the Great's lieutenant, Ednyfed Fychan, from whom they were descended. Much of the history one comes across in the North Wales countryside is of that durable period. But even in later, more fragile times, one name, when dropped, resounds with a clang. Penmynydd is the family seat of the Tudurs.

The Tudurs *(Tuduriaid)* of Penmynydd were not royal.

Perhaps through Ednyfed's wife, Gwenllian, they could trace their descent back to Hywel Dda and thence to the dynasty of Gwynedd. The English monarchy had a more direct link with Llywelyn the Great and those royal ancestors through the Mortimer family. Ironically it is likely that the House of York, and consequently Richard III, had more respectable Welsh blood than his rival, Henry. But if they were not royal they were certainly distinguished. The Tudurs of Penmynydd fought for Glyndŵr, being his kinsmen. Maredudd Tudur, of that period, gained an office in connection with the diocese of Bangor; and his son, Owain Tudur, went with forces of Henry V to France. He probably distinguished himself at Agincourt; and was given the post of clerk of the wardrobe in the Queen's household, after Henry's early death.

The new king, Henry VI, was an infant, and the Queen then aged only 21. She was Catherine of Valois, daughter of Charles VI of France. How the relatively humble Welshman managed to persuade this daughter and widow of kings to marry him remains a mystery. It was illegal and rash, and had to be kept a secret. It seems they kept the secret for fourteen years, during which time three sons were born. When the news broke, in 1436, the Queen-dowager went into a nunnery, where she died in 1437. At about the time of her death Owain was called before the Council, arrested, and sent to Newgate.

Owain escaped shortly afterwards, was recaptured and escaped again. He remained an embarrassment to the king who finally pardoned him and sent him home to Ynys Môn in 1439. The king also recognized the existence of his Tudor half-brothers, giving them titles, in 1453. Edmund, the eldest, was created Earl of Richmond, and it was arranged that he should marry Margaret Beaufort, the Duke of Somerset's daughter. (It was through this liaison that the Tudurs acquired their position of representing the House of Lancaster. Margaret's grandfather, John Beaufort, Earl of Somerset, was, like Henry Bolingbroke, a son of John of Gaunt, Duke of Lancaster.) Poor lady, she was only 14, and pregnant, when her husband died. They were at

Pembroke at the time, and there, in Pembroke Castle in 1457, the boy was born.

The Wars of the Roses were by then in full flood and Owain Tudur of Penmynydd, supporting the Lancastrians, was beheaded at the age of 76 at Hereford, after the Yorkist victory of Mortimer's Cross. His grandson (born an Earl) was then 4 years old. As a Lancastrian heir he was in constant danger for the next twenty years, and was smuggled into Brittany in 1470 (by his uncle, the Lancastrian Earl of Pembroke), when the defeat at Tewkesbury ended all hopes of a recovery.

The Lancastrian line had in fact died out, when Henry VI died without an obvious heir. But Henry Tudor, through his mother, was the nearest thing to an heir which it had. He was second cousin once removed to Henry VI (as well as being the son of Henry's Tudor half-brother), whereas Edward IV and Richard III were the previous king's third cousins. In one way and another, he represented competition. The Duke of Brittany was constantly tempted by the Yorkists to hand over the boy, and once very nearly did so.

When Edward IV died and Richard III succeeded, the Lancastrian cause seemed to be reviving. The new king was distrusted by the nobility, many of whom fled to France. Henry Tudor (the name, incidentally, was pronounced, and often spelt 'Tidder') and his uncle were now in France, and it was with two thousand followers that they finally set sail from Harfleur landed at Milford Haven and during the first week of August in 1485.

It was an invasion. It was an attempt, largely organized by the staunchly Lancastrian Earl of Pembroke, to oust the Yorkist monarchy. But it was the native Welsh on whom the Tudurs relied for their support, and the quick passage through Wales during the late summer of 1485 was the means by which they raised their army. Henry advanced fast, and had reached Shrewsbury without opposition. Bosworth is about 12 miles (19 km) west of Leicester, and it was there he met the king.

On the walls of the house at Penmynydd are the Tudur

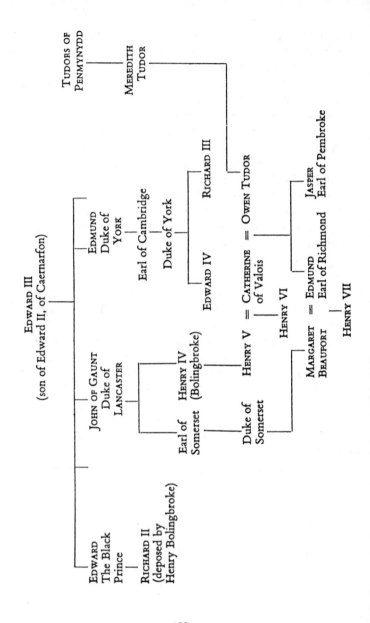

EDWARD III
(son of Edward II, of Caernarfon)

EDWARD The Black Prince

RICHARD II
(deposed by Henry Bolingbroke)

JOHN OF GAUNT Duke of LANCASTER

Earl of Somerset

HENRY IV (Bolingbroke)

Duke of Somerset

HENRY V = CATHERINE of Valois = OWEN TUDOR

HENRY VI

MARGARET BEAUFORT = EDMUND Earl of Richmond

JASPER Earl of Pembroke

HENRY VII

EDMUND Duke of YORK

Earl of Cambridge

Duke of York

EDWARD IV

RICHARD III

TUDORS OF PENMYNYDD

MEREDITH TUDOR

arms. And in the fourteenth- and fifteenth-century parish church nearby (which sits small and peaceful under its raucous rookery) they reappear, on the lovely alabaster tomb of Gronw Fychan and his wife. The church is now unfortunately kept locked, and consequently the old Tudurs can only be seen by luck or effort. There they lie, in their fourteenth-century clothes, he in his full armour, his moustache neatly laid outside his chain-mail, his feet on a lion; she in the flowing folds of her alabaster dress, with necklaces and clasps, her feet resting daintily on two little dogs. Though the pedigree is a little hazy, it seems they were the grandparents of Owain Tudur, great-grandparents of Edmund, and great-great-grandparents of Henry VI. The tomb of these very substantial people was built in about the year 1385, a century before the battle of Bosworth field.

For such a consistently flat place, it is remarkable how varied Ynys Môn's slopes can be. The few miles of the Menai Straits in this eastern end, between Beaumaris and Menai Bridge (*Porthaethwy*), display a scenic character which one would never have anticipated, quite unconnected with the rest of the island. The steep, wooded banks over the water might be above Maggiore or Como, and some of the fine houses along this shore might also. It is a very exclusive stretch of water, and as attractive as any millionaire could wish.

Wherever one is in Ynys Môn there is a view. In many ways the island's primary function is as a platform from which to look out at Caernarfonshire. All the time one can see the flanks of the mountains of Snowdonia (*Eryri*), and the cloudbank gathered over them. And the sky, of which there is so much, billowing with cumulo-nimbus drifting east.

Ten

ARFON AND LLŶN

One hot day in the Italian countryside the Emperor of Rome fell asleep. He had been hunting with a retinue of thirty-two kings, when the afternoon heat overcame him. His chamberlains set their shields over him as a canopy, and he slept. And as he slept he dreamt. He saw himself going on a sea-journey, at the end of which an island came into sight (the fairest in the world) and at the far side of the island a rugged terrain of towering rocks. Reaching this far shore he saw, from the mountains, another island. But nearer at hand a river flowed to the sea, and at its mouth was a castle. It was the fairest that mortal had ever seen; and he went down to it and entered. Two auburn-haired youths were playing a game with golden pieces on a board of silver. A white-haired man sat in a throne of ivory. At his feet there was a girl.

She rose to meet him, and he sat down with her. 'And when he had his arms around the maiden's neck, and his cheek against her cheek, what with the dogs straining at their leashes, and the shoulders of the shields coming against each other, and the spear shafts striking together, and the neighing and the stamping of the horses, the emperor awoke.' But poor man, he had fallen in love. 'Not one bone-joint of his was there, nor the middle of a single nail, to say nothing of a part that might be greater than that, but was filled with love of the maiden.' He was the saddest man that mortal had ever seen.

For a week he could neither eat nor drink. All he wanted to do was sleep, because in sleep he could see her again. At last he told his dream to his wise men, and on their advice messengers were sent out in the direction which he had taken in the dream. And they came at last to the island of Britain. Crossing it they came to Eryri, and from the rugged heights looked down on Arfon and Môn. And they saw the Afon Seiont flowing out the sea, and at its mouth a castle.

The story, unlike other *Mabinogion* ones, has a happy ending. Macsen Wledig, the emperor in question, came to Arfon and found in the castle where, at the mouth of the Seiont, Caernarfon now stands, the fair Elen who became his bride.

Caernarfon Castle occupies the spot, but the story was written probably a century before the present medieval fortress was built. 'The Dream of Macsen Wledig' represents, perhaps more than any other tale, the way in which historical events become transmuted when they enter folklore. The theme of the man who falls in love during a dream and finally finds, in waking life, his beloved, is a common international tale in Europe and Asia. In Greek mythology Medea fell in love with Jason in the same way. Into this framework real people and real places have been pressed. Elen was Helena, much loved in Britain, the wife of Constantius and mother of Constantine I. Macsen is the Spanish-born adventurer Magnus Maximus, who, in 383, proclaimed himself Emperor, while serving with Theodosius's army in Britain. He took the whole of the British army to France to attempt to remove the western emperor Gratian. And he succeeded. Gratian was killed; Maximus set up rule at Trèves. In 387 he gathered yet more British troops and set off to conquer Italy. In 388 Maximus and his Britons took Rome. Theodosius, however, appeared with the imperial army from the east, and in the same year Maximus was executed.

The Romans came to Caernarfon and built their fort on the banks of the tidal Afon Seiont in AD 77 or 78. It was part of Agricola's campaign to subdue Ynys Môn. The story in the *Mabinogion* (although purporting to explain how they came to be there) really concerns their final departure, 300 years later. To raise an army large enough to invade Italy it was clearly necessary not only to take all the legionaries, but also every able-bodied man who could come. Gildas again puts his finger on the problem:

After this, Britain is robbed of all her armed soldiery, of her military supplies, or her rulers, cruel though they were, and of her vigourous youth who followed the footsteps of the above-mentioned tyrant and never returned. Completely ignorant of the practice of war she is, for the first time, open to be trampled upon by two foreign tribes of extreme cruelty, the Scots from the north-west, the Picts from the north.

We know what happened next.

The Roman called their fort after the river, latinizing it as Segontium. It lies a little outside the present town, on the road to Beddgelert. The road actually crosses through the southern end of it, but a large part of the northern section of the fort is fully excavated and open to view. More clearly than anything I know, it presents the rather frightening orderliness of the Roman mind. All the lines are straight, all the buildings purposeful and laid out with the minimum waste of space.

What we see today is not, of course, Agricola's original military post. That was made of wood, and surrounded by an earthen bank. The stone fort so neatly laid out by the Beddgelert road was started about AD 100, under Trajan, continued under Hadrian during the 120s, and was still being added to in the fourth century. It seems to have fallen out of use during the mid-second century, probably due to the need for manpower for the building of Hadrian's Wall. Its high period is during the third century, but it became unused again for some decades from 290. The final rebuilding coincides with the time when Maximus was serving in Britain; and it was evacuated, never to be used again, in the 380s, when he left.

Caernarfon was, then, by no means invented by Edward I. Indeed when he arrived it was an established administrative town, a 'Castle-in-Arfon', the seat of Princes, with a motte-and-bailey court and thriving port. The parish church (now a mainly fourteenth-century building), which stands near the Roman fort, is on the site of a chapel used by Llywelyn ap Gruffudd.

Edward arrived in 1282, and by 1287 the whole castle and

186

garrison town had been substantially established. The castle was probably mainly completed by 1299, but work on it continued well into the next century. By the 1310s the walled town was inhabited by sixty English families: burgesses of the Borough (like Conwy) granted its charter by Edward in 1284. Like Conwy, the castle is the work of James of St George, and like Conwy also it is a single-walled castle, not the concentric type which was by then becoming common. Like Beaumaris it was never quite finished. A jagged piece of wall still sticks out into nowhere on the south-eastern side of the King's Gate, and on the south side of the Prison Tower, nearby, a planned gateway between the two halves of the castle was never built.

The castle was built around the original motte (which was removed during the late nineteenth century) where the former Welsh castle had been. While it was being built Edward had a temporary wooden structure erected on the spot. And it was there, in 1284, that Eleanor gave birth to their first son.

The proto-investiture of this Prince of Wales of course never took place. It was not until 1301, after the Welsh revolt of the 1290s, that the King made Edward of Caernarfon the Prince of Wales. He took this step because the title was at that time vacant. It was a title which had been officially recognized since Llywelyn ap Gruffudd concluded a peace with Henry III, at Montgomery, in 1267. Llywelyn had already, in 1258, assumed the title of Prince of Wales. In return for an annual payment of homage (in a form, cash, which Henry desperately needed) Llywelyn was to be allowed to rule over much of Wales. He lost this privileged position on the accession of Edward when, in 1274, he declined to attend the coronation.

When Llywelyn met his unfortunate death the position of Prince of Wales remained empty for eight years. The Welsh revolted under Madog ap Llywelyn in 1294; and Edward experienced this at first hand, being forced to retreat hurriedly to the shelter of the walls of Conwy. It is surprising that he still left the title available, and not until six years after the end of the uprising thought of filling it with his own successor.

Edward of Caernarfon became Edward II in 1307. Not a happy figure, he antagonized his barons by his incompetent rule and excessive favouritism. He was deposed in 1327 and, later that year, murdered. In the meantime he perpetuated the form set by his father by appointing his eldest son Prince of Wales. Since then it has gone on.

Work on the castle had more or less stopped in 1292; but after the revolt, in which it was taken and held by the Welsh, it was fortified further during the summer of 1295. It is perhaps the most elaborate of British medieval castles, built with an eye on decoration. Bands of different-coloured limestone (some probably from Penmon in Ynys Môn, some from part of the Menai Straits) form patterns in its walls, and on some towers red sandstone also added to the ornamentation. There is something almost smug about its well-dressed, meticulously laid stones. Yet for all its ornamental nature it was functional as a fortress. Glyndŵr failed to take it in 1401 and again in 1403-4.

When the Civil War moved into Wales (following the fall of Chester to the Roundheads in February 1646) Caernarfon Castle became the royalist headquarters in North Wales. General Mytton besieged the castle and town early in that year, and, after some weeks of hardship, Caernarfon surrendered to Parliament at the beginning of June. At the Restoration, in 1660, Charles II ordered that it should be pulled down. Somehow this command seems to have been ignored.

Nothing much happened to the castle then until the end of the nineteenth century, when it came in for a good deal of restoration. In 1908 it was taken over by the Office (later the Ministry) of Works, and it was they who put the roofs and floors in for the Investiture of 1911, thus giving the misleading impression that much of it is still inhabitable. The rooms provided by this renovation now house an excellent military museum.

In spite of traditions to the contrary, no investiture of a Prince of Wales had ever taken place in Caernarfon Castle before 1911. It was normally performed, if at all, over the centuries, in the House of Lords. It happened that in 1911 David Lloyd George was the Member of Parliament for Caernarfon. Indeed he had been since 1890 and was to remain so until 1945, when he became an Earl and in the same year died. Although he did not become Prime Minister until 1916, in 1911 he was already a prominent political leader and, it seems, able to exercise some influence over the King.

This magnificent affair cost what would now be nearly two million pounds. In harder times, the replica of it so brilliantly produced in 1969 probably cost rather less. Between the seventeenth century and 1911 public ceremonies of investiture had lapsed; but that of 1969 was undoubtedly the first to be public in the absolute sense. It had a global audience. Apart from the twenty-five thousand people in the streets of Caernarfon, the comfortable millions were able, at various distances, to watch every twitch of the face muscles of the royal participants. Caernarfon became a film-set for the purposes of colour television, and was probably nicer to look at for a year or so than it will ever be again. North Wales shone for a summer at the centre of popular publicity, smiled on by the mass media, all cleaned up and glittering with new paints for its brief season of importance in the world of entertainment.

Afon Seiont originally washed the south wall of the castle, at its flood. The quay, now a car-park, was built in the early nineteenth century. The west side of the old town still looks out on to the water, and the wall stretches there intact from the castle to St Mary's Church. The walls are slightly dwarfed elsewhere by modern building, since the town, unlike Conwy, has spread outside them almost as if they had not been there. The hub of the town now is Castle Square, where the market takes place, a wide expanse surrounded by some decently dignified buildings. But the area within the walls still feels, with its narrow streets and densely packed buildings, very much like a walled town, the old original settlement, like the pedestrian alleyways into which one dives through an arch in the battlements of Dalmatian or Arab towns, but of course rather more prosaic. Although the wall is still practically complete, and the street pattern identical to that of Edward's borough, very few old buildings actually remain even in this old-seeming area. Some seventeenth-century buildings in the High Street still stand, but in an altered state.

The rest of Caernarfon is a fairly unattractive shopping and administrative centre, beset with traffic like any other haphazardly planned town. It mostly cowers beside its two awe-inspiring monuments: the grandiose battlements of the castle, and, alongside it, Lloyd George. Giant, bronze and angry, he faces the square, waving a rhetorical fist.

At this south-western end of the Menai Straits the distinction between the land and water slowly becomes blurred. Newborough Warren sticks out on the Ynys Môn side, and its counterpart of the landward side is Morfa Dinlle. If these low jutting pieces of land are little more than elevated sandbanks, the sandbank known as Caernarfon Bar is almost a piece of land. The sea foams over it viciously, marking the boundary between the Straits and the Bay.

The end of Morfa Dinlle is so far from the land, surrounded on three sides by tide, that it is easier to approach it from the sea. Few people consequently see Belan Fort, which stands on sand with its edges nearly in the water. It was built in 1776 by Thomas Wynn (another branch of the Wynn family), who later became the first Lord Newborough. He built it to protect the western entrance to the Menai Straits from the French, and a few years later, then the Lord Lieutenant, he went to the unusual length of raising his own private army with which he garrisoned Belan. There were four hundred of them, and they were provided entirely at his own expense.

Once again, down Morfa Dinlle, we come into the country of myth. Dinlle, the name itself, relates it to the hero-god Lleu: Din-Lleu. Lleu Llaw Gyffes was the son of Arianrhod, an intimidating lady who had been supposed at the time to be a virgin. His uncle (and, the tale implies, his father), Gwydion, hid him immediately after his birth. The boy grew up to be the main hero of the long and complicated *Mabinogion* story, 'Math son of Mathonwy'. 'They came to Dinas Dinlleu. And there Lleu Llaw Gyffes was reared . . . '

The coastline here is flat and dull, the beach long and straight. It is not broken until the outlines of Bwlch Mawr and the Rivals *(Yr Eifl)*, several miles away. Here Gwydion brought up Lleu Llaw Gyffes at Dinas Dinlle, close by Llandwrog, on the shore. Since there is a large hump there on the flat coast there is no mistaking it.

It is vast. It is a high, steep, complex mound of unnatural appearance in the wide and open country. Assuming that it was at one time circular (which is not necessarily so) half or nearly half of it has already fallen into the sea. It is composed of two circles of ramparts, an outer wall halfway up the hill, an inner wall at the top. Inside the huge enclosure made by the inner wall there are signs of other earthworks or constructions. On the north side the inner wall is built so steeply that it is still extremely difficult to climb. In its scope and layout it is similar to other forts, but most of them are on the top of hills. In places the soil has fallen away, revealing that Dinas Dinlle is not, as might have been thought, an example of a large-scale earthwork, but is probably constructed of stone, actually of rounded seastones in the same way as the walls bounding the fields nearby. If the earth could be cleared away perhaps it would appear as an example of dry-walling as impressive as the citadel at Mycenae. On the beach below one can spot, by their even size and different colour, many of the stones which formed the remainder of the fort. Although Dinas Dinlle has not been properly excavated, finds, mostly Roman coins, seem to point to the period of the second and third centuries AD.

The sea sweeps in with the wide bright breakers of an Atlantic coast, like County Clare. From the top of the fort one can see all there is to be seen of the home of the other member of this misty family – 'Caer Arianrhod'. Gwydion took Lleu there to confront his sister Arianrhod with their offspring. It seems that even then it could be approached directly by ship.

Now it is even safer; it is under the sea.

The nature of Caer Arianrhod (the form it takes on the map) is known only in the form of rumour, and evidence of its ever having been, as it traditionally was, a town, is strangely elusive. People have reported remembering having heard, when young, of somebody, unfortunately unknown, finding some pottery on the reef, but the age of the pottery was never ascertained. Even Ashton, who recorded its plan in his *Evolution of a Coastline*, was looking down at it through the water. Archaeologists in rowing boats have circled it at low tide, without being able to land; and little can be achieved by an archaeologist in a rowing boat. Some fancied they saw masonry, others saw no reason for supposing it to be any more than 'a denuded drumlin', an oval lump deposited by passing ice, from which the sea has washed away the clay. But it is called Caer Arianrhod, both in the story and today, and it is there to see, whatever it really is. A line of stones far out at sea, appearing as a long, even, hard, straight line, such as might have been a breakwater or wall, quite a distance from the lowest point of the tide, with a larger stone, in about the middle, standing above the line.

A little farther south, at Clynnog Fawr, we are on firmer ground. There is, in fact, something very sound and strong both about the name and the place. The church of St Beuno at Clynnog is, for a small Welsh village, unusually substantial. It is also rather later than most, which explains the fine Perpendicular windows. Beuno, in fact, lagging a little behind other saints, founded it in the early seventh century. Tradition asserts that he was buried there, and a chapel in the south-west corner marks the spot. The church which stands so solidly on the site today, however, is all later than 1480 (the chancel and transepts being of that date) and mostly of about 1500. Beuno's tomb traditionally had healing properties, and was still, when Pennant came this way in the late eighteenth century, resorted to by ailing pilgrims.

It is just beyond Clynnog, past the bulk of Bwlch Mawr and

its offshoots, where a gap between the hills allows the road to cross the neck of the peninsula, that Arfon becomes Llŷn. The names refer to *cantrefi* (the plural of *cantref*), originally meaning a hundred towns. In most rural *cantrefi* in North Wales there are probably not even a hundred villages, and it is hard to see how there ever could have been. But a *cantref* is something more than an administrative division. It marks a distinction in one's view of life, an almost tribal territorial relationship. And whether one comes from Arfon, Llŷn, Eifionydd or Ardudwy is seldom a matter of doubt, even to second or third generation exiles.

The division of Wales into its basic units was firmly established even before the arrival, in England, of the Normans; it has persisted largely because it was based on both natural and historical regions, and partly, of course, because the later county system which Edward I brought with him followed, to some extent, the boundaries already laid down. The largest unit, the *gwlad*, was a kingdom. North Wales was Gwynedd and Powys, with their respective dynasties. These were subdivided into *cantrefi*, which might perhaps best be described as localities. Each *cantref* was split again into a small number of *cymydau* (the plural of *cymwd*, anglicized as 'commote', meaning something like neighbourhood).

The three peaks known as the Rivals (*Yr Eifl*) (which dominate the view as one approaches the peninsula), mark the entrance to Llŷn. And here, although in this area of early habitation practically every summit of any size is crowned with a hill-fort, is one of the most impressive Iron Age forts of all. Tre'r Ceiri, home of the giants. It is so well-preserved that it looks recently built, as though only temporarily evacuated by its population, and contains besides the two lines of defence, the clear foundations of about one hundred and fifty huts. Both the huts and the battlements (which, most visible on the seaward side, have a lower inner level providing a wall-walk) are beautifully built, masterpieces of dry-stone walling. Unfortunately this splendid citadel is so remote, high on its steep 1,500-foot (450 m) hill, that for most people it is inaccessible. Were this not so it would perhaps be better known. The climb however provides the added reward of a staggering view: Snowdonia *(Eryri)*, Ynys Môn and Holyhead *(Caergybi)*, the whole of Llŷn and Eifionydd, and, across the bay, the mountains behind Harlech.

A cairn of Bronze Age style lies at the summit of the mountain, in the north-western corner of the walled enclosure. The huts which dot the area of a remarkable variety, round, oval, rectangular, in some cases semi-detached. It must have been a Welsh equivalent of Knossos. Finds date from the mid-second century until about AD 400.

Just below the Rivals *(Yr Eifl)*, lies the quarry village of Trefor. Self-contained, on the way to nowhere, it came into existence in this remote spot purely to house and provide for the quarry workers. The mountain (the seaward Rival, *Eifl)* represents a sort of smaller version of Penmaenmawr, once a source of high-quality granite (once again, not correctly granite, but a mixture of quartz and porphyrite), but now become inactive, being, perhaps both because of its size and the particular characteristics of its stone, rather limited in economic scope. Trefor stone, which came in various colours, including pink and blue-grey, has been much used for monumental purposes. One of its more unusual uses was for curling stones.

Almost inaccessible beyond the quarry, a little valley under the Rivals *(Yr Eifl)* bears a name and an association linking it, once again, with the stream of early history, Nant Gwrtheyrn is translated as Vortigern's *(Gwrtheyrn's)* valley; and traditionally this is where the unfortunate high-king of Britain, replaced at Dinas Emrys by Ambrosius *(Emrys)*, came to die.

The road runs down through the gap towards Pwllheli, and a lane leaves it to pass behind the Rivals *(Yr Eifl)* and follow the peninsula's north coast. This is Llŷn. Its slopes, bare of trees in the sea wind, probably provided, more than anywhere, a foothold for the earliest people. Blocked from the anglicized north-east by the substantial barrier of the mountains, and simply too far away to merit anyone's interference, the end of Llŷn remained throughout history, and to a large extent still remains, a country on its own. Its settled population is firmly related to the land it lives on. Every inch of the long promontory has been cultivated for centuries, a living picked out of the rocks, stones which largely composed it built up into walls to harbour the important soil. Every cove and cliff-foot is milked of its lobsters and crabs, and the silky green sea which lies at the bottom of all its slopes yields, profusely, a slippery harvest of mackerel.

The sea off the cliffs of Llŷn is as clear as the Aegean. One gets dizzy looking into its clean depths. When the trawlers haul in Caernarfon Bay close in under the peninsula, one can see, from the deck, the net creeping up like a monster, fathoms down, crawling towards the boat through the soft water; its fat cod-end finally lying peacefully submerged alongside, waiting to be gathered.

The people of Llŷn have lived this self-contained life for so long that they probably have nothing to fear now from the influences of the outside world. Their way of life seems indestructible. In a world where everybody knows everybody else, being in any case, related to them, it is the stranger who is at a disadvantage, not the native. Wide-eyed monoglot children gape with wonder when it is explained to them: he's an Englishman. As recently as July 1971 a *Times* reporter estimated that there were about twelve elderly non-English speakers left in Llŷn. One of them, whom he interviewed, explained that she had managed well enough not speaking any English for about ninety years. Their grandchildren, brought up in Welsh, will of course learn a little English when they go to school. And indeed they will need to, since the days are gone now when the farthest anyone ever went was to Pwllheli on a market day. But it will probably always be unusual and a little odd to hear anything but Welsh being spoken in the stony small-farm country of the peninsula's backbone.

Perhaps it is this bond between the language and the way of life which reinforces the feeling of the durability, the continuity, of Llŷn. Only, elsewhere, in such places as the Aran Isles, can one find, intact, the survivors of the pre-Norman, pre-English, even pre-Roman Iron Age Celts. All that is left of them is the language, and the settlements of these few exposed western headlands.

Not that tourism has failed to penetrate. The coast has its one or two holiday villages. Nefyn and Morfa Nefyn (though neither of them really seaside towns) have been popular family-holiday spots for at least a generation. But it is a short season; and the interior remains, even in the August rush, largely undisturbed. In the case of Nefyn there seems even to have been a retreat. It was, by the end of the twelfth century, a town of some importance in North Wales, and was chosen by Edward I as the place at which he celebrated, with a full-scale feudal tournament, his conquest of Gwynedd. This remarkable event, in 1284, was perhaps the only thing of note which ever happened in Nefyn, or ever will. There is no sign there now of pomp or pageantry.

Morfa Nefyn, though even smaller, is more nearly on the sea, to the extent of almost succeeding in being a resort. At one extremity of the bay lies Porth Dinllaen, a harbour fully sheltered by its rocky headland, with an almost inevitable promontory fort well placed at its neck. The little village by the water, including an inn, looks as if it might well have arisen there by mistake. And in fact it was under a misapprehension that the inn and the pier were built. Porth Dinllaen, in 1839, narrowly escaped becoming the port for Ireland. If it had happened that this sheltered inlet, instead of Holyhead, had been chosen as the embarkation point for the important mail, then presumably Stephenson would have been obliged to tunnel through the Rivals (Yr Eifl) rather than bridge the Straits, and Telford would have had to build another road. The effect which this would have had on both Ynys Môn and Llŷn may be judged by comparing Holyhead with Porth Dinllaen. It was only by a single casting vote that this attractive tiny hamlet has retained its isolation.

Between Porth Dinllaen and Mynydd Mawr at the peninsula's end are farms and villages, lanes, stone walls, crags, bays and beaches (such as Porthor, known as Whistling Sands), one more hill-fort (on round Garn Fadryn), several pubs (at, for instance, Sarn), a chambered tomb, some hut circles and at least three churches. It is, in fact, a typical stretch of north-west Wales. Through it one comes, with, inevitably, the feeling of having attained some goal, to the heather-covered slopes of the headland, Braich y Pwll. It was, for centuries, a pilgrimage. Resting at Clynnog and Nefyn, the pilgrims made their way down to the end of the land, to the holy island. It still has the air, as perhaps all places which have been intensely sacred have, of offering a destination. Like one's first glimpse of Delos, climbing to a high point of another headland, the basking whale of Bardsey *(Ynys Enlli)* coming into sight elicits the feeling 'There it is'. As if it were something one had been looking for.

Ynys Enlli correctly (but more commonly known through the ages by its Viking name, perhaps Bards Eyre, island of bards), lies 3 miles (5 km) off the headland and about twice as far from the nearest landing place. A vicious tide-rip makes the crossing at all times long and hard, and often quite impossible. It was the home of holy men since the early sixth century, and its charisma as a goal of pilgrimage derives from its being the reputed burial place of twenty thousand saints.

Most people will get no nearer (like Moses) to this promised land than the view of it. Where the cliffs of Braich y Pwll dive to the sucking sea, one looks out hopelessly across Bardsey sound *(Swnt Enlli)* to the dozing, wallowing island. This is the end of the land, the end of the land-bound journey. It is, all too visibly, the end of the world in which most people live. Beyond is hermit's country, the world of mystics. We know what it is like, but it is not for us.

We know what it is like, in this case, chiefly because it has been described by someone who lived there for fourteen years. Brenda Chamberlain's *Tide-Race*, a book which leaves one soaked in spray and encrusted with salt, describes the island as it was during the 1950s, when a community of about twelve people farmed its slopes and fished its sea. Perhaps one day before very long all that too may be over, as much a part of the past as the twenty thousand saints. Lord Newborough (in whose family it had been since the sixteenth century) sold the island privately in 1971. At present a small community of people remain, and continue to farm and fish it.

The early Celtic monastery on Ynys Enlli appears to have been succeeded by a medieval (Augustinian) one from about the eleventh century. All that remains of this now is a ruined thirteenth-century tower. The other buildings on the island are farmhouses rebuilt in the late nineteenth century; and, at the southern tip, the lighthouse.

No doubt the choice of such inaccessible places for religious foundations in early times was due mainly to the dangers suffered elsewhere. And Ynys Enlli probably owed its rise to prominence, and a few thousand of its saints, to the Saxon attacks on inland monasteries. Its numbers would undoubtedly be boosted by the refugees from the massacre of monks near the Welsh border, in the early seventh century. Its fame in later times would arise from what was even then its antiquity. Two pilgrimages to Ynys Enlli were equivalent to one to Rome. The journey cannot ever have been anything less than hard.

Eleven

LLŶN AND EIFIONYDD

Under the shelter of the headland squats what must qualify as the paradigm Welsh village, being at the same time the most village-like and the most Welsh. The traffic jams of the summer weeks seem hardly to have affected it at all, when one dares, out of season, to approach it again. A stranger in the street stands out as conspicuously as a giraffe, drawing eyes, one feels, from behind those net curtains in the tiny windows of the one cluster of grey cottages. In the pub they look at you with the unspoken question written in their faces, longing, but not being able, to ask who you are and why, and where you have come from and for what purpose to their small world, in Aberdaron in the winter.

Under the headland, and almost in the bay, with its two low islands and its wide strip of sand, Aberdaron crouches. It feels, and is, remote. The road ends here, with a short, bright village street, and then suddenly the sea. For those few weeks the coaches and cars swarm through it, the families crowd its beach, and it adapts without much effort to the world of souvenirs and ice-cream. For the rest of the year it is a small harbour-village at the end of Llŷn.

Aberdaron is sheltered, in its private bay, facing south, and in fine weather a mild and sunny place. But one always feels aware there of being so close to the waves of southerly storms. At the edge of the village the church and, precariously, the churchyard face the potential weather, the sea and its gales. Sand has piled high on the seaward side, making the church, from some angles, look half buried. Once it was some hundreds of yards from the coast. Some of the churchyard had by the nineteenth century already started to fall into the sea, and it is only held together now by a strong sea-wall. High tides lick at it and their waves spatter its gravestones. And through the centuries its parishioners must have struggled out of the single Norman doorway in the west wall into the spray and driving rain of countless south-west gales. Or stood, frozen to granite, in the open churchyard sloping above the sea, for grim winter burials.

St Hywyn, to whom this (and no other) church is dedicated, came to Llŷn in the late fifth century, and became associated with the monastic community of Ynys Enlli. The early Celtic church he built at Aberdaron was, of course, made of wood, and like so many others was only replaced by a lasting stone structure in the late twelfth century. This, a simple Norman church which is now most of the north nave of the present one, was enlarged during the fifteenth century. It fell into disrepair in the 1830s, after a century which had been hard times for the Church in Wales. Happily it was carefully restored during the 1860s, and serves its function now as effectively as ever, its vicar during the 1970s being none other than the poet R.S. Thomas.

The pattern of long sandy beaches curving between rocky headlands (the tops of them a springy turf under one's feet) establishes itself at this far-westerly tip and continues all along the south coast of Llŷn. The long sweep known as Porth Neigwl (but in English, Hell's Mouth, into which a strong and heavy surf often rolls) is perhaps the best example of these spacious beaches, stretching as it does all the way to the peninsula's other extremity. If Braich y Pwll is the equivalent of Land's End, then Mynydd Cilan is the Lizard. And to continue this analogy, the area is also slightly less distinguished scenically.

Most people come to Abersoch from the other side. It is not only difficult, but rather perverse, to cross this headland from Porth Neigwl and come down into the village from behind. Most people, historically and today, come to it from the Pwllheli side. And it hardly seems an exaggeration to use the phrase in both its senses, because I have the firm impression that most people, at some time or other in their lives, have been to Abersoch.

Possibly to the rich young Midlanders who constitute so large a part of the present-day invasion, it would seem unlikely that the place had not been discovered suddenly by their generation, made accessible by the advent of the car, and made desirable by the universal ownership of sailing dinghies and speed-boats. So modern and smart is it now that they would find it hard to realize that it has been, for all its persisting old-Welsh-village façade, modern and smart for generations, and began to be so when their grandparents, for their part, were rich and young.

To the real discoverers of Abersoch 'before the war' means 1912. You should have seen it before the war. The overdressed and fading figures in the albums inhabit an empty beach, down to which they come each day with their hampers and rugs from the cottage which they have adventurously hired for the two months of the summer. How they found it is a mystery. Why they thought it worthwhile to make the journey by train to Pwllheli and then by bus (getting off to enable it to climb Llanbedrog Hill) into this lonely, off-the-map place.

It was an adventure worthy, perhaps, of the time; and belonging to those who also turn up in more distant places, posing beside familiar monuments, but always wearing their stiff-collars and boaters, their big hats and stays and long dresses. You sent the servants on ahead, to the Abersoch cottage, with the trunks. A hamper regularly arrived from home during the summer, with edible goods which no one would expect to find in distant Wales. Cousins and their friends came to stay. It is strange to find that in this same place, where the first car-owners proudly paraded their enormous machines, the descendants and equivalents of these people now flock with their MGBs and their Lotuses. There is one overwhelming factor which distinguishes this new Abersoch generation from the last and the one before that. They are, like so many other categories of people, drastically more numerous.

Part of the secret of the place is the climate. Sunshine beats down for endless sandy summer afternoons, beating on the roofs of the beach-huts stacked against the slope, on the green but crowded south Caernarfon sea, on the hot sand lined with drawn-up yachts, on the brown and busy people. It is an imitation Côte d'Azur, but without the French and their inconvenient language; St Tropez-in-Llŷn. Part of its secret also is the anchorage, a safe and almost wind-proof bay which has become one of the largest small-boat centres in the country. Part of it of course is tradition. They go where their friends go, to have the security of being amongst others of the same type.

Wales is unpredictable, and Abersoch is one of its surprises. One would never expect to find these large businessmen in shorts parking their Bentleys in these lanes, or climbing the steps from the jetty to the yacht-club towards a gin-and-tonic overlooking the thirst-making sea, at the end of a long Welsh afternoon; and the purr of sports cars and speedboats, the sweep and splash of skis. It is part of a confident and expansive order of things which is, to put it mildly, incongruous in stony, chapel-going Llŷn.

Pwllheli is the area's market town; a small, not specially beautiful, well-established place. Pwllheli is the point at which the ordinary lines of communication with the outside world reach the border of Llŷn. It is the place to which the outlying farmers come religiously on market day, to sit most of the afternoon in the dark pubs and exchange information. It might have appeared grey and even drab were it not for the clear light, which would make any place look fresh and clean. This light, as sharp and bright as that of a Greek island, characterizes the whole of Llŷn and coastal Eifionydd. It makes the walls and cottages, the turf and rocks, immediately present, there in front of one's eyes with a salience which leaves the colourless and indistinct features of the ordinary inland world seeming only half-experienced. Even these unremarkable streets and shops stand out in three crystal dimensions.

Pwllheli flourished as a port (particularly during the last decades of the eighteenth century) until the middle of the nineteenth century. Its shipbuilding industry then began to be replaced by that of Porthmadog, the port which Madocks suddenly invented in the 1820s. The harbour, from which slate, corn and, during the times of large-scale emigration of the late eighteenth and early nineteenth centuries, the inhabitants of Llŷn and Eifionydd, left for the Atlantic, eventually became largely silted up. Pwllheli began to build accommodation for visitors about the middle of the nineteenth century, and by the 1890s was a flourishing resort. It spread, at that time, away from the harbour to what was, and is, known as the South Beach. This, a stretch of sand about 4 miles (6.5 km) long, reaching as it does along the coast to Llanbedrog Head, is still a popular seaside.

When I first went to Greece a friend advised me to visit the town of Patra, because it was ordinary. There was nothing specially interesting or unusual about it, and in order to get to know a country one should see an ordinary modern town there. Perhaps something similar could be said about Pwllheli, which is certainly as Welsh as Patra is Greek.

The road from Pwllheli to Cricieth runs along a flat and uninspiring coastal plain. There is nothing of interest about it until, halfway between the two towns, one suddenly and unexpectedly drives past what seems to be a sort of large internment camp. But looking again you fail to find the guard-towers at the corners of this high and impenetrable fence, and if machine-guns scan the low, faceless huts, they are well hidden. Even more surprisingly there seems to be little sign of the internees, whom one expects to see processing round in circles for their daily exercise.

Only the overhead chair-lift which swings above the camp gives it away. Behind that formidable fence are interned a holiday camp's happy holiday-makers.

In addition to the chair-lift to the beach they are conveyed by their own narrow-gauge railway. Two kindly retired steam railway engines amuse the children. There is free water-skiing instruction, a roundabout, a 'French' bar and a 'Spanish' bar, and all the usual fun and games. Visitors have a choice between all-in, bed-and-breakfast, or self-catering terms. and the additional temptations of cafeterias, snack-bars, grill-rooms, chip-shops and restaurants. Thrown in are amusements, the indoor and outdoor swimming pools, the sporting competitions, the ballroom dancing.

It is, again, a strange anomaly. The last thing one would expect at this southern end of Llŷn is this large injection of rowdy fun-and-games people. Perhaps fortunately for the surrounding area the fence works both ways. It not only keeps out the marauding tribesmen; it keeps the pink and jolly families in. Isolated behind it they seem to feel little need to come out. So many cheerful people spilling over Chwilog and Llanystumdwy would have a devastating effect.

At this point Llŷn becomes Eifionydd: an area which covers the southern part of the peninsula's thick neck, the coast and its hinterland as far as Porthmadog. Strictly speaking it was not a *cantref* (like Llŷn and Arfon) but a commote which, together with Ardudwy, formed the large *cantref* of Dunoding; but it is quite distinct enough to stand on its own, as it normally does. Hundreds of tiny villages with names longer than their streets dot the rolling land. A maze of narrow lanes threads among the fields and farms, a network pattern developed haphazardly in the course of natural evolution. In the distance, from some places, one can see mountains. It is a very beautiful country, a sweeping, open landscape under an expansive sky.

Even the tiniest hamlet in this area, and indeed in this sort of area everywhere in North Wales, has its chapel. And to understand fully what is involved in the people's way of life one really has to understand why. Nonconformism and the Welsh way of life are inextricably entangled. To a large extent those big, austerely empty, featureless, high light rooms, surprisingly fresh and airy inside their massive grey shells, are used for the worship of a monoglot God.

One feels in the villages of Eifionydd that it is somehow right that this should be so. The English language penetrated later and less strongly into this area than in other parts of Wales. And what was always felt to be the greatest threat to national identity, and an incongruity which fell far short of satisfying its purpose, was the English church. It will be remembered that one of Glyndŵr's aims was to set up an independent Church of Wales. Since the original conquest, Wales had not had its own church. Comparison with Scotland, where Presbyterianism had been established in the seventeenth century, and which had, in any case, its own official Church, was eventually inevitable.

Nonconformism began to develop into a concise movement in Wales during the eighteenth century. Not that Wales had ever conformed: the Celtic Church was a worry to successive early Popes, and Pelagius, the first successful heretic (whose appealing doctrine, that man was not damned by Adam's fall but able to save himself simply by being good, scarcely seems like heresy today) was a Brythonic Celt. But during the eighteenth century a system of absentee-landlordism on the part of bishops (some of the bishops of the Bangor diocese, for instance, never went there) had led to the deterioration, and secularization, of church life in Wales. The need for religion which seems to be inherent in the temperament of the people, was thwarted of an outlet.

Methodism began to gather strength in the 1730s, originating as a form of religious revival. The movement became Calvinistic, rather than Wesleyan, probably because of the temperament of the people involved. By 1811 the Welsh Methodists were ordaining their own ministers. The appeal of the movement (unpopular at first, and discouraged by the landowners and the established church), gradually became strong amongst the people. The emotionalism of it suited them, the passionate sermons and strongly-worded hymns. Crowds of thousands gathered to the travelling preachers at the remote places and odd hours of the night or early morning which their persecutors forced them to adopt. Because the aristocracy had, since Tudor times, become increasingly Anglicized, the movement, as a part of Welsh culture, relied on a peasant following. This in itself perpetuated and emphasized the differences between the squires (who remained Anglican by religion as they were English by language) and their tenants, and added greatly to the sense of popular identity which came with Methodism.

With its overtones of austerity, severity, and the fatalistic acceptance of God's will, it had, in any case, much to offer to the inhabitants of a rough and windy land, whose only contact with that century's material advances had been, in all too many cases, the contribution of their labour or rent to the prosperity of some great family. Poverty, abstinence, respectability and chapelgoing became, for these various reasons, an essential feature of Welsh life. It is perhaps no accident that the tall hats which, earlier in the twentieth century, the women still wore to chapel on Sundays, were the last remnants of the once-universal Puritan tall hat.

Not is it by chance that this same movement eventually produced that mixture of liberal politics and Home Rule demands which has developed into today's political Welsh Nationalism. The area of Llanystumdwy and Cricieth is inevitably associated with one of the originators of this trend.

There are of course many people in North Wales today who are the children of men with whom Lloyd George had a mutual acquaintanceship. North Wales is anyway dotted with the birthplaces of famous people; but, perhaps because the country's greatest export over the centuries has been people, they were mostly men who were destined to achieve their fame elsewhere, and not come back. H.M. Stanley, born at Denbigh (Dinbych), made a name for himself by an encounter at Ujiji, on Lake Tanganyika. A small and otherwise insignificant cottage on the outskirts of Tremadog was where a certain unsuspecting woman, in inauspicious circumstances, gave birth to Lawrence of Arabia. But Lloyd George, of Llanystumdwy, although he would probably never have become famous if he had never left, remained faithful throughout his life to the area in which he was brought up.

He was the son of a schoolmaster, and was actually born near Manchester. His father died while he was an infant, however, and he and his mother went to live with her brother at Llanystumdwy, close to Cricieth. His uncle was a shoemaker, and a part-time Baptist minister. David was educated at the village school, and when he was 16 he went to work for a solicitor in Porthmadog. Five years later he started his own practice in Cricieth, and worked as a solicitor there and in Porthmadog for the next five years. At the early age of 27 he won a by-election at Caernarfon, becoming the Liberal Member for Caernarfon Boroughs.

Lloyd George was a Welsh Nationalist. It was a chapel-based party, with Welsh disestablishment as its aim. This at that time was also part of the Liberal Party's programme, and so the Nationalists joined the Liberals. But Lloyd George was more extreme in his opinions than his position even at the left wing of the Liberal Party would indicate. He wanted complete severance from England, true Home Rule for Wales. In 1886, four years before he was elected, he had been one of the founders of a group called Cymru Fydd, the remote ancestor of the present Plaid Cymru. His advocacy of separatism became unpopular, and the movement failed in 1895. He tried unsuccessfully to form another group in 1899.

Lloyd George kept his constituency for fifty-five years. When he gave up office after an illness, in 1931, he spent more time in Cricieth, where he lived in a large white house called Bryn Awelon, up a lane on the Caernarfon side of the town. It was probably during this later period that so many people's fathers got to know him and he them. He seems to have been an accessible and friendly figure, and became, to his inconvenience one of the sights of Cricieth which visitors to the town had to see.

Afon Dwyfor runs down into Llanystumdwy, through a narrow wooded valley; and it was from the name of this river that David Lloyd George took his title, 'of Dwyfor', when, only two months before his death, he relinquished his Caernarfon seat to become an Earl. He lies buried not, as he might have been, in Westminster Abbey, but at Llandystumdwy, where, on the steep bank of the river, a fine, imposingly simple memorial commemorates him.

Meanwhile the Welsh Disestablishment Bill, which Gladstone had launched soon after Lloyd George joined his party, was delayed by the war, and not finally put into force until 1920. By then of course the chapels, which partly owed their original success to the Englishness of the Church of Wales, had become deeply rooted in Welsh village life, and remain so; a powerful element in the education and outlook of the communities.

Cricieth, with its long promenade and wide beach, its several good hotels, and, picturesquely on a promontory of rock, its crumbling castle, is in many ways an ideal small resort. Except in unfortunate weather, when the drizzle sweeps its exposed front very dismally, it is attractive as a town, laid out with some order and consistency. The town is originally older, like Caernarfon, than its Edwardian charter; but only a few sixteenth- and seventeenth-century houses remain of the old Borough. Most of the present town was purpose-built as a watering-place during the nineteenth century.

Cricieth Castle, which so suitably adds its jagged outline to the top of the round rock, was not built by Edward I. It was standing there, in substantially the same form, when he founded the Borough around it in 1284. It is one of the few pre-conquest castles, like Dolwyddelan, and Dolbadarn, and was built during the earlier part of the thirteenth century by the Princes of Gwynedd.

When Llywelyn the Great died there was some doubt about the succession. He had two sons, one (Dafydd) by his wife Joan, and an elder illegitimate, but wholly Welsh one, Gruffudd. It seems that Dafydd felt himself to be in an insecure position, as he imprisoned his half-brother in Cricieth Castle in 1239. It also shows some foresight, if the date is correct, since Llywelyn did not die until 1240. But Dafydd had already been chosen by him as successor, and it may have been clear that this was against the wishes of the people.

Gruffudd was eventually released, after interference by King Henry III, and found himself transferred to an even safer imprisonment in the Tower of London. There he fell during an excape attempt and broke his leg. It was, however, his son, Llywelyn ap Gruffudd, who succeeded Dafydd, and became the last Welsh Prince of Wales.

Llywelyn ap Gruffudd seems to have made frequent use of Cricieth Castle. He imprisoned a rival there in 1259, and a letter from him to Edward I in 1273 or 1274 is addressed from Cricieth. Edward came to Cricieth and made some alterations to the castle shortly after Llywelyn's death. The inner gatehouse was raised – it now forms the most prominent feature of the ruins – but other improvements seem to have been small-scale. Consequently what we have is mainly the shell of the seat of the two Llywelyns. It is thought that the inner ward would be the work of the earlier, the outer ward added by the later.

Cricieth Castle did not have a particularly dramatic later history. It was missed by Madog's revolt, and fell to Glyndŵr in 1404. On this occasion it was largely destroyed, and has remained in that state ever since. Consequently it also missed the customary change of hands which Welsh castles underwent during the Civil Wars.

Black Rock Sands *(Traeth Morfa Bychan)* stretch to the east, forming the next bay beyond Cricieth, a few miles of hard, clean sand, Black Rock Caves under the headland, and, living up to its name, Black Rock itself. The coast flattens, behind, becoming Golf Course country; across the bay Harlech rock stands out, and, in the distance, the long bulk of Cadair Idris. The broad estuary of Afon Glaslyn lies between its sand spurs, Morfa Bychan and Morfa Harlech, forcing the road to curve inland towards Porthmadog. Traeth Mawr, which Madocks stole from the sea, stretches northwards to Beddgleert, and we have been here before.

Part Four

Ardudwy

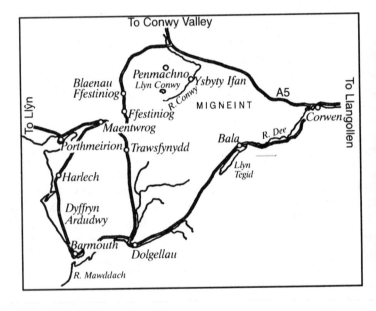

Twelve

OVER THE WATERSHED

From the point at which the Conwy valley and the Lledr valley joined, and, together, turned north towards the sea, a line drawn south to Dolgellau passes through 23 miles (38 km) of almost completely empty country. In the eastern section of Ardudwy and its approaches there are no towns. Two small villages and a couple of wild moorland roads are all that interfere with this wide expanse of utter wilderness. From a high point in the middle of it, say above Cwm Penmachno, you can see it stretching away, ridge after ridge of moor, unbroken between Dolwyddelan and Bala, inhabited as far as one can see by not even a sheep. For those troubled by the population problem it provides instant relief.

The two valleys which drain this high land to the north flow down into Afon Conwy, each of them containing a road, a river and a village. One of these rivers is in fact the infant Conwy itself, which runs with suitable gurgling and prancing through the moorland from it source, Llyn Conwy, and, gathering confidence, proceeds down a long, straight, even-sided upland valley to Ysbyty Ifan.

'John's Hospital'. In or about 1180 the Knights of St John of Jerusalem established a Hospice and sanctuary in this remote valley, the purpose of which was to provide safety and hospitality to travellers over the moors. It seems that Llywelyn the Great extended their lands, together with the privilege of sanctuary, to take in most of the valley and the area of Llyn Conwy. The hospital, famous for its hospitality in the Middle Ages, appears to have degenerated during the late fifteenth century to become a den of thieves. The right of immunity remained, now abused, after the religious purpose had disappeared. Sir John Wynn describes it:

. . . there was continually fostered a wasps' nest, which troubled the whole countrey, I mean a lordship belonging to St Johns of Jerusalmen, called Spytty Jevan, a large thing, which had privilege of sanctuary. This peculiar jurisdiction, not governed by the King's Lawes, became a receptacle of thieves and murtherers, who safely being warranted there by law, made the place thoroughly peopled. Noe spot within twenty miles was safe from their incursions and roberies, and what they got within their limits was their owne . . . In this estate stood the hundred of Nantconway when Meredith removed his dwelling thither . . . in the beginning of King Henry the Seventh his time.

Maredydd ap Ifan, Sir John's ancestor, had, as we have seen, moved to Dolwyddelan Castle from his home near Traeth Mawr, complaining of the turbulent conditions there: 'for if I live in mine house in Eifionydd, I must either kill my own kindred or be killed by them'. He would prefer, he said, to fight with outlaws and thieves than with his own blood and kin. It was largely due to the arrival in the district of this ancestor of the Wynns that the area of Ysbyty started to become less dangerous.

Ysbyty now is a compact and sturdily-built riverside village, a number of solid brown-grey buildings, including an old mill, still with its wheel. This, built during the middle of the nineteenth century, lapsed from its corn-grinding function in the 1930s, and from then until the early 1960s provided the whole of the village with electricity.

The Hospice of Ysbyty Ifan was dissolved along the monasteries, and nothing remains of the religious foundation now. The present church was built (on the site of the original one) in 1858. It contains, however, some original memorials, including alabaster effigies of three members of a great family. They are in a very poor state of repair, but one of them (now without his feet) was Rhys ap Maredydd, none other than the standard-bearer of Henry Tudor at the Battle of Bosworth, on that occasion when the Red Dragon flew again and the long-delayed prophecy of Dinas Emrys came true. This ruined alabaster torso of the man whom Richard III personally hacked down in his effort to come to grips with his Welsh rival, lies alongside the effigies of his wife and son. This son was Cardinal Wolsey's chaplain and cross-bearer, unfortunately now without a head, but recognizably still wearing his surplice. It seems strange to find these eminent people at remote Ysbyty Ifan, forlornly lying, mutilated, on the floor.

Parallel to Afon Conwy running through Ysbyty Ifan is Afon Machno running through Penmachno. In a similar way the river runs down on shingle through its birch-groves, forming the self-contained and isolated valley. But Afon Machno comes not from open moorland but out of its high, hanging cwm, where, at the very end of a long and empty valley, is the smallest and most distant settlement of all, at Cwm Penmachno. Once justified by its surrounding slate-quarries, it lies now, trapped in encircling hills, heavy with an end-of-the-world peace.

Penmachno itself is not all that much larger, a shop, a pub, a church, a school, a chapel or two and a number of terraces of squat grey cottages. That it was an early settlement of some importance is indicated by the discovery, in the churchyard and nearby, of five early Christian tombstones. One of them, by mentioning the Consul Justinus, dates itself fairly accurately at AD 540. Another, of the fifth to early sixth century, not only bears the primitive Chi-Rho monogram (the Greek letters XP, being the first two of the word 'Christos', put together in the form of a cross with a round head) but mentions the person commemorated as lying 'in hoc congeries lapidum' – in this heap of stones, which indicates that the Bronze Age custom of building a cairn over a burial still existed in remote parts of Wales well into Christian times. A third, also of the fifth or early sixth century, bears a reference to Venedotia, the Latin name for Gwynedd, and includes on its side the word *magistrat* – , an unusual case of a Brythonic native bearing the title

'Magistratus' in post-Roman times. The church which contains these relics of its predecessors was built in 1857, and has now been practically rebuilt in the 1970s.

Penmachno owes what little subsequent fame it has had to being the birthplace of the great Bishop Morgan, who was probably born, in 1545, at the house called Tŷ Mawr, Wybrnant which still stands, in very much its original state, in the hills above the village. A window commemorating this man who gave Wales its first translation of the Bible was added to the new church in 1859.

All around Penmachno, above the Bishop's birthplace, stretch acres of untracked forest, a wild high area planted and replanted through the centuries, and now intensively worked by the Forestry Commission, which provides for Cwm Machno its main means of existence. Out of the head of the valley on the other side, and up out of the trees, rises a small road, emerging on to open, unfenced land, with wide views for miles to the south, over Y Migneint. It joins the road which comes up from the very top of the Conwy stream, and in this plateau between the two valleys lies Llyn Conwy. This expanse of water opens in a shallow dip in the moorland, grouse-shoot country, heavily clumped with heather, flat and exposed to the rainclouds which sweep over it. Larks spring out of it loudly from the early summer.

In the distance the gentle bulky outlines of the two Arenigs rise over the moor; blue-grey smooth-flanked mountains, dominating the expanse of the Migneint. This area which lies between them and the Uwch Conwy (Upper Conwy), called Y Migneint, meaning an area of bog, is in fact a cotton-grass and heather moorland rich in botany and views. Y Migneint is, in the true sense, a moor: that is, an area of poor, acid, peaty soil on which an undisturbed ecology of moss, heather and moorgrass perpetually work out their cycles. Spagnum sponges up its incipient streams, and rushes and reeds add a rare vertical perspective to the patches where water settles in the peat's hollows. Alternative rush and heather zones mark out its structure of peat-ridges and boggy hollows. The spongy ground squelches, everywhere thick with plant-matter.

This area of what we would probably normally describe as heath, is the largest example of this kind of land in Wales. Lying at over a 1,000 feet (300 m), its endless rolling views (given proportion by the tops of the Arenigs, hull-down over the horizon) provide an airiness, an open exposure to the sky, verging perhaps on loneliness. One feels that only in mid-Atlantic could one be more alone.

Even those familiar with the Migneint in all its moods find it difficult to explain the fascination of what is, after all, a large, flat, empty area. A great expanse of almost nothing. But whether on those thirsty days when the ground smells of warm peat, the cotton-grass dotting the hollows with white, and the larks bursting, invisibly, high in the bright sky; or under heavy nimbus trailing across the bell-heather on the humps, threatening rain and darkness; or on crisp and glassy days when the Arenigs loom pure white, a brief slanting sun clarifying the frozen reeds and crackling grass: in all seasons one feels aware that the place has its own distinctive character.

The peat moors stretch on and on above the Ffestiniog valley, broken only by the occasional lake in their hollows, until finally one larger than the others intrudes, at Trawsfynydd, and the land rises again on the other side as a mountain, bounding the moorland on the western side.

The *Mabinogion* crops up from place to place throughout North Wales, and no part of it is so firmly located on the ground as the tale called 'Math son of Mathonwy'. Although we have already met the principal characters, Gwydion and Lleu Llaw Gyffes, on the coast near Dinas Dinlle, no part of North Wales is so firmly established as being the scene of their tale as the Ffestiniog valley and the area, around Trawsfynydd, immediately above it.

Gwydion (whose name may connect him with Woden and Odin) was perhaps a god whose cult became localized in north-west Wales, and who later became humanized in the country's mythology. He appears in the *Mabinogion* as a sort of magician, involved in the affairs of the kings of north and south Wales. What we know of him now (just as what we know of Brân, the owner of the magic cauldron) comes from a fourteenth-century manuscript containing material first written down probably during the eleventh century, and coming, presumably, from very much older verbal sources.

Before the birth of Lleu Llaw Gyffes, Gwydion had caused a war between the north and south of Wales, by stealing the sacred pigs of Pryderi, a south Wales prince. A chase ensued, and finally a battle and a truce, which took place at Dolbenmaen, now a cross-roads village just off the Caernarfon-Tremadog road. The two armies travelled under truce across Traeth Mawr (where, until Madocks reclaimed it, a road ran across the sand when the tide was out) and when they reached Y Felenrhyd (a ford of Afon Dwyryd, between Maentwrog and Penrhyndeudraeth, in the Ffestiniog valley) 'the men on foot could not be restrained from shooting at each other'. And there, at the ford of the river, Gwydion and Pryderi fought hand to hand, 'and by magic and enchantment Gwydion conquered, and Pryderi was slain'. And at Maentwrog, the tale states, 'was he buried, and his grave is there'.

The Vale of Ffestiniog is lush and wooded now, as it must have been then (whenever then was), and the particular corner of it which is Maentwrog has a warm, brown, fertile feeling about it which is in great contrast to the country slightly east and north. This is assisted now by harmonious architecture, using the local dark brown stone, of a southern-mountain character, not unlike that of Bavaria or the Italian Tyrol.

There in the churchyard at Maentwrog is something known as Twrog's Stone. It is a monolith, a rounded pillar, partly over-built by the new church. Whether it is supposed to be the grave of Twrog, or brought there by Twrog, or found there by him when he came, or simply the site of his first church, is not clear. It is agreed that the stone is probably prehistoric, whatever that they mean. Assuming that excavation would reveal its true length to be about five feet, it bears a strong similarity to the pillar in the chamber of Bryn-celli-ddu, which marks the centre of that burial mound. Could it be that Twrog's Stone is all that remains of a burial chamber, and that its presence there was what led to the positioning of the original church? If that were the case we could have two views about Pryderi: either this was Pryderi's tomb, or the mention of Pryderi's burial here was a reference to the existence of a burial mound at this spot.

Arianrhod, as we have seen, was not a good mother. Gwydion brought up Lleu Llaw Gyffes, their son, at Dinas Dinlle, and the only contribution his mother made was to lay a series of curses on him. One of these was that he should never have a human wife. Undeterred, Gwydion and Math made a wife for him out of flowers. The recipe is simple: you take the flowers of the broom, the meadowsweet and the oak. The ingredients are to be found growing on many North Wales hillsides in high summer. Having given her human form they further established her identity with a name, and they christened her Blodeuwedd.

Now that they had provided him with a wife, they decided that what he needed next was land. So Math (the king of Gwynedd) gave him 'Cantref Dinoding' – 'and that is nowadays called Eifynydd and Ardudwy. The place in the cantref where he set up a court was the place called Mur Castell, and that in the uplands of Ardudwy'.

This place is known now as Tomen y Mur, and stands high on the shoulder of a hill looking out over Trawsfynydd. As far as anything certain is known about this remarkable site, it is known that it was at one time a Roman camp, and that the mound which forms its most conspicuous feature is said to be a medieval Norman motte. One cannot help wondering, however, if there is something older than a medieval motte within that mound. It looks so like the burial mounds in Ireland, which also, in their later years, served as a ready-made basis for a fortified motte. Roman baths exist nearby, and even a so-called amphitheatre.

There is, however, little visible sign now of a Roman fort at Tomen y Mur. What is most striking about it now is the situation. It surveys the country around in a way reminiscent of the hill of Tara. Although only on a gentle rise, it stands exposed on all sides. A long area of reed, marsh, and rough land, rises slowly to the east, and on the other side lie the grim grey hills over the cold expanse of Llyn Trawsfynydd. It can have changed little in lay-out since Lleu Llaw Gyffes and Blodeuwedd lived there; except, that is, in one respect. Tomen y Mur looks down today upon a disused nuclear power station, and the lake beside it is in fact artificial.

Trawsfynydd power station has blended now with its grey background, forming a bulky and unlovely outcrop in that high bleak valley. It is even, in a way, splendid, adding a sort of monstrous insult to the injury which the place suffers from wind and rain. The situation of Tomen y Mur and its wild surroundings are on the whole desolate and grim, subject to fearful weather, a bad place to get caught by rain. The square, sinister bulk of the power station suits their mood.

The end of the story of Lleu Llaw Gyffes moves no great distance from Tomen y Mur, his home. His wife invited in a stranger while he was away visiting Math, his overlord, and immediately fell in love with him. He was evidently similarly affected by her. 'Nor did they delay longer than that night ere they embraced each other. And that night they slept together.' Wife and lover together, in Lleu's absence, plotted to kill him when he returned. Never trust a woman made of flowers.

It happened that, like other heroes, he could only be killed in a certain way, which, Delilah-like, she persuaded him to tell her, with the rather feeble excuse that her memory was better than his. Since his death could take place neither on horseback nor on foot, neither indoors nor out, it was necessary to arrange for him to stand under a canopy with one foot on a bath-tub and the other on the back of a goat. It is a theme of being between two worlds, two elements, two dimensional schemes, which seems to have had particular mythological meaning.

Only at the joining-points of the structure of reality can one free oneself from the normal world; hence ambiguity is the sphere of the supernatural. In such a way the mistletoe became sacred because it was neither a plant (with roots in the ground) nor something other than a plant. It evaded the categories with which, with a psychological need for order, early men structured the world.

And so Blodeuwedd and her lover plotted this bizarre death. They set up a bath-tub on the banks of Afon Cynfal, and somehow got the ingenuous man to have a bath in it. Asked to demonstrate in what position he might die, he obligingly did so. It could, as Blodeuwedd herself icily remarked, have been easily avoided. 'He arose out of the bath and put on his breeks, and he placed one foot on the edge of the tub and the other on the he-goat's back . . . ' And so, neither clothed nor naked, neither on dry land nor water, neither on the ground nor on horseback, he was poised, ready.

Whatever the explanation of this strange episode, it took place, the story insists, under the lee of a hill on the bank of Afon Cynfal, which is crossed by the road from Ffestiniog to Trawsfynydd. A fast-flowing, sizeable stream with a clearly defined and steeply-sided valley, broadening in its lower stretches and meandering in its upper. Above the bridge it comes down among the hills, bordered by clumps and lines of trees, on one side of it a convenient series of knolls, behind one of which the lover waited with his spear.

Blodeuwedd must have known that it was only a matter of time. Gwydion had made her with his own hands, and could presumably unmake her again at will. She heard that he was on his way to Tomen y Mur, and left the court with her maidens and crossed the mountain and Afon Cynfal in its upper cwm. An element of absurdity attended her to the end. Terrified of pursuit, the maidens walked looking backwards, and in this way walked into Llyn y Morynion ('lake of the maidens'), one of those lakes up there in the shallow depressions of the moors. It is easily done. Blodeuwedd herself was turned by Gwydion

219

into an owl, and you can hear her still bemoaning the fact. The lover died the same death as Lleu, who, resurrected by Gwydion, threw a spear so hard at him that it pierced the stone with which he tried to protect himself. 'And there the stone is, on the bank of the Cynfal river in Ardudwy, and the hole through it.' It seems, however, that it no longer is.

The contrast between the rich and mild Ffestiniog valley and the wild open country of Tomen y Mur and Llyn y Morynion is repeated by that between the top and bottom of the valley itself. One comes down out of the grim excrescences of Blaenau Ffestiniog (distinguished, apart from its unemployment problem, by the surprising fact that it was here, in a grey terraced house, that the novelist John Cowper Powys chose to retreat for the duration of his later life), and into a totally different world. From that of slate to that of flowering greenery. Rhododendrons grow wild on the hillsides, luxuriantly, even high above the mountain wall. Everything thrives; cows stand comfortably in lush meadows. It is as wholesome and acceptable as Austria. One looks out over it almost wistfully: a soft foam of distant trees, in dairylands forlorn.

One point of interest marks, or, according to one's tastes, mars, the upper end of this valley. Just below Blaenau, at Tanygrisiau, the Central Electricity Generating Board has one of its (at present) rare pump-storage schemes. If it is enabled to pursue its plans it seems we may be seeing more of them, in increasing numbers, throughout our mountain areas, as we have seen at Dinorwig, near Llanberis. The system, which no doubt seems especially beautiful to technologists, relies on the fact that at some periods electricity is cheaper (because it is in less demand) than at others. The mechanism then consists of two parts: a reservoir high on a hill, and another reservoir at its foot. Water stored in the top one flows to the bottom, in the process creating electricity; at off-peak periods some of this electricity is used to pump the water back again to the top. The operation has about it an element of endlessness, of self-regeneration, which Sisyphus would have recognized. As a system it seems practically foolproof. As a use of mountains and lakes, however, it has its snags. The top dam is in this case large and visible, and however attractively designed and camouflaged it may be, it is still a big departure from the natural hillscapes which, in some people's views, the National Parks are intended to preserve. Moreover the demands of the system when used as part of the regular supply, require that the level of both lakes must be constantly changing, and while a new area of water might be argued to be a local asset, a part-time area of mud could hardly be represented as anything of the sort.

Up the sides of the valley, among the clumps of indigenous scrub-oak, and through largely untamed country, runs the Ffestiniog railway. This early narrow-gauge track, originally built to carry the slate down from the upper end of the valley (where quarries flourished from the beginning of the nineteenth century) to the quay at Porthmadog, was one of the first of its kind to go over (in 1836) from horses to steam. It began to carry passengers from its early days, and now provides visitors with what is undoubtedly one of the best ways of seeing unspoilt Welsh scenery, of which there is enough in the ten slow miles of its journey to satisfy the most deprived romantic.

At Tan-y-bwlch, above the valley opposite Maentwrog, the National Park Committee has established a headquarters and Study Centre, occupying an old private house and its grounds including 106 acres (40 hectares) of woodland, which provides a focal point for activities in the Park which Snowdonia has so far lacked. Snowdonia National Park has suffered, in fact, in the past, through being shared between three counties, the planning departments of which were individually responsible for their pieces of it, and were only advised, not instructed by a joint Advisory Committee which had, in effect, no powers at all. This administrative entanglement has been the labyrinth in which much goodwill and many good ideas got lost.

When National Parks were first conceived and designated,

in the 1940s, it was firmly intended that each park should be treated as a single and separate unit, and that for this purpose each should have its own planning board, with its own planning officer and staff. These would operate independently of the surrounding County's normal planning department. County councils, however, are territorially possessive creatures, and it turned out that in only two areas (the Peak District and the Lake District) were they willing to be coerced into relinquishing their parks, and pieces of parks, to new and independent authorities. It seems that their attitude arose largely (and still arises) from a feeling that such bodies would represent a diminishing of their own powers. Put more rationally, the argument might be that they would tend to act in the national, rather than the local, interest. Perhaps the surprising and unfortunate thing about this attitude is that it should be felt that there is a necessary and natural conflict between the two.

What is even more surprising (in view of the obvious advantages, for implementing the principles and purposes of National Parks, of each park being planned and administered as an integrated unit) is that the county councils somehow managed to pursue their dogged line even in the face of strong ministerial opposition.

For decades the Government and its advisers and commissions continued to press, with increasing plaintiveness, for their original requirements to be put into effect. Finally this view was strongly supported again in 1971, on the occasion of the reorganization of local government, by Sir Jack Longland's report to the Countryside Commission. Longland argued that the subordination of Park Planning Committees to their respective county councils

has meant that they have not developed a vigorous life of their own, or achieved a record of action, more particularly in providing facilities for recreation, comparable to those of the Parks with Planning Boards. They are unlikely to fulfil all the main purposes of National Parks, under their present method of administration, which accords a relatively low priority to Park affairs.

The County Council Association replied briefly to Longland's attack, pointing out that the general economy of a park and hence the provision of services and facilities were important factors affecting its attractiveness. Parks should not be allowed to become 'merely museums for the few.' Consequently progress was necessary, and would have to be intelligently and sympathetically planned. 'This,' they conclude somewhat arbitrarily, 'can best be achieved by having one local authority responsible for all aspects of the national park and its surrounding area.' The emphasis is on economics, and the suggestion seems to be that only a County Council would be sufficiently realistic in its attitude to ensure that a park does not cease to be 'an area in which people live and work in reasonable economic conditions.'

So great is the association's political influence (rather than their logic) that it was they, apparently through sheer determination not to concede, who in effect finally won this particular round of the long fight. What actually resulted was an attempt at compromise, a rather uncomfortable agreement between the Countryside Commission and the County Councils Association to the effect that the park administration within the county councils, the National Park Committees, should have more delegated power; but would nevertheless still be reliant on the county councils for the majority of their membership, and for their staff. One wonders, however, to what extent the supposed conflict on which this basic agreement rests is real. It is assumed, but not proved, that the provision of employment is incompatible with the preservation of natural scenery, and that it is therefore impossible for an area to be both beautiful and prosperous.

Not even Snowdonia's politest friends would claim that the planning and administration of the Park had, during the first decades of its existence, been a success. The National Park lies in the counties of Gwynedd and Conwy, principally the former, and the makeup of its Board reflects this: nine Councillors from Gwynedd, three from Conwy, with a remaining six members (outnumbered two to one) appointed by the Secretary of State. County councils (for whatever reason) traditionally, and sometimes patently, do not like National Parks. They have obligations and duties with which such nationalized amenities may indeed tend to conflict. They have certainly got closer and more urgent calls on their priorities, on their staff, resources, time and finances. Their members are elected by local people, whose day-to-day activities may seem to be affected adversely, if at all, by the preservation of landscape beauty, of buildings and places of architectural and historic interest, and by the provision of access and facilities for the public enjoyment of all this. They have enough real and immediate problems and needs of their own, without the worry of dealing with the nation's recreation.

Down below Tan-y-bwlch the lower Ffestiniog valley is separated from Traeth Mawr, stretching north, by a projecting spur, across which runs a little-used lane, through humpy, tufty, rocky sheepland, an area as unmistakably North Wales as the Loire valley is France. The other side of this, off the Beddgelert road, the Croesor valley runs decisively into the hills, up into its cwm under Cnicht. This mountain, which, with its two neighbours the Moelwyns, forms the end of the chain that began with Moel Siabod in the north, stands pointed and apart over the flat valley. It insists, by its steep-sided and sharp peak, on a comparison with the Matterhorn. The name Cnicht, is actually not Welsh, but an old spelling of the Saxon word 'knight'. Apparently the peak is somehow considered to resemble an armed knight.

The tiny Croesor village in its cwm typifies remote Welsh mountain hamlets, and it and the area have, for a long time, been highly-prized retreats of artists and writers. These valleys – with their old, crouching farms, their stone walls growing on the hillsides, mud-thick cart tracks winding up them, slopes and ridges rising everywhere into the higher mountains – are somehow highly inhabitable. The comfortable feeling one has there is not just that of being surrounded by uncontaminated nature. It is the feeling that the area and human populations have an old and well-established relationship; that it has been lived in, worked, changed, made by man, not over centuries but over millennia. One suddenly realizes that the structure of the hills themselves, cleared, levelled, walled, built on, show the influence of man. It gives, perhaps, the feeling of being part of a continuing process, an almost organic cycle of events.

The Beddgelert road out of the Glaslyn valley joins the Ffestiniog valley at Penrhyndeudraeth, where, on a slope over-looking what is left of the estuary, Bertrand Russell spent the last decades of his long life, and in the end turned out, like all men, to be mortal. It was from Penrhyndeudraeth that Khrushchev, Kennedy and others received the telegrams which may have contributed to their avoiding nuclear holocaust during the Cuba crisis. The small, low-lying grey village with its wide streets and air of uneventfulness hardly looks the place to be involved in such global matters. Lord Russell's house is some way outside the village, above the Porthmadog road; a gentle and unpretentious building, under protective trees.

Between the two estuaries – Afon Glaslyn and Afon Dwyryd – a highly-favoured headland stick out in to the water. Towards the end of it, on a sheltered bay, is one of the most successful flights of fancy anyone has had. Whatever else it is, Portmeirion is unique.

It was at no state accidental, and in fact had been planned and imagined by its creator, Sir Clough Williams-Ellis, for many years before he finally acquired the site. This private headland was previously owned by his uncle, and tenanted by a woman who had lived there amid increasing jungle as a well-defended recluse. The area (once, long ago, a small village) had become fashionable during the mid-nineteenth century, when landscape gardeners had planted what are now majestic trees and spectacular rhododendrons. The growth of the present complex has been gradual; at first it started as no more than a hotel and a few small cottages. The old house by the sea was converted to a hotel, and the jungle cleared, in 1926. Additions to the design then came one by one, the Watch House perched on the cliff, the Campanile (partly built from the ruins of a twelfth-century castle which once stood nearby, and partly the clock-tower of a London brewery), the Chantry on the slope of the hill. Time seems to have been unimportant. Purchased buildings sometimes waited twenty or thirty years for re-erection. The process still continued nearly fifty years later, although the last major item to be added was the Colonnade which was brought from Bristol in 1959. It is thus the achievement of a lifetime, and the confident expectation of continuity which this patience implies is, itself, a symptom of the unshakeable belief, belief in certain principles and belief in one's own opinion, with which the thing had been carried out.

It has, over the years, as the retreat of film-stars and writers and politicians, gathered its own ethos. In keeping indeed with its brittle brilliance is the fact that Noel Coward, secluded in the Watch House, wrote *Blithe Spirit* there during that one famous week. Remembered too by its regular and its long-serving staff is the visit of the late Duke of Windsor, then Prince of Wales, and his entourage, in the pre-war heydey. But neither a factual description nor its personal folklore anywhere approach the question of what Portmeirion is.

Much has been said about it, often contradictory, and, like any aesthetic judgement, so relative to one's tastes and standards as to be meaningless. It is mannered, contrived, precious, whimsical and self-conscious. It is an architectural ode to joy, a celebration of man's latent exuberance. Much of the tartness, of course, arises from envy. We all have a hankering, like god, to start creating things. God found the temptation too much for him, and so, given the chance, would we. Most of us never get this chance, and almost no one else today can exercise creativity on a total scale, the creation of a self-contained environment, like Madocks's Tremadog. The ideal creative expression of social man is a village. Portmeirion combines this social element with one which is on the more personal plain of art. It is an artefact.

One's first instinct is to laugh, and this, it turns out, is not far from the correct response. It seems that the mistake that many people make is to approach the place with reverence rather than relish. The thing is a sophisticated joke. As such it treads the treacherous boundaries of whimsy, and like any such arch joke it is perilously fragile. To the wrong person (one, for instance, without the faculty for smiling wryly) or the right person in the wrong mood, it could be maddening. Above all it poses a question. Where is the line of taste drawn, above which lies good taste and below which bad? Where does a witty conceit become a banal pun? And into which category fits such a pleasantry as the *Amis Reunis*, a boat lying alongside the quay which, it turns out, is not a boat but a boatlike part of the quay? On this level – the fine distinctions of aesthetics – Portmeirion is perhaps something worth serious consideration. It is serious, in any case, to the extent that all good jokes are serious. But it would be wrong, and against the intentions of its creator, to take it too seriously as anything else, as architecture, design or town-planning. In his description of his work on it the words 'levity', 'lawless', 'light-opera approach' crop up in significant positions. It was for fun. It was intended, if for anything precisely formulated, to amuse.

But amusements of this sort are essentially particular. Such an elegant equivocation as the hybrid *Amis Reunis* reminds me of, for instance, the playful rococo contortions of Nabokov's prose, a conceptual sleight of hand which, one knows, leaves some people writhing with delight and leaves others floundering. Many of the effects are in the deadpan, meticulous style of Rex Whistler's *trompe l'oeil* tricks, a display of skill and imagination almost irritatingly extreme, to which the reactions of some would be an incredulous, admiring chuckle, and of others a puzzled wondering of why he bothered. Why, indeed, do they bother? For those who feel the need to ask the question there can be no answer. To them it must seem like an in-joke from which they are excluded.

To me it succeeds. I find it a highly likeable contrivance; urbane, spirited, and shamelessly epideictic. And added to the softening effect of the refusal to be solemn which pervades it, is the peace and softness of its setting. This estuarial calm (the ducks and waterbirds across the tidal sands), reinforced by the faintly privileged, élitist air which, whatever popular and democratic claims may be dutifully made, underlies the assumption on which the thing is based, firmly imposes relaxation. A notice, in keeping with the exclusiveness of both the site and the sense of humour, implicitly encourages would-be visitors to turn round and go back before getting anywhere near, on the grounds that it is desirable to restrict their numbers. And at night when the day-visitors have gone, leaving the secluded water-front to the silence and the sea-birds, the residents and hotel guests find themselves absorbed into the atmosphere of what is, basically, a civilized day-dream.

Thirteen

HARLECH DOME

The daily ebb and flow of the tide is a microcosm of its greater movement, and in and out it comes over the centuries, now submerging a broad and fertile inhabited plain, then marooning high and dry and overlooking acres of land a one-time port. Perched on the edge of cliffs overhanging what still looks as if it should be the sea, now a wide flat plain of checkerboard fields, Harlech seems a little absurd. From what is it trying to escape, clambering high on to those crags, shunning the low and spacious lands at their feet? The whole thing is suddenly clear when one sees the castle's Water-Gate at the foot of the rock, now separated from any water by a famous golf course. And one realizes that then, a mere seven hundred years ago, the high tide licked at the rock itself and, it is thought, Afon Dwyryd, the estuary of which now reaches Tremadog Bay some 4 miles (6.5 km) farther north, once partly encircled Harlech.

Harlech now is little more than a village, old and solid but very small, and out of all proportion to its fame and the massive solidity of its castle. The area around teems with prehistory, and it is unlikely that so prominent a water-side spot would have been neglected at earlier times. The fact that the place ('Harddlech') rates a mention in the *Mabinogion* is perhaps a clue that it was of early importance. After the burial of Branwen on the banks of Afon Alaw in north-west Ynys Môn, the seven men who escaped from the Irish war set off with the head of their leader, Brân, to bury it on the White Mount in London. They paused (for seven years), to break their journey in Harlech, and spent the period feasting. The time passed quickly because they were entertained by three birds, the birds of Rhiannon, which sang them 'a certain song'.

And of all the songs they had ever heard each one was unlovely compared with that. And far must they look to see them out over the deep, yet was it as clear to them as if they were close by them; and at that feasting they were seven years.

Moreover the story mentions that it was 'at Harddlech in Ardudwy, at a court of his' that Brân himself was sitting, 'upon the rock of Harddlech overlooking the sea,' when the message first came from Ireland that the Irish king wanted to marry Branwen.

It is possible, but not likely, that such association arose after the conquest, and that Edward's army, arriving from Caernarfon and by sea in the spring of 1283, found the place empty. From then on, however, we know where we are. The castle took a few years longer to build than Conwy, starting in the same year, but cost a little over half as much. It was substantially completed by 1290, in time to resist the siege of Madog and his rebels in 1294-5. Glyndŵr brought it back again into prominence, and seems to have been unusually persistent in his attack on it. In 1401 he failed to take it (as he failed to take Caernarfon), and tried again, this time with the help of troops from France, in 1404. By then the garrison was in a poor physical and moral state. They were weakened by illness, and had started to desert. An internal rebellion took place in the castle in 1404, after which the remnants of the garrison surrendered.

Glyndŵr failed to take Caernarfon, and his supporters had been ousted from Conwy by Hotspur in 1401. It was by a process of elimination, therefore, that he made Harlech his headquarters. From 1404 it became not just his military centre but his home. There he called his Council, appointed Ministers, held a Parliament, and, Owynus Dei Gratia Princeps Wallie, concluded a treaty with the French. Reading his letter to Charles VI one can have no doubts either of his good intentions or his confidence in his ability to bring them about.

. . . that the Church of St David's shall be restored to its original dignity, which from the time of St David, archbishop and confessor, was a metropolitan church . . . that our chapels, etc., shall be free, and shall rejoice in the privileges, exemptions, and immunities in which they rejoiced in the times of our forefathers the princes of Wales.

Again, that we shall have two universities or places of general study, namely, one in North Wales and the other in South Wales, in cities, towns, or places to be hereafter decided and determined . . .

His wife, his daughter, his son-in-law Sir Edmund Mortimer, and the four Mortimer children all joined the Prince at Harlech. Four years later the citadel fell; Mortimer had died in the meantime, and the other members of the family were taken prisoner, eventually to end their lives in the Tower of London. And Glyndŵr himself disappeared.

Harlech became a Lancastrian stronghold during the Wars of the Roses, and was, in 1468, the last fortress to fall to the Yorkists. It had in the meantime withstood a long and painful siege, and it was at this period, perhaps its prime, that it acquired its song. The authorship of the words of 'The March of the Men of Harlech' is variously attributed, and there are, in any case, several different versions of them, but the tune is traditional.

The castle had fallen into disrepair, like Conwy, by the sixteenth century, but was refortified and held for the King during the Civil Wars. Oliver Cromwell's brother-in-law, who was a local resident called John Jones, besieged it but failed to take it. Eventually, in common with all the other castles, it surrendered to General Mytton, falling in the spring of 1647, five months after Conwy and nine after Caernarfon. And that, inevitably, was the end of its active life.

All Edward's castles are unique, designed to fit their site and, it seems, playing on the range of possible variations of the type, individual members of the genus 'late thirteenth-century castle'. Both Conwy and Caernarfon are single-wall castles; Beaumaris is the only true double-walled, concentric example. In Harlech we see the idea being played with, an incipient outer wall, too slight to be the real thing, forming the first step towards concentricity. It is, perhaps, an extension of Conwy's east and west barbicans, spread to enclose the whole castle; and the plan of Beaumaris is a mere change of emphasis, growing naturally out of Harlech's transitional step.

The main feature of Harlech Castle is its imposing gatehouse, occupying the bulk of the eastern side of the castle and forming the entry from the outer to the inner ward. It was not just and elaborate defensive structure, but also contained the majority of the castle's principal rooms. It thus had the function of being not just a gatehouse but a sort of keep, towering over the inner ward into which it projected. The inside of the castle now is rather bare, and much imagination is needed to picture the crowded and busy complex which the guidebook's description implies. From outside it is of course deservedly famous. It sits confidently and squarely on its rock, and looks even more massive and uncompromising through having lost all its merlons and finials, the only touch of delicacy it might have had.

The hinterland of Harlech is composed of a large dome-shaped fold, which rises, in the form of a long ridge or chain of mountains flanked by shelving plains, between the Trawsfynydd-Mawddach valley and the curved coastal strip. It is hard to penetrate even on foot, except at the one or two notable points, and veined by countless rock-walled lanes which, after bewildering meandering, come to their sudden conclusions in a hill-side farmyard under the mild gaze of a few shaggy, steam-breathing Welsh Black cattle, and the expressionless acceptance of a fatalistic mountain farmer.

Two roads in particular run into this upland area east of Harlech, both of them leaving together from Llanbedr, on the main road south. They split a few miles inland, one to the right and Cwm Nantcol valley, the other to the left and Cwm Bychan.

One would hardly recognize the cottage-like building on a bend at the left of the road to Nantcol as being a chapel, let alone as being that archetypal chapel of Curnow Vosper's painting, which has, somehow, settled itself permanently into the popular imagination. Wales is, to many people, old settles and dressers, and a print of *Salem*. At that time (early in the twentieth century) Salem Chapel's interior was, it seems, well-attended by ladies in tall hats and coloured shawls, with weather-beaten chapel-going faces. It never will be again, now that the people in the picture are dead and the clothes become a tourist gimmick; but that Sunday scene in Salem hangs securely, preserved, on many Welsh and English walls.

Past Salem Chapel one rises, by the wooded Nant Col, out into mountain pastures, the long chain of mountains gradually opening ahead. On the right the slightly separated round bulk of Moelfre; ahead Y Llethr, the long ridge of which runs south to form the main slope of the Dome; and to the left, until the lane turns to face them, the two Rhinogydd, the higher to the north. Between them is the sharp gap called Drws Ardudwy, the door through which the men of Ardudwy must have retreated to their homeland after their raids on the inland valleys.

On one of these raids, a legend records, the men of Ardudwy penetrated as far as the Vale of Clwyd, from which they carried off not, as one would expect, the cattle, but the Clwydian women. On that occasion they failed to regain the Drws, since the pursuing men of Clwyd overtook them as they crossed the moor above Ffestiniog; and there, once marked by an area of upright stones, and labelled on the map as Beddau Gwŷr Ardudwy, 'the graves of the men of Ardudwy,' is the place where they met their end. The story also offers an alternative explanation of the name of that moorland lake, Llyn y Morynion, which the *Mabinogion* cites as the lake into which Blodeuwedd's maidens accidentally walked while fleeing from

233

Gwydion. The captured ladies of Clwyd, the legend improbably claims, had become infatuated with the men of Ardudwy who were carrying them off, and, on seeing them slain, they all rushed into the lake. It seems that the truth about the naming of Llyn y Morynion may be that, over the years, so many parties of maidens have drowned in it that really no other name would be appropriate.

All the way up this valley into the hills one passes substantial farms, prosperous with sturdy Welsh Black cows and square, absurdly woolly mountain sheep, the farmed land reaching right up into the cwm, almost as far as Drws Ardudwy itself. The most extreme of these farms, where the road comes to an end, is Maesygarnedd, famous for having been the home, in the seventeenth century, of the man who married Oliver Cromwell's sister, Catherine. Colonel John Jones, improbably for the inhabitant of so remote a place, influenced history by being one of the men who signed the death-warrant of the king. He lived to see his work undone, and was executed at the Restoration.

Some of the sheep on these upland farms will be seen to have horns. Those familiar with hill-farming might take these to be the ewes, since in fact in several breeds of mountain sheep the ewes are horned. As it happens the pure Welsh mountain sheep is not one of these: the rams wear magnificently convoluted headpieces, which, huge and heavy, look exactly the sort of thing with which one could successfully blast the walls of Jericho. The Welsh mountain ewe is small and hornless, active and extremely agile, almost impossible to keep in a field for long, but well able, on a wild piece of mountain, to look after herself. They produce minute white lambs, to which they are exceptionally good mothers, and hiss and stamp their feet with convincing fierceness if they feel that they or their infants are threatened. As a breed it is extremely ancient, probably one of the original Celtic breeds, just as the cattle, the hardy and productive Welsh Blacks, are probably closer than other breeds to the pre-Roman British cattle.

The road to Cwm Bychan similarly rises alongside a river, the brown and stony Afon Artro, through oak-woods and mossy coppices, and out eventually into still more wide mountain valleys, this time with both the Rhinogydd on the right. The lake, from which Afon Artro issues, lies under echoing rocks, trees softening its lower end and giving it a mellowness and hospitality which its wild situation could have lacked. The whole valley-head is unspoilt, secluded, a trough sheltered by the curving walls of the range. And at its upper end, beyond the lake, the farmhouse still sits in secure isolation, as far away from anywhere as one could normally be.

The Lloyds of Cwm Bychan (whose ancestral home it was) retained, until they relinquished it in the nineteenth century, an independence equivalent to their location. They were, we are told, staunch supporters of the Jacobite cause. One wonders how anybody knew. It would be easy to support any cause with unequivocal staunchness from Cwm Bychan, and it is hard to see how the Jacobites would have benefited, or their opponents suffered, from the unserving loyalty of the Lloyds. Pennant set the seal on their fame by riding up to visit the Cwm Bychan Lloyd of his time, and found the squire hospitable, profuse with goat-meat and beer.

The family lay in their whole store of winter provisions, being inaccessible a great part of the season by reason of snow. Here they have lived for many generations, without bettering or lessening their income, without noisy fame but without any of its embittering attendants.

Up from the head of the cwm opposite the squat house rises a path which becomes the remarkable construction known as the Roman Steps. They are, in fact, probably not Roman, and for much of the way not really steps, but a paved pack-horse trail rising from the valley to the pass. The route leads up easily through the heather, evenly paved in stretches, until it approaches the entrance to the pass itself. It is at this top end that the 'steps' are at their best, at the start of the narrow gap, under the crags of Rhinog Fawr which rises over it on the right. The ground steepens and then flattens out, and the pavings become more regular and carefully set. It is a fine and expert piece of building, and has attracted admiration for centuries. Initials and dates in the 1890s can be found, testifying, presumably, to the place's popularity with Victorian sightseers.

This section of the paved way is unfortunately very easy to miss, and many who go to see the Roman Steps probably return having seen only the poorer stretches of them. It is necessary to bear in mind their position, to the right above the footpath, and to branch off the path, taking a right fork, at some point before it climbs the last slope towards the defile.

The *bwlch* to which this ancient trackway leads – Bwlch Tyddiad – looks out on to a different region. Miles of forest and mountain stretch away, which only the map knows to be in fact the area sloping down towards Trawsfynydd. As a crossing from one country to another the pass is a gift, and anyone who ever wanted to migrate from the plateau on the seaward side of the Harlech dome to the Ffestiniog moorlands or the upper Conwy would have certainly used it. A Roman road runs near the Trawsfynydd to Dolgellau road, down from the fort at Tomen y Mur. (It is in fact Sarn Helen, the long Roman paved way which crosses North Wales from north to south, called after Helena, mother of Constantine, who recurred in Welsh mythology as the wife of Macsen.) At whatever date were built the steps which remain so impressively today, it is almost certain that they would have had a predecessor. Pack-horse trains undoubtedly crossed the mountains through the Middle Ages and more recently. And before them the Romans must have left their lowland roads in their constant search for minerals. Inevitably – since such passes are rare – they would have found themselves using a track beaten by men and animals for centuries before they came. When the first pastoral tribesmen moved their flocks they must have passed through Bwlch Tyddiad. The steps cannot be dated; but footpaths are amongst the oldest things. They precede fortresses and buildings, hut circles and cromlechs. They are as old as feet.

The walk to Bwlch Tyddiad is beautiful and easy, and the view, through rather featureless, breaks open suddenly as one reaches the crest, with evocations of great arrivals and discoveries, of Xenophon and the Greek army sighting the sea, or Cortez on his peak catching the first glimpse of the other ocean.

Dyffryn Ardudwy is the name of the village south of Llanbedr, and of the country between the ridge of the dome and the sea. The Rhinogydd (one rounded, one flat-topped and craggy) and Y Llethr with its long continuation, bound the area definitively on one side. A large plateau stretches below them, vast and empty but dotted with ancient stones. Two fine burial chambers stand behind the school at Dyffryn Ardudwy. And in the little simple stone church at Llanbedr is a stone bearing that most ancient and numinous design, the double spiral. How it came there or where from nobody knows. But one can be fairly sure that the carving pre-dates by millennia not only Llanbedr's church but Christianity itself.

At Tarxien, in Malta, the sign appears on the decorated blocks of a Copper Age temple. It recurs at Mycenae carved on ivory plaques, engraved and painted on jars; and again at Knossos is everywhere, ornamenting jars and ritual objects, and runs in a band through the mural of the hall of the double axes. One solitary whorl has strayed, lost, on to the steps of the amphitheatre at Phaestos. Undoubtedly the wall of long slabs around the Irish burial mounds (also, like all these examples, dated at between 2000 and 3000 BC) best exemplifies it in its finest form; and at New Grange in particular, the most elaborate of them, it positively cries out to be understood. Emblematic, it is said, of death and rebirth, the form proposes the cyclical nature of things, the renewal which arises from every conclusion. The indented screw draws your tracing finger in, compulsively, to the narrowing centre; whereupon, with a reliable but endlessly impressive magic, the coil in relief proceeds to lead your unchecked finger out.

Here along the sandhill coastline of summer afternoons the tide has been flowing again. This time it is preceded by drifting sand, and the poor little church of Llandanwg sits half buried, its eyes scarcely above the heaping waves of the dunes. The tips of tombstones show here and there, and many are as conclusively buried as their owners. Sand pours over the dune and drifts as high as the top of Llandanwg's doorway. In the summer come voluntary workers with spades and brushes, and, so that the church can be used for summer services, take it all away. In the winter the wind comes and puts it all back.

Llandanwg may perhaps count itself lucky. It has not yet gone under the sea. From the coast at some points a little to the south, and better from the slopes of the dome itself, one can see, at some stages of the tide, a line of stones running at right angles to the coastline out to sea. It is called Sarn Badrig, and local legend identifies it as one of the embankments which protected, or failed to protect, Cantre'r Gwaelod. Science shakes its head, amused and scornful; but is able to give no other explanation of this 14 mile (22.5 km) long stretch of stones, which, if natural, is remarkably straight.

Cantre'r Gwaelod is far from being the only legendary country under the sea, but it is in many ways the most appealing. The 'bottom cantref', it was, true to its name, the most low-lying and therefore the first to go. Like such doomed places it was beautiful, like Pompeii, Atlantis and Lyonesse, and the people lived a luxurious and carefree life. One of them, Seithenin, was in fact so carefree that he became a drunkard, and it was unfortunate for the inhabitants of that land that it was this man who was responsible for tending the lock-gates and embankments which kept out the prowling sea. The ruler of the country at the time was Gwyddno, and it was his son, Prince Elffin, nephew of Maelgwn Gwynedd, who, some time later, made the mistake of taking his bard Taliesin on a visit to his uncle at Deganwy.

Bereft of his drowned inheritance Elffin appropriately took to fishing, and tended a weir on Afon Dyfi where it ran into what was by then the sea. It was there, south of Cadair Idris, that he found Taliesin, a beautiful child, who, when found, was sown up in a leather coracle and stranded in the weir. Elffin was not fortunate by nature, but this was a lucky catch. The child (like Moses, Perseus and Mordred, set adrift by a destructive parent, only to be found and cared for, eventually, like Oedipus, by a prince) immediately surprised its elders by a display of precocious wisdom, like Ambrosius, Apollo, David, CuChulainn, and Christ.

The found child was in fact an inspired being, and the story also tells his prehistory. The witch-goddess Ceridwen (who lived on an island in Llyn Tegid, the lake of Bala) was brewing in her cauldron a mixture which would give knowledge and inspiration. The finished product was intended for her son Afagddu, who, rather like his name, was extremely ugly; she had decided that the only remedy for his being the ugliest person in the world was for him also to the cleverest. And so she had set about concocting the brew.

It had to simmer for a year and a day, and while Ceridwen collected the necessary herbs to add to it during this period she hired a boy, little Gwion, to stir it for her. Late in the year three drops splashed from the cauldron and burnt his finger, which he naturally sucked. Doing so he acquired knowledge and understanding of everything, past, present and future; and at once ran from Ceridwen's foreseen vengeance. Such supernatural knowledge is, as Odin, Prometheus, and Adam found, not to be acquired without arousing the anger of the immortals. She pursued him, and the two, with their now equally-matched magic arts, went through a series of metamorphoses in the course of the chase – she a greyhound, he a hare; he a fish, she an otter – until eventually he had become a grain of corn on a threshing-floor, and she, as a hen, swallowed him.

Returning to human form she found herself pregnant, and nine months later gave birth to Taliesin. He was too beautiful to kill, and so she threw him (in his coracle) into Afon Dyfi, where he flowed to the sea and Elffin's weir.

The story was included in Lady Charlotte Guest's translation of the *Mabinogion*, and through Thomas Love Peacock's version, *The Misfortunes of Elphin*, it became widely known. But its source is found only in a sixteenth-century manuscript, and although the unknown origins of this may be, almost certainly are, very much older, it lacks the authenticity as Welsh tradition which the other *Mabinogion* stories have, and so has been omitted from the modern version of the collection, the excellent and probably definitive translation by Gwyn Jones and Thomas Jones. This consists basically of stories found in the manuscript known as *The Red Book of Hergest*, which was compiled between 1375 and about 1425. Some of these stories are clearly very old, and as they stand at the moment their material seems to belong mostly to the twelfth and perhaps mid-eleventh centuries. The earlier of them, including the so-called 'Four Branches' (to which the stories of Branwen and of Math, which we have encountered, belong) seem to deal with hazily-remembered gods and folk-heroes. Some which appear to be slightly later deal with more romantic, less primeval figures. 'The Dream of Macsen Wledig', for instance, tells the story of Magnus Maximus in confused form. And four stories deal, in a similar vein, with Arthur. Of these three belong to the same tradition, and the same period, as the works of Chrétien de Troyes, and so close are they to his stories that it is hard to avoid the conclusion that both he and they were translating from a lost original. One other tale of the *Mabinogion* tells of what appears to be pre-Roman Britain, the king Lludd who founded the city of London; and who, eventually, became the Lud after whom a gate of the post-Roman city is named Ludgate, and also (through Geoffrey of Monmouth) probably that similar ancient British king, King Lear, who had such trouble with his daughters. One tale of the *Mabinogion* remains and stands alone, playing no part in the Four Branches, in the Arthurian tradition, in Welsh proto-history, or, since it takes place in a strange and other-earthly dimension, in a topographical description of North Wales. 'Culhwch and Olwen' is a long, muddled, often ridiculous and grotesque tale of giants and adventures. Arthur and his henchmen ride through it as remote and primitive figures, far from their later forms in medieval romance. It is an unwieldy saga, but brings its magic with it intact; the most obviously ancient of the eleven stories which go to make up the *Mabinogion*.

Down the long coastal strip, where sand-dunes flow down into what was once that large *cantref*, the stone-walled slopes become increasingly overgrown with caravans. Caravan camps, acres and thickets of them, begin to crowd the seaside. A crop more reliable, a flock more abundant, than anything which the stony land has ever produced. They even threaten to mingle with the gravestones of Llanaber churchyard. Were it not for this distinctive feature, these small fields from which the rounded stones have been gathered and piled into a jig-saw pattern of high, prominent walls, would be more than a little reminiscent of the wild coast of Connemara. But the caravans dominate its natural character, and it is now, uncompromisingly, a holiday seashore.

Llanaber church (the parish church of Barmouth, *Y Bermo*, but nearly two miles outside the town) is as near to architectural perfection, within the limits of its function and style, as would be possible. It is set, alone, on the edge of a slope to the sea, crowded into a corner by its hundreds of tall gravestones, and from the outside looks no more than a long, low and unpretentious country church. But it is in the Early English style, and Early English architecture (rare in Wales) has a cool, restrained interior which seems to represent – more than an aesthetic achievement – an attitude of mind. The slim elegance of single lancet windows and the clean light of the clerestory. The human proportions and the way in which, without fuss or effort, the whole effect falls within the range of the eye.

In spite of its immediate and compelling feeling of consistency, Llanaber has in fact been much modified and added to. The total effect is a fortunate one, made up of largely random parts. It is in fact not, as it seems to be, completely in that civilized, light, uncluttered style. You come into it through a fine Early English doorway, but are faced at once with fat Norman pillars. From these spring Early English arches, which lead the eye up to a sixteenth-century roof. But the bulk of the church belongs to the first part of the thirteenth century, and it tilts slightly to prove its age.

Llanaber church contains two early tombstones, both thought to belong to the tenth century; but one inevitably becomes a little blasé, and no stones in this vicinity could seem impressively old compared to that propped obscurely against the wall behind the back pew in the small, dark church of Llanaber.

Fourteen

DOWN TO AFON MAWDDACH

REMEMBER Tryweryn. Water, it is often said, is the most inflammable substance in Welsh politics. Reluctance to part with it can hardly be due to any shortage, since there is more than enough to spare, but simply stems from resentment at the thought that it all goes to feed the insatiable thirst of English cities, without doing any appreciable good to the area on which it happens to fall. There is some reason in the claim that the place which suffers from the high rainfall should be the place which benefits from any results; and that Wales is as entitled as any other mineral-owning country to cash in on the possession of this valuable raw material, as entitled to exploit its monopoly as anywhere endowed by a chance of nature with some precious commodity which everybody wants.

Antediluvian Tryweryn was a tiny village in a valley, a few houses and a church and a churchyard, together with a number of outlying farms. It was not especially beautiful, a lonely farming valley enclosed by long slopes, over which, along the contour, ran the Ffestiniog to Bala road, the road which comes down from the moors. Now Tryweryn is the subject only of patriotic graffiti, crying out in white paint from grey roadside walls. It all lies under the lake.

One comes down from Y Migneint, between the two Arenigs forming a gateway, one mild and humpy, one severe and looming; and finds oneself driving above the shoreline of the vast and soulless sheet of Llyn Celyn, where the valley used to be. The reflective surface of the water reveals nothing.

Perhaps it is only a knowledge of the facts that makes the lake look unnatural, sitting awkwardly, ill-fitting, in its shallow-sided valley, an occasional lane or wall disappearing suicidally into it. The eye never seen innocently, always through the distorting lens of awareness. Perhaps to a stranger

Llyn Celyn might look beautiful, a generous plain of cooler light contrasting with the dark surfaces of the hills, an aid to perspective, giving size and proportion to the landscape. Others see a valley arbitrarily blanketed by the characterless void of water.

Several of the farmhouses which formed the community did in fact survive, and, now looking slightly lost, stand perched on the banks of the water. The social effect on them has been as great as the physical, an effect of isolation. Neighbours were once a few fields away, and the scattered community would have been able, at least in principle, to come together at some central spot. Now it is a long way round the lake to the next farm across the water. A barrier more consequential than distance now isolates them.

Llyn Celyn (as it is called, after Afon Tryweryn's tributary, the Afon Celyn, and the village of Capel Celyn) has a potential capacity of 16,400 million gallons (74,620 million litres). No pipelines issue from it as bait to dynamite and reminders of the destination of its contents. Instead the requisite amount of water is simply discharged through the dam into Afon Tryweryn. Since this is where it would have been going anyway, one may wonder for a moment where the need for the dam comes in. The answer is, of course, that in Britain it rains a good deal more at some times of the year than at others, and that the human consumption of water continues throughout the year, and in fact probably varies in inverse ratio to the rainfall. About five times as much rain falls in the United Kingdom as is needed to supply the population with water, but most of it fails to land when and where it is needed. That is why it comes in handy to have 16,000 million gallons of water held back for a sunny day.

Such large impounding reservoirs can really only be built in a limited number of places, requiring as they do the combination of the factors of height above sea level (to allow the supply to be effected by gravitation), and impermeable bedrock, a large and uncontaminated catchment area, a capacious watertight basin in conjunction with a strong and impervious defile, and of course a high rainfall.

From Afon Tryweryn the water released from the Llyn Celyn reservoir flows, as it would have done anyway, in to the Dee *(Afon Dyfrdwy)*, which it reaches near Bala. This channel then carries it, with an efficiency which the engineers evidently felt unable to improve on, towards the county of Cheshire and its eventual destination. Two miles upstream from the Chester Weir it is retrieved from the river, at the rate of up to 65 million gallons (295,750,000 litres) a day, by the Corporation of Liverpool, its new owners. It joins the aqueduct bringing water from Lake Vyrnwy *(Llyn Efyrnwy)*, in Mid-Wales, at Norton Water Tower, and they proceed together to the Prescot Reservoirs near Liverpool's eastern outskirts.

Below the dam the valley softens, a close and wooded contrast to the open spaces out of which the road and the river have come. It leads down through fields and copses, and comes unexpectedly into Bala from behind, pitching one suddenly into the busy street of a small town.

Bala is a Welsh country town, juggling the two elements, town and country, in fairly equal balance. In spite of its solid urban structure (the hefty facades of public buildings, the planned look of its streets) it is a very rural place. There is a farm so close on its outskirts as to be effectively in the High Street, and always those men with low caps and tall sticks standing talking on the corners or sitting in a row on the street bench. There seems constantly to be a cattle-truck rolling through its main street, and the people standing in discussion on the pavement more often than not are wearing gumboots. A few paces in any direction takes you out into the fields.

There is not a great deal to do in Bala, and consequently the main occupation there is standing around and talking, always in Welsh. In spite of the air of purposelessness, however, and in spite of its being so self-contained and in the middle of nowhere, Bala has none of the feeling of depression which relatively isolated places often have. The chatter on the pavements is lively and cheerful.

The town is known for a number of things. Traditionally, and still, it is a great shooting centre, catering for both the international syndicates and the locally-based groups. It was visited twice by George Borrow, who carefully recorded every detail of his stay at the fine old inn in the main street. 'I "trifled" over my brandy-and-water till I finished it, and then walked forth to look at the town.' He does not seem to have found a lot to do in Bala, and a modern traveller would probably find himself similarly occupied – but not, perhaps, consider it worth while to tell us so. Borrow was not much busier on his second visit: 'My dinner concluded, I trifled away the time till about ten o'clock, and then went to bed.'

The town has been notorious for centuries for its riotous fairs, which it still holds. And, rather by contrast, it was, outstandingly one of the early centres of Methodism. Thomas Charles of Bala (whose statue stands in front of a chapel in a side street) founded not only the Bible Society, but also both the Calvinistic Methodist body and the Sunday School movement; the latter, as much as Calvinism itself, has been a decisive influence on Welsh cultural life ever since. A crucial moment in the nonconformist movement came when, after years of failing to persuade the church to ordain Methodist preachers, Charles himself ordained the first eight ministers, at Bala, in 1811.

Bala's other piece of history is its mound, the 'Tomen' of Bala. In George Borrow's time it was the spot to which 'the idlers of the town' resorted. Before that it was almost certainly the motte of a medieval castle, probably one of the seats of the Princes of Powys. Before that one may speculate. It is, as Borrow puts it, one of 'that brotherhood of artificial mounts of unknown antiquity, found scattered, here and there, throughout Europe and the greater part of Asia,' which, he says, 'seem to have been originally intended as places of sepulture, but in many instances were afterwards used as strongholds . . . ' This is perhaps as much as one can say of the

Tomen of Bala, now enclosed by a wall and planted with hedges like a public park.

The wide main street is lined with mature trees, which would give it a fine boulevard atmosphere if they had not in the past been savagely, horribly mutilated by the local authority. This act of civic barbarism is the only piece of nastiness in Bala, and it would perhaps be unfair to mention it were it not for the commonness of the habit of trying to reduce a town's greatest asset to a row of gaunt and ugly sticks. When it is essential that trees should be pruned, the work should be done only by people who understand them.

Bala is old and well-established, but possibly the town now owes its reputation to its position on a lake, Llyn Tegid, now the property of the Snowdonia National Park and a fast-developing recreational centre.

Llyn Tegid, the largest natural area of fresh water in Wales, is almost an inland sea. It stretches away at such length that one can never form any coherent impression of it. It is not a wooded, secluded, steep-sided or wild lake, but simply a long stretch of water. The River Dee *(Afon Dyfrdwy)*, flows both into it and out of it, originating in the hills to the south-west.

The road leaves the lake and the small meandering Dee *(Afon Dyfrdwy)*, and passes under the bulk of the Arans, a big double hump on the left. And one realizes at some point below Aran Mawddwy (which is, in fact, the highest Welsh peak south of Snowdon) that all the streams have started to run the other way. A river develops out of these, Afon Eiddon, which accompanies the road down towards Dolgellau. Ahead occasionally are views of Cadair Idris, a long stretch of ridge blocking the southern horizon. It is something about the roll and texture of the country, not any line or boundary, that makes it Mid-Wales. The demarcation takes the form of a continuous merging, and the decision as to where exactly one side of the transition stops and the other begins is largely arbitrary.

Nevertheless Dolgellau is, in terms of the distinction

between North and Mid, a border town. It has the solid rock-hewn definition of the north; and it has the mellower, softer character of the middle. A concise and substantial town, built of local rock in large blocks, it still looks brown and soft, hunched over its soft brown river. Dolgellau has a close community and is self-contained, with the air of being populated mostly by prosperous yeomen. Once (like Llangollen) a centre of the woollen weaving industry, which, run by water-power, flourished during the eighteenth and nineteenth centuries, for a brief period in the mid-nineteenth century involved in mineral working, it now functions as a market town, shopping and administrative centre for the area to the south.

The town is old, mentioned by Leland, Camden, and Pennant, and the bridge (parts of which may even be medieval) dates from 1638. Glyndŵr held a Parliament there, although Machynlleth, a similar town farther south, where his magnificent Parliament House still stands, seems to have been more a centre of his administration. Dolgellau contains, very much in keeping with its sound and substantial nature, some excellent old hotels. Wordsworth visited one of these, and as a result wrote one of his better poems.

> *If you ever go to Dolgelley*
> *Don't stay at the Lion Hotel.*
> *You'll get nothing to put in your belly*
> *And no-one will answer the bell.*

The authenticity of these heart-felt lines may, however, be in some doubt, since they have apparently been omitted from de Selincourt's otherwise comprehensive edition of the poet's collected works.

But perhaps Dolgellau's chief feature is, even more than its bridge, the mountain. Cadair Idris rises over it, like Mont Blanc over Chamonix or the Matterhorn over Zermatt, looking magnificently mountainous and very much bigger than it is. Dolgellau is essentially a town at the foot of the mountain. And indeed Cadair Idris is a suitable counterpart, a mountain worth being at the foot of. It is said to have been called after Idris the son of Meirion (who gave his name to the district of Meirionydd) the son of Cunedda, that early general who came down with his army and his sons to rid North Wales of the Irish. Idris, a grandson of Cunedda, would thus be a cousin of Maelgwn, King of Gwynedd.

It is Afon Wnion, a combination of several streams, which flows through Dolgellau. Afon Mawddach itself comes down another valley from the north, coming down with the Trawsfynydd road to join Afon Wnion near the village of Llanelltyd. To a great extent this valley is typical of the general pattern, in which, again and again, a road runs down from high land beside a fast-flowing, tree-surrounded river. It is an inevitable pattern, a result of the structure of the country, being imposed by the basic quality of North Wales, which is its mountainousness. To it the area owes a great deal of its best and most characteristic scenery. The high land attracts the clouds and provokes the rain; streams drain it; running together they fill a river. Then down the valley which the river has carved, between its slow accumulation over level moorland and its meandering across silted lowlands, a road inevitably joins it. They run together round the rough spurs and outcrops, the one providing entertainment to the other. Of exactly such a type are the upper reaches of Afon Mawddach with its falls and pools, before it starts to level off, and that stretch of the A487.

The glacial valley into which Afon Mawddach comes from these uplands can best be seen from the hillside to its east, where, vertiginously crossing the steep slope above it, the three mile circuit called Precipice Walk overlooks it. This, long ago cut into the high slope by sheep crossing the mountain, is now laid out with pedagogue notices as a Nature Trail, the work of the Snowdonia National Park Information Service. Look out there and you will see plantations, oakwoods, and upland pastures; look down here and you will see bell-heather and ling in an acid soil. The macro and micro cultures of our land are painstakingly spotlighted for us.

Precipice Walk is on the cluster of hills occupied by the Nannau estate, and indeed one could not approach it without being aware both of this and of the presence of the monumental block of the present house. Nannau (where a house was first built in 1100) is one of the old seats of the Vaughan *(Fychan)* family, a dominant and ancient line in this part of Wales. Their ancestors were well-established here in Glyndŵr's time, and in fact one of the owners of Nannau added to that hero's reputation for possessing supernatural arts by trying, and failing, to shoot him with an arrow at point-black range. Glyndŵr was wearing chain mail, and it was his treacherous host (as might be expected) who came to a bad end.

From the start of the Precipice Walk, looking north, one sees a very extensive acreage of coniferous plantation, and this (however hard the Nature Trail's notices try to draw one's attention to the little human settlement of Llanfachreth and the few remaining rough fields) dominates the view. There one hears, in the otherwise total silence, the distant drowsy purr and buzz of the busy chain-saws. This is Coed y Brenin, a systematic plantation dating from 1935, and named in honour of George V. Somewhere amongst it lie some of Wales' more successful gold mines, and the area is rich not only in seams of gold but several other minerals.

Cymmer Abbey stands below Nannau, where Afon Mawddach finally reaches the estuary's head, now no more than a few elegant standing walls, delicate arches leading into and out of nowhere. It was founded in 1198, a Cistercian house, being given its charter, like Conwy, by Llywelyn the Great. Now it stands beside a large farm, and, inappropriately in such a fertile and unspoilt spot, caravans have begun to grow thickly around it.

Here the winding Afon Mawddach really starts, and runs in its flat valley through low-lying fields between the two steep sides which enclose it, for more than seven miles of crow-flight to the sea. Ruskin said, along with so much else, that there was in Britain only one more beautiful walk than the walk from Barmouth *(Y Bermo)* to Dolgellau, and that was the walk from Dolgellau to Barmouth *(Y Bermo)*. Perhaps he was exaggerating; there are probably walks as beautiful even in Wales. Certainly he had an enviable turn of phrase. And certainly Afon Mawddach meanders very attractively around the wooded spurs of the valley.

It swings, for instance, in towards the southern slope, and is caught for a moment at Penmaenpool, where an old wooden bridge branches over a placid loop of the river. G.M. Hopkins, who featured ('In the Valley of the Elwy') in the first chapter of this book, now, with appropriate symmetry, recurs in its last, having written a long but lesser poem called 'Penmaen Pool, for the Visitor's Book at the Inn.'

Who long for rest, who look for pleasure
Away from counter, court or school
O where live well your lease of leisure
But here at, here at Penmaen Pool?

The Mawddach, how she trips! though throttled
If floodtide teeming thrills her full,
And mazy sands all water-wattled
Waylay her at ebb, past Penmaen Pool.

Then even in weariest wintry house
Of New Year's month or surly Yule
Furred snows, charged tuft above tuft, tower
From darksome darksome Penmaen Pool.

And even, if bound here hardest home,
You've parlour-pastime left and (who'll
Not honour it?) ale like goldy foam
That frocks an oar in Penmaen Pool . . .

Gold mines again lie in the hills above Bontddu, halfway down the estuary. They had been in use for centuries, and perhaps reached their peak of production during the 1860s. It is from the mine above Bontddu that royal wedding rings have come to be traditionally made. But royal weddings unfortunately happen with insufficient frequency to keep a gold mine going.

Afon Mawddach straightens, broadens into a tidal inlet, when full lying fjord-like between the wooded foothills, empty a shining sea of sand. At the northern neck the mountains press against the water, the farthest extremity of the ridge called Llawllech (which runs down all the way from Y Llethr and the Rhinogydd) almost jutting into the sea. And one enters Barmouth *(Y Bermo)* with very little room to spare, by a twisting and tilting road under dramatic red cliffs.

The name Aber Maw has undergone two changes over the centuries. It has been anglicized, and it has also been vernacularized. Probably it has been a subject of amusement that the English have misunderstood and mispronounced the name to such an extent that they call it Barmouth *(Y Bermo)*. If so, the joke has only gone halfway. The Welsh, for some equally obscure reason, call it Y Bermo.

Under the name Aber Maw it has been in existence for a considerable time. Giraldus, on his trip through Wales, noted it. It reached its peak of popularity, of course, during Victorian times, resorted to by the romantics and academics, including Tennyson, Wordsworth, Shelley, Ruskin and even Darwin. Much of the town must then have been brand new, or even under construction. The larger part of it dates from the second half of the nineteenth century. But such a first impression is misleading, and Barmouth *(Y Bermo)* in fact possesses a feature rare, perhaps unique, in Wales. It has an old quarter.

The old town represents the physical remains of the old port, and is clustered (like the old quarters of other ports, Vigo, Naples, Lisbon, or like Plaka around the Acropolis) steeply on a rocky slope. The buildings jut and cling, interpenetrating, locked together like the strata of the rock into which they are cut. The windows of one look directly at the tops of the chimneys of another. In some you enter from behind by what would otherwise be a second-storey window. Steps and chimney-like passages wind in and out around them; and eventually one emerges through the terraced backyards and past people's windows, to look down precipitously on to the whole of old Barmouth (Y Bermo).

The headland above the highest houses, and other property in the area, once belonged to a Mrs Talbot. This fact might not have been of much interest had she not been also a friend of Ruskin's. Inspired by his interest in social reform, and in particular his sincere desire to remedy the social problems of housing and house-owning, she presented him with some of the old cottages on the rock, with which he formed the Guild of St George's an experiment which went some way towards the idea of housing-subsidies and controlled rents. Probably it was again under Ruskin's prophetic influence that Mrs Talbot helped to found the National Trust, by giving to it, in 1895, its first property. The top of the craggy headland above the old town, a breezy expanse of mountainside with fine views over Y Bermo and the sea, known appropriately as Dinas Oleu, the fortress of light, is 'to be kept and guarded for the enjoyment of Y Bermo for ever.'

Y Bermo, now is a seaside town with several different facets. Stacked impressively against the rocks, it faces a mild, broad shore; on the one hand the severity of a stone Welsh town set against crags, on the other the world of fairylights, cockles and donkey-rides. These two aspects also involve a sharp seasonal contrast, a pair of extremes with hardly any happy medium between them. In the summer both town and beach tend to become too full for normal movement; in the winter, in spite of its gentle climate, it is perhaps equally uncomfortably empty. This sort of schizophrenia is present to some degree in most holiday places, but seldom is the change so sharp from a quiet and inactive piece of Welsh townscape to a noisy and busy summer resort.

Y Bermo is both of these, and also, quite separately, a fishing-port. In that capacity it specializes in lobsters, so that besides the sand and the amusements there is also a small and busy quay to look at, cluttered with apparently several thousand lobster-pots. A minor fleet of wooden boats lies alongside, and the force of men which they employ is busy there, perpetually winding up ropes, and (since lobster-fishing is not exactly a time-intensive job) unwinding them again.

Perhaps no town could be entirely at ease with such a combination of functions. The result, in this case, is that out of season Y Bermo looks as if it has come to the party wearing the wrong clothes. Real fishermen, in smocks and seaboots, seem hardly comfortable in bars the ceilings of which are draped in fishing nets, port and starboard lamps identifying their respective corners, trawl floats hanging in clusters like fruit, port-holes in a clinker-built bar, and lobster-pot stools.

In 1860 Afon Mawddach was bridged, giving the town its most famous and easily recognizable feature, Barmouth Bridge *(Pont y Bermo)*. The railway arrived triumphantly along it from Tywyn and Mid-Wales, to put Y Bermo on the map. The long wooden bridge contains a footpath, and one can at least be glad that the injury to the estuary has not been compounded by the addition of a road. The issue is, in any case, debatable. This long walk out over the water gives pedestrians a chance to look up Afon Mawddach, reaching inland, and at Cadair Idris and the hills around it, which they could otherwise not possibly have. The feeling that it mars the long, logical run of expanding water towards its outlet, the visual relationship between the river and the sea, the continuity of water opening to the horizon, depends, both physically and mentally, on one's point of view.

What is quite certain is that, since it is there, there are few better places to stand and look at the scenery of Wales, as, under you, the Mawddach either flows in up its creek, or out towards its perch and sand-bar, to end, where North Wales itself inevitably ends, in the sea.

CONCLUSION

TIME IS CHANGE

At Capel Garmon and Bryn-celli-ddu are stones left by the first lonely builders, too early even for our comprehension. At Pen-y-gaer and Tre'r Ceiri one finds the Iron Age defending itself in its tribal, pastoral groups. At Segontium was interposed the relatively brief flowering of Roman order. At Dinas Emrys and Deganwy the Dark Ages loomed, struggling with a burden of magic and ignorance, the giant figures of Vortigern (*Gwrtheyrn*), Ambrosius (*Emrys*), Maelgwn and Taliesin jutting from the obscurity. At Dinas Brân we enter the world of the early medieval romance, when knights went riding into the forest looking for adventure and finding mystery. At Conwy is encountered the full pride and power of the high Middle Ages, the confidence which permitted the crusades. Glyndŵr has left little in North Wales in the way of physical traces, but it is hard not to remember him at Harlech, which he left much as he found it; and his life and disappearance, symbolic now of the death of an ideal, perhaps mark the point at which this simpler world ended and the modern age began. Certainly at Gwydir we are at the complicated, multi-national political Europe of the Renaissance. It is only a step, historically, from there to Tremadog, and the sight of the lessons of the eighteenth century's civilized life being applied to the new power of sudden industrial expansion. We saw, in Llandudno, the effect of the coming of the railways together with the coming of Victorian prosperity, which in its turn relied for its maintenance on such devastation as that which still surrounds Blaenau Ffestiniog. And in Rhyl the modern equivalent of this expansion, arising from universal car-ownership and (with all the accompanying implications of power stations and giant industrial enterprises) the spread of enough wealth to maintain a city of bingo halls.

Britain's history is built into its geography. And in the sketching of a portrait of this patch of the island inevitably lines of family resemblance come to light. But there can perhaps be few areas of this size in which so much of the past of British civilization is still apparent, still, as it were, on the surface. This, together with a similar social durability, is one of the factors which identify the area. The really extraordinary thing about it is its resilience, its dogged continuity. No sudden destructions overtook it, shattering earthquakes or (except in the legendary drowned *cantrefi*) inundations. Unlike Knossos it never completely collapsed. Unlike Venice and Istanbul it never shrank back from the wider circles of former glory into its sad, crumbling nucleus. It remains almost exactly what it was: an independent-minded country, small, minding its own business, measuring time not with the sudden, separated jumps (and halts) which characterized the development of its southern counterpart, but as a continuous flow. We can see now that the process has been going on, during those four thousand years, in a natural, evolutionary progression.

Will this continue? What prospects are there for an indigent area on the edges of the megalopolis? We know that the whole process of change has been speeding up. For the first few hundred million years of the earth's existence hardly anything happened. The whole of our history and prehistory, including the rise and fall of all great civilizations, has taken place, hectically, within a microscopic fraction of that time. Once change moved at glacial speed. Perhaps in not many years to come it will be actually observable with the naked eye, the sudden rush of the exponential curve as it approaches the vertical. Can North Wales continue at its present steady pace, now that time flows so fast that many countries, like Alice and the Red Queen, have to run flat out in order to stand still?

Certainly the difficulties are obvious enough. Migration has turned a diminishing population into an increasing one. Seasonal overcrowding aggravates the pressures on an ailing infrastructure. Tourism has become Wales' first industry. The National Park, with facilities limited by its nature, frequently reaches saturation point. The multiple use of land to some extent (perhaps insufficiently and too late) helps to relieve the pressure: caravans in the orchards of small-holdings, soft drinks for sale at the farmhouse, Farm Trails, footpaths, picnic sites. The Forestry Commission has at last begun to understand how great could be its contribution to the relief of this sort of pressure; caravan sites, tents, car-parks and perhaps much more could be swallowed wholesale, turned invisible, by the vast social deserts of the forests.

The causes of the problem, if it is a problem, were of course economic. It is cheap to live in the country, but the countryman, now that our media present a national and urban-orientated culture, has been given urban expectations. At the basis lies the fallacy that money has a value distinct from what you can buy with it. That wages in the cities are only higher because life in the cities is more expensive is not a relevant point if, as it often is, richness is viewed in terms of turnover and not of profit. In many villages of North Wales the ideal goal has traditionally been, therefore, to leave. To the previous generation it was choice between leaving or working in the quarries. To this it has been a choice between leaving or not working. To the next, perhaps, there will be a proper choice.

The elements which have kept Wales alive have, consequently, been economic too. Tourism is worth millions of pounds a year, whatever doubts one may feel about its unreliability and its built-in problems. Industry has been successfully enticed into certain areas, and it certainly brings money. Those who have made their money elsewhere find, ironically, that what they want to buy with it is the very thing which, to the emigrant, is without commercial value: the ability to live in Wales. Certainly changes inevitably result, in the surface fabric and in the basic structure of North Wales. To live at all it must change, but still one feels that in many places better planning might have enabled a more natural, organic growth. The urbanized village is no more a survival of anything than is the dying hamlet. But perhaps again such death and renewal is part of a country's history, its life-story being a series of resurrections. And perhaps in post-Phylloxera years it would be not only futile but ungrateful, for even the most pedantic connoisseur, to criticize a vine for being grafted.

Nevertheless we cannot help being conscious that we are living in a period of transition faster-moving and more cataclysmic than most. Perhaps the Dee (*Afon Dyfrdwy*) is barraged, placing North Wales minutes from the doorsteps of Merseyside; an Expressway sweeps through the whole of the area, making Ynys Môn and Llŷn, for the first time ever, within anybody's easy reach. Towns are by-passed, new bridges built, oil terminals constructed, dams imposed on the scenery, until one can hardly keep track of each year's progress. Whether it is good or bad depends so much on the standards from which it is viewed. When our ancestors quarried at Blaenau Ffestiniog it was to them a great commercial achievement, shifting and selling all that slate, and what they didn't want they tipped unhesitatingly out on to the hillside. As to the effect on the visual environment, they never gave it a thought. And they would perhaps be surprised and hurt if one were to criticize them for it today.

Now we are more self-conscious. Now we look more carefully at everything we do. The great industrialists can hardly move without a sociologist and a landscape architect at their elbows. Even so I would suggest that progress (which none of us of course would care to do without) exerts on a country like North Wales two pressures, one of them visible and the other not.

The visible one is plain enough. Narrow lanes grow into wide roads, council houses in slate-quarry areas are roofed with tiles, composite blocks replace granite, the line of urban development creeps out of the towns and up the valleys towards the hills, the visitors bring, with their money, their tin cans and plastic cups, their orange-peel and paper bags, and their cars, which, while giving welcome employment to a few hundred petrol-pump attendants and car-park ticket-sellers, occupy an inconvenient proportion of the summer-time roads.

At least if you can see it you can assess it. No car-park gets built or factory sited without consideration of the view, and planners and architects all press for higher standards of design, more consideration for the setting, and the use, wherever possible, of appropriate materials. If visible progress destroys North Wales it will at least be against considerable resistance.

The images are corny but concise: it is the invisible fungus spore which brings a rot, the invisible bacillus which provokes an epidemic.

Among the destructive influences the most insidious, and therefore perhaps the most dangerous, is the introduction of the suburban attitude. During the past century and a half there has come into existence a new type of being, urban man. Conditioned to an exclusively urban set of values, he sees the phenomena of the countryside in simplified terms. All cattle are likely to be bulls; hay exists only in bales. The idea that grass is a growing crop is inconceivable to him. Grass is for having picnics on. All this is clear enough, and we have become accustomed to it. But the off-shoot, the half-caste, suburban man, is less easy to recognize and to be ready for.

A caravan in a field is still a piece of the country. Fifteen caravans in a field is harder to accept as such, and (for their inmates) it becomes necessary, while ostensibly living the simple life, to deal with one's neighbours. First you put up a little spiked green fence, staking out around your caravan your claim of field, not so much with the practical intention of keeping anybody out, as as a territorial gesture, a recognition of their existence. A Saturday morning in summer then reveals the full swing of the wheel, the absurd and sad spectacle of men in shirtsleeves busily mowing their patch of countryside, the purr and throb, in a fifteen-caravan field, of perhaps a dozen motor-mowers. Backwards and forwards they hurry, competitively, restoring this rough and untidy nature to the conditions which they have come to regard as right. They are busy suburbanizing the countryside.

So too those who acquire an old, squat Welsh cottage, a thick-walled hovel which has outlived its practical purpose of breeding generation after generation of prolific Welsh children, set about at once converting it to what they think an old Welsh cottage should be. Quaint and pretty and cottage-like, it at once, for the first time in its long life, looks completely out of place.

The individuals move into the countryside their elements of suburban life, the painted cart-wheel in the garden, the coach lamp beside the door, the old lamp-post by the pathway, the rustic poker-work house-name on the gate. But it is not left to them. The county councils contribute with their chain-link fences along the road, just as the Welsh Office's Ancient Monument Department strikes, with its neatly mown grass and its well-pointed, tidy ruins, at the very quality essential to our ancient monuments, their antiquity. And an army of people moves into the villages and valleys to persuade and flatter them into tidying themselves up. Tidy Village competitions and Litter Drives and an armoury of other weapons are brought to bear, by the suburban attitude, on the deplorable, uncivilized natural state which our countryside would otherwise be in.

Perhaps those who imagine that not leaving rubbish where it falls, and generally keeping things clean and smart, is in any way part of the natural way of life of a rural area, should sometime visit a North Wales farmyard, and observe the accumulation of agricultural detritus which, together, goes to make up its particular atmosphere. The chaos of old machinery and fertilizer bags, broken gates and tin drums, fencing posts, lumps of timber, pieces of corrugated iron and recumbent water-tanks, which grows in the corners of the stackyard and against the shippon wall, is symptomatic not of a slovenly and uncouth nature, but of the fact that this is a place which is lived and worked in, and distinct from something set out for inspection, for show.

Being prettily painted, neat and tidy, spick and span, has nothing to do with North Wales as it really is. Perhaps the villages which have in fact kept best are those organic and human places, full of rusty iron and children, which would perhaps be marked by people with righteous minds as the Worst Kept Villages of all.

The change in attitude, the trend towards the suburbanization of the countryside, is undoubtedly part of the change in population. But, as often, it is affected most by the unwillingness of colonists to be content to practise, themselves, the principles which they so devoutly believe to be virtues. They take it to be a duty to impose them on their neighbours, making them aware of guilt for sins they never knew existed, setting them standards which they had always been happy to do without. The English outside England are by nature missionaries; and it would perhaps be unwise to suggest that all missionaries should be eaten.

The country is, then, probably well-protected against environmental vandalism and the more obvious ugliness of development; but not against the destructive force of the suburban standards which come with the money brought by the industrialists, the tourists, and the new residents. North Wales, like Maréchal Villars, probably knows by now how to defend itself from its enemies, but may need help (if at all) in defending itself from the best-intentioned of its friends.

GLOSSARY

SPELLING

For a long time the spelling of Welsh place-names remained something of a matter of choice, and indeed local variations can still be seen on signs and even maps. Efforts were made during the 1970's, 1980's and 90's to achieve some standardization, and these efforts still continue, with the result that many once-debatable variants now have an accepted and correct form. This result is largely due to the publication by the University of Wales Press of a 'Gazeteer of Welsh Place-Names', which lays down the standard form, and which underlies the spellings of place-names used in this edition.

THE MUTATIONS

Most languages (including the older forms of English) have changes in the spelling of their words to represent different genders and cases. We are accustomed to these changes coming at the ends of words, and so react with some dismay and bewilderment to finding them at the beginning. The first letters of some Welsh words change for various reasons, among which is the word's being feminine and preceded by the definite article, or its being an adjective following a feminine noun. This may seem to those not used to it to be an awkward form to use, and indeed it is not unknown for Welshmen to get it wrong. What certainly becomes apparent at once is that it places an additional obstacle in the way of people needing to use a dictionary. In the brief glossary that follows some words are therefore given twice, and, since the commonest mutations are perhaps those which involve *c* changing to *g*, *m* and *b* changing to *f*, *t* to *d*, *p* to *b*, and *g* dropping out, anyone looking up in a dictionary a word beginning with *g*, *f*, *d*, *b*, or with another letter such as *w* or *l*, is advised to try again under *c*, *m* or *b*, *t*, *p*, and *g* respectively. This may seem a rather laborious procedure, but it is easier than learning the rules for mutations and the gender of every noun.

Aber	mouth of a river
Afon	river
Bach (fach)	small
Bardd	poet
Bedd	grave
Betws	oratory (from 'bede-house')
Blaen (pl. *Blaenau*) head	
Bod	dwelling
Bont (see *Pont*)	
Braich	arm
Brenin	king
Bryn	hill
Bwlch	pass
Bychan	small
Cader (or *cadair*) chair	
Cae	field
Caer	fort
Cafn	trough
Cantref (*can:* 100; *tref:* town) a regional division	
Capel	chapel
Carnedd	cairn
Caseg	mare
Castell	castle
Ceiri (a form of *cewri;* singular *Cawr*) giants	
Celli	grove
Clogwyn	cliff
Coch (goch)	red
Coed	wood
Craig	rock
Crib	crest
Croes (groes)	cross
Cwm	a bowl-shaped valley

Cŵn (singular *ci*) dogs
Cymro (pl. *Cymry*) Welshman
Cymru   Wales

Note: initial *d* is sometimes mutated to *dd*

Dau (fem. *dwy*) two
Dinas (sometimes *din*) city, fortress
Dol   meadow
Drws   door
Du   black
Dyffryn   valley
Dysgl   dish
Eglwys   church
Fawr (see *Mawr*)
Fôr (see *Môr*)
Fynydd (see *Mynydd*)
Ffrith   mountain pasture
Ffynnon   well
Gaer (see *Caer*)
Glan   bank
Glas (las) blue-green
Glyn   valley
Goch (see *Coch*)
Gorsedd throne (and hence the bardic institution)
Groes (see *Croes*)
Gwaelod bottom
Gwyn (wyn) white
Gwynt   wind
Las (see *Glas*)
Llan   originally an ecclesiastical enclosure; hence a church or parish
Llus   bilberries
Maen   stone
Mawr (fawr) big
Moch   pigs

Moel	a bare mountain
Môr (fôr)	sea
Morfa	sea-marsh
Morwyn (pl. *morwynion*) maid	
Mynydd	mountain
Nant	stream, hence a stream-valley
Pen	head
Pentre	village
Plas	mansion
Pont (bont)	bridge
Porth	harbour
Pwll	pool
'R (see *Y*)	
Rhos	moor
Rhyd	ford
Sarn	causeway
Sych	dry
Tal	front, forehead; hence headland
Tan	under
Tomen	mound; originally a dung-heap, from *tom*, dung
Traeth	beach
Traws	cross
Tre	town
Twll	hole
Tŷ	house
Wyn (see *Gwyn*)	
Y (*yr* before a vowel and *'r* after a vowel) the, of the	
Yn	in
Ynys	island
Ysbyty	hospital

BIBLIOGRAPHY

BACKGROUND

Ashe, G., *From Caesar to Arthur*, 1960, London, Collins.

Ashe, G., *The Quest for Arthur's Britain*, 1968, London, Pall Mall.

Chadwick, N.K., *The Druids*, 1966, Cardiff, University of Wales Press.

Daniel, G., *The Megalith Builders of Western Europe*, 1962, London, Pelican.

Embleton, C., *Snowdonia*, 1962, Sheffield, The Geographical Association.

Gildas (ed. and trans. H. Williams), *The Ruin of Britain*, Cymmrodorion Record Series No. 3, 1899, London, Nutt.

Powell, T.G.E., *The Celts*, 1958, London, Thames & Hudson.

HISTORY

Davies, H.R., *The Conway and Menai Ferries*, 1942, Cardiff, University of Wales Press.

Dodd, A.H., *A History of Caernarvonshire*, 1968, Denbigh, Caernarvonshire Historical Society.

Tacitus (trans. H. Mattingley), *On Britain and Germany*, 1965, London, Penguin.

Tucker, N., *Conway and its Story*, 1960, Denbigh, Gee & Son.

Rees, W., *A Historical Atlas of Wales*, 1959, London, Faber & Faber.

— *The Calendar of the Wynn Papers*, 1926, Aberystwyth, National Library of Wales.

ANCIENT MONUMENTS AND BUILDINGS

A Survey and Inventory by the Royal Commission on Ancient and Historical Monuments in Wales and Monmouthshire:
Anglesey, 1937, reprinted 1968.
Caernarvonshire (3 vols.) 1956, London, H.M.S.O.

Bezant Lowe, W., *The Heart of Northern Wales* (2 vols.), 1912,
1927, Llanfairfechan, Caxton Press.

✓ *Conway Castle and Town Walls*, 1968 (Official Guidebook),
London, H.M.S.O.

MYTHOLOGY AND EARLY LITERATURE

Geoffrey of Monmouth (trans. Lewis Thorpe), *The History of the
Kings of Britain*, 1966, London, Penguin.

Gruffydd, W.J., *Rhiannon – an inquiry into the First and Third
Branches of the Mabinogi*, 1953, Cardiff, University of Wales
Press.

Jackson, K., *The International Popular Tale and Early Welsh
Tradition*, 1961, Cardiff, University of Wales Press.

✓ Jones, G. and T. (eds. and trans.), *The Mabinogion*, 1957, London,
Dent (Everyman).

Loomis, R.S., *The Grail, from Celtic Myth to Christian Symbol*,
1963, Cardiff, University of Wales Press.

Malory, Sir Thomas, *Le Morte d'Arthur*, 1947, London, Dent
(Everyman).

Rees, A. and B., *Celtic Heritage*, 1961, London, Thames &
Hudson.

Williams, G., *The Burning Tree – poems from the first thousand
years of Welsh verse*, 1956, London, Faber & Faber.

MOUNTAINS AND MOUNTAINEERING

Carr, H.R.C. and Lister, G.A., *The Mountains of Snowdonia*, 1925,
London, Lane & Bodley Head.

✓ Cambell, B., North, F.J. and Scott, R., *Snowdonia*, 1949, London,
Collins.

Poucher, W.A., *The Welsh Peaks*, 1965, London, Constable.

Young, G.W., Sutton, G. and Noyce, W., *Snowdon Biography*,
1957, London, Dent.

Snowdonia – National Park Guide, 1960, London, H.M.S.O.

✓ *Snowdonia – Forest Park Guide*, 1969, London, H.M.S.O.

LITERATURE

Borrow, G., *Wild Wales*, 1920, London, Oxford University Press (World's Classics).

Chamberlain, B., *Tide-race*, 1962, London, Hodder.

Firbank, T., *I Bought a Mountain*, 1940, London, Harrap.

Hopkins, G.M., *Poems*, 1964, London, Oxford University Press.

Thomas, R.S., *Pieta*, 1966, London, Hart-Davies.

Watts-Dunton, T., *Aylwin*, 1950, London, Oxford University Press (World's Classics).

INDEX